ESSAYS ON
EURIPIDEAN DRAMA

ESSAYS ON
EURIPIDEAN
DRAMA

BY
GILBERT NORWOOD
FORMERLY FELLOW OF ST. JOHN'S COLLEGE
CAMBRIDGE
PROFESSOR EMERITUS OF CLASSICS,
UNIVERSITY COLLEGE, TORONTO

UNIVERSITY OF CALIFORNIA PRESS
BERKELEY AND LOS ANGELES
CAMBRIDGE UNIVERSITY PRESS
LONDON
UNIVERSITY OF TORONTO PRESS
TORONTO

UNIVERSITY OF CALIFORNIA PRESS
BERKELEY AND LOS ANGELES, CALIFORNIA

CAMBRIDGE UNIVERSITY PRESS
LONDON, ENGLAND

UNIVERSITY OF TORONTO PRESS
TORONTO, CANADA

To
MY WIFE

PREFACE

THIS book fulfils a hinted promise made in the latest edition of *Greek Tragedy* (1948), which here and there it corrects. But the constituent essays were conceived and first written at widely separated times; and, as regards one of them, this fact has perhaps some little importance.

My preface to *The Riddle of the Bacchae* stated that its argument occurred to me as an undergraduate. But I hesitated to increase the reader's distress by revealing that another play also had during the same period inspired me with novel views; and kept the *Supplices* theory hidden, not least because I could hardly believe it myself. In due course a brief statement was written and every few years exhumed for what should by that time be the cold eye of objective criticism. It became clear that the play as it stands could not be fathered upon Moschion, or any other dramatist in his right mind. The theory of a patchwork origin that in the end took shape as the only credible explanation of our text, but may nevertheless at first repel some readers, is at least (they are assured) not the outcome of a fancy wantonly indulged. Whatever ingenuity I may command has been applied to seeking a solution less eccentric; but the farrago before me has proved otherwise intractable. The whimsical element in Euripides' genius and art, studied in the opening essay, helps to explain the palace-miracle of the *Bacchae* far better than I explained it long ago: to excuse our fundamentally irrational *Supplices* it does not suffice.

My thanks are offered to Messrs. Methuen for permission to use translations first printed in *Greek Tragedy*. The helpful kindness of my friends and colleagues Professors R. J. Getty, G. M. A. Grube, and W. P. Wallace has been most valuable. The dedication of this book is an attempt to voice my gratitude for assistance varied, able, and untiring, without which it could not have been completed.

G. N.

TORONTO
October 20, 1951

CONTENTS

I. TOWARDS UNDERSTANDING EURIPIDES　　*page* 1

II. THE *BACCHAE* AND ITS RIDDLE　　52

III. GOD AND MAN IN *HIPPOLYTUS*　　74

IV. THE *SUPPLICES*　　112

INDEX　　183

I

TOWARDS UNDERSTANDING EURIPIDES

This title has been chosen in order to disclaim all thought of covering the whole subject. We shall discuss only those features of Euripidean dramaturgy that need fresh attention.

From what standpoint, in what mood, should we address ourselves to this study? Perhaps no other ancient poet's work forces these questions so urgently upon us. Compared in this respect with him Aeschylus and Persius, even Lycophron and Lucan, are easy: however we vary in promptness and depth of apprehension, we all agree about their methods and claims on our esteem. But Euripides has evoked astonishingly diverse judgements from critics consummate in learning, acumen, even poetic genius: Goethe himself urged any modern student who would censure our poet to do so on his knees;[1] twenty-one centuries earlier Philemon the dramatist exclaimed that if there were a future life he would hang himself to see Euripides; Swinburne wrote venomously of this "botcher",[2] a word that Walter Headlam did not scruple to repeat as regards one aspect of his work;[3] whereas Verrall looked upon him with the liveliest admiration, we are told that Jebb, Sophoclean as he was, "could not speak of Euripides without pain in his voice, and seldom, without necessity, spoke of him at all".[4] Something has uniquely gone wrong. Euripides, it seems, is no classic after all, a classic being a writer who, let mankind change its perspective as it may, retains unshaken and unequivocal repute. Concerning him we are no more agreed than were his Athenian

[1] Eckermann, *Gespräche mit Goethe,* March 28, 1827: "Wenn ein moderner Mensch wie Schlegel an einem so großen Alten Fehler zu rügen hätte, so sollte es billig nicht anders geschehen als auf den Knien."

[2] *Works* (Bonchurch ed.), vol. XV, p. 252: "It was all I could do . . . to win from him [Jowett] an admission of the charm and grace and sweetness of some of the shorter and simpler lyrics which redeem in some measure the reputation of the dreariest of playwrights—if that term be not over complimentary for the clumsiest of botchers that ever floundered through his work as a dramatist."

[3] *Class. Rev.,* vol. XVI (1902), p. 440: "In this department [use of the chorus] of the playwright Euripides, who sneers at him [Aeschylus], is himself the clumsiest botcher in comparison." [4] J. Burnet, *Essays and Addresses* (1929), p. 49.

contemporaries, and less agreed than later antiquity. Chaucer and Ronsard, to mention no greater names, are more firmly established. Why cannot the world make up its mind concerning Euripides? The fault may —let us face it—be his. But it may be ours, wholly or in part. Perhaps a fresh discussion will at least make clearer the reasons of our disagreement, possibly thus reducing their number and their power to disconcert or mislead.

Our point of view must be subjective. Accumulate as we will all the knowledge available concerning the Greeks and their literature dramatic and non-dramatic, concerning other peoples also and their writings, with whatever additional learning seems even possibly relevant, we must in the end voice our own minds. Anyone who airily asserts that it will never do to judge an ancient Greek by "our modern notions" relies on a mischievous half-truth. If, for example, we shrink from saying that Cadmus and Tiresias in their scene of the *Bacchae* are "most laughable", as Pentheus calls them, we should leave Euripides unopened. Indeed, as regards tragedy, we can make short work of this uneasiness about modern notions: Aristophanes' idea of Aeschylus (so far as it goes) closely resembles our own; and even what he says about Euripides never bewilders us. When all is said, the entail of Western culture has not been cut: we stand yet in the great succession.

The dangers besetting subjective study of Euripides are in our day well realized: they have, indeed, been displayed in a fiercer light than usually illumines the more secluded bypaths of Helicon. Verrall's essays on Euripidean dramaturgy[1] were generated by an idea so obvious to him that he never thought of defending it: whatever struck him as absurd must have been absurd in the fifth century before Christ and consequently impossible for tragedians then at work. And so, observing that if we take Euripidean drama at its face value we achieve results insufferable to us, he propounded new explanations of it, derived from nothing less than a law. "On the Euripidean stage whatever is said by a divinity is to be regarded, in general, as *ipso facto* discredited. It is in all cases objectionable from the author's point of view, and almost always a lie."[2] This doctrine was set forth and applied with a skill so formidable, a wit so engaging, a prose style at once so vivacious and urbane, that it could not be ignored. His writings received frequent and hostile examination, resulting in a verdict that his treatment of elements to which he objected had produced con-

---

[1] Especially *Euripides the Rationalist* (1895) and *Essays on Four Plays of Euripides* (1905).
[2] *Euripides the Rationalist*, p. 138.

clusions more objectionable still.¹ That is on some matters true; but not on all. There is no Euripidean Principle, no Law of Euripidean Dramaturgy: each play must be studied by itself, in the light of its own manner.

Nevertheless, subjective we must be, however hard we try to forget our twentieth-century preoccupations. We cannot forget them; moreover, they cannot be entirely wrong. Our chief danger is the very fact that started Verrall upon his adventures: the deceptive modernity of Euripides. Each of us feels again and again—for some, indeed, that sense is almost continuous—as if he were our contemporary. The sublimity of Aeschylus, the serene grandeur of Sophocles, the sustained tragic mood of both, make such intimacy impossible. Who would care to lunch with Atossa or Ajax? But Admetus, Jason, Phaedra, Hermione, Xuthus, and many others, especially Orestes so horribly fascinating whenever he appears!—with them we have surely forgathered times without number. So of the situations in which they move: imagination easily transmutes Troy and Argos, Corinth and Thebes, into the cities whose streets we daily tread. But this kinship may imperil criticism by luring us into an assumption—the more dangerous because unconscious—that Euripides can be, must be, judged by our standards, perhaps even our fashions, without misgiving or reservation: that, because the current view of a given Euripidean play saddles it with some fault that Jonson or Racine would never have dreamed of committing, therefore we must jettison that current view and tumble the dubious play until we can restate its plot and meaning in terms that would satisfy those later playwrights, with Boileau, Bradley, and so many others into the bargain. That method should be ruled out. We may seek to explain away, and if we fail may condemn, incidental self-contradictions; but features affecting a drama's whole structure, such as the fission of *Andromache* or *Heracles*, must be accepted as part of its author's deliberate plan, whether we approve it or not. We can legitimately censure, at the end of *Cymbeline*, the King's astounding attitude to the Roman domination; but we have no right to denounce the juxtaposition of ancient Britain and Renaissance Italy.

The danger of objectivity (on the other hand) has been displayed with melancholy completeness in the world's most celebrated critical treatise. Aristotle's *Poetic* repels at first reading by its icily aseptic air and odd dislocations; after we have learned the reasons or excuses for these

¹ E.g., Burnet (*ut sup.*, p. 54) writes that Euripides' plots "are his own creation, and it is inconceivable that he should have set himself to make these plots seem incredible". As to "his own creation" see the context, about the Arthurian legend as employed in the early French *chansons*, etc. So explained, the phrase is true, an important note on Aristotle (*Poet.* 1451ᵇ) and Antiphanes (fr. 91).

deterrents, it continues to repel. He commits the basic error of treating an art as if it were a science, rarely conscious that he is no longer engaged on the *Historia Animalium*. We owe him a huge debt of gratitude for much that he tells us; and we pay him in full but with little joy. When he offers as an example of a dramatist's inconsistency the fact that in *Iphigenia at Aulis* the heroine when a suppliant "is utterly unlike her later self",[1] he suggests a zoologist who should remonstrate with a rabbit for suddenly sprouting horns. Far more disconcerting, we find no treatment of religion, not as a theme of tragedy—an omission that might pass for certain reasons—but as a formative influence, nay, as the very source of tragedy among Greeks: only the curt phrase that it "originated with the authors of the dithyramb".[2]

Worse still is the famous sentence: "After passing through many changes tragedy found itself and stopped."[3] By "stopped" he of course does not mean that no plays were thereafter written: to mention but one poet, his own fellow student and pupil Theodectes won high repute and is coupled by him with Sophocles.[4] He means that the tragic form itself developed no further: because (he assumes) no development was possible. But why should he assume this? Why abolish Shakespeare and Racine before they are born? He has but created a chimera bombinating in a temporary vacuum. Choerilus of Samos[5] penned his charming lament, that the poetic field was now fully occupied, at the very time when Aeschylus was inventing a new kind of poetry altogether. But, further, the very phrase "found itself" (or "attained its natural form") raises a question basically important for all types of art. Aristotle implies that somehow, whether by a law of Nature or by divine ordinance or by the conditions under which the soul meets and ponders its experience, a Platonic Idea of Tragedy exists independently of the men who compose tragedies:[6] something that

---

[1] 1454ª31 ff.

[2] 1449ª9 ff. It is useless to suggest that perhaps Aristotle did better in some lost passage. He is concerned here with origins, and we have a right to protest against his leaving a subject thus.

[3] 1449ª14 f.: πολλὰς μεταβολὰς μεταβαλοῦσα ἡ τραγῳδία ἐπαύσατο, ἐπεὶ ἔσχε τὴν αὑτῆς φύσιν. A distinguished critic has recently paraphrased this in a still more regrettable form. Lionel Trilling writes: "We must consider that technique has its autonomy and that it dictates the laws of its own growth. Aristotle speaks of Athenian tragedy as seeking and finding its fulfillment, its entelechy...." *The Liberal Imagination* (1950), p. 257.

[4] 1452ª22–9: comparison of *peripeteia* in *Oedipus Tyrannus* and in *Lynceus*.

[5] Fr. 2 (Kinkel).

[6] This disastrous assumption was crisply asserted by A. W. von Schlegel also: "So hat dieser Dichter [Euripides] ... das innere Wesen der Tragödie aufgehoben." *Dramaturgische Vorlesungen*, VIII, in *Sämmtliche Werke* (Leipzig, 1846), vol. V, p. 137.

stands waiting to be realized in matter, after which no further development can supervene. That no such pattern of tragedy exists can easily be proved, if we grant that *Agamemnon, Oedipus Tyrannus, Hippolytus, Phèdre,* and *Macbeth* (let us say) are all great tragedies: for the modern plays contain no chorus, which is vital to the ancient; and the ancient by no means always end in the hero's death or in sorrow, as do the modern. Yet stay! Would Aristotle have approved the modern plays? We cannot be sure; but shall certainly remark: "If he would not, so much the worse for his authority as a critic." The truth obviously is that he writes not only as a scientist but as a Greek scientist: 'Sophocles was a consummate playwright, *Oedipus Tyrannus* the highest achievement of tragic art; no other kind of tragedy is so estimable or capable of such heights, wherefore Euripides is a poet of equivocal distinction.'[1]

But, quitting Aristotle with the usual blend of reverence and exasperation, can we discover elsewhere traces of a recognized standard or ideal? Aristophanes at once comes to mind. His genius and critical skill,[2] his lively interest in tragedy and wide knowledge of it, his date and the fact that perhaps his finest comedy contains an elaborate examination of Aeschylean and Euripidean art: all this makes him a perfect witness. If a definite conception of tragedy was held by cultivated fifth-century Athenians, or existed only in Aristophanes' head, the *Frogs* would reveal it. But what do we find? Censures, no less pungent and instructive than delightful, of Euripides' music, prologues, and analogous elements with, be it noted, never such a rebuke as 'You ought to work in Sophocles' manner.' That Aristophanes, in this vitally important connexion, neglects Sophocles[3] shows his artistic discretion: that master clearly defied both the parodist and the buffoon, even the critical comedian; whereas Aeschylus, for all his splendour, and Euripides, for all his brilliance, alike offered delicious opportunities. But even so, why not come to the root of the matter, plot-construction—which Aristotle calls "the tragic drama's soul"[4]—and arraign Euripides for such ostensibly fundamental blunders

---

[1] 1453^{a}28 ff.: ὁ Εὐριπίδης εἰ καὶ τὰ ἄλλα μὴ εὖ οἰκονομεῖ ἀλλὰ τραγικώτατός γε τῶν ποιητῶν φαίνεται. Similarly critics are fond of saying that Dreiser is a fine novelist but "cannot write" and that Van Gogh is a masterly artist but "cannot draw".

[2] It need scarcely be remarked that underneath his magnificent foolery an intellect both powerful and serious is again and again at work.

[3] Obviously his death occurred between the first conception and the production of the *Frogs*. When Aristophanes heard the news he not only grieved as a man but ground his teeth as an artist. Sophocles in Hades sorely threatened his scheme. But he extricated himself neatly: ὁ δ' εὔκολος μὲν ἐνθάδ', εὔκολος δ' ἐκεῖ (82), in particular, is perfect.

[4] *Poet.* 1450^{a}38 f.

as episodic scenes,[1] for lack (that is) of the unity obtaining in Sophocles, of course, but no less conspicuously in Aeschylus, whom the comedian puts forward as his victim's antagonist? Throughout the *Frogs* Aristophanes disregards this topic:[2] he implies that each *part* of a Euripidean play is in the abstract sound enough, but that the poet has bungled his treatment of it. Here is no standard of tragedy, only of the poetic (and musical) style appropriate thereto. The scholiasts do better, often giving examples of good or bad "economy". On *Hippolytus* 659, for instance, we read: "This is an admirable feat of economy: by means of Hippolytus' absence the poet gives Phaedra opportunity to hang herself and libel him by means of the letter." Such notes are probably derived from Peripatetic scholars who followed up Aristotle's remark on "bad economy". They certainly point to what we have in mind, but are by no means enough to warrant our attributing an elaborated system of tragic art to those scholars. Possibly they evolved one; but in any case they are too late to be relevant here.

In our own day a great English scholar has declared for a very definite and articulated scheme. Dr. Gilbert Murray maintains that standing elements in Dionysiac ritual are mirrored in the structure and events of Euripidean tragedy.[3] For example, after an impressive list of theophanies in extant plays—*Hippolytus, Andromache, Supplices, Ion, Electra, Iphigenia in*

---

[1] Ar. *Met.* 1909ᵇ19: ἡ φύσις οὐκ ἐπεισοδιώδης, ὥσπερ μοχθηρὰ τραγῳδία.

[2] Nor does he discuss characterization, being content to censure the wickedness of sundry Euripidean people, though of course they are often perfect works of art.

This essay contains comparatively little about Euripides' power as a delineator of character, because it has been treated so often. But two vital remarks must be quoted. E. R. Dodds writes: "The *Medea*, the *Hippolytus*, the *Hecuba*, the *Heracles*: what gives to all these plays their profoundly tragic character is the victory of irrational impulse over reason in a noble but unstable human being. *Video meliora proboque, deteriora sequor*: it is here that Euripides finds the essence of man's moral tragedy. Hence the scientific care which, as an ancient critic remarks, he devoted to the study of ἔρωτάς τε καὶ μανίας—the dark irrational side of man's nature." (*Class. Rev.*, vol. XLIII (1924), p. 99.) W. Schmid has noted that in Aeschylus and Sophocles the characters are driven by a daemonic pressure that stands above all personal interests, but in Euripides by self-preservation, direct or indirect. This, he says, is the much blamed and praised realism of Euripides (quoting the Sophoclean οἷοι εἰσίν). (Müller's *Handbuch der klassischen Altertumswissenschaft*, Abt. VII, Teil 1, vol. 3 (Munich, 1940), p. 768.)

[3] See his "Excursus on the Ritual Forms preserved in Greek Tragedy" (pp. 341-63 of Jane Harrison's *Themis*). He summarizes his contentions thus (p. 363): "Something like the old hierophant reappears at the beginning, something like the old re-risen god at the end; and, as we have seen, it is in plays of Euripides, and most of all in the very latest of his plays [*Bacchae*], that we find in most perfect and clear-cut outline the whole sequence of Contest, Tearing-asunder, Messenger, Lamentation, Discovery, Recognition, and Resurrection which constituted the original Dionysus-mystery."

Tauris, Helen, Orestes, Bacchae, Iphigenia at Aulis,[1] *Rhesus*[2]—he continues: "If this were free and original composition the monotony would be intolerable and incomprehensible: we can understand it only when we realize that the poet is working under the spell of a set traditional form."[3] But by no means all the eleven instances can bear the weight Murray lays upon them. The *Supplices* theophany gives no support at all to his thesis: moreover, it is foolish and obtrusive, for which reasons it has often been condemned. Can we believe that anything in *Helen* is seriously concerned with any kind of religion or religious feeling except—if it is an exception—Theonoe's respect for her dead father? In several of the other plays, especially *Andromache* and *Rhesus*, the deity enters chiefly in order to wind things up with an air of pomp. Assuredly the frequency of these divine appearances arrests our attention; but in the absence of any other evidence for the traditional spell of Dionysiac religion, is it not more reasonable to suppose them the free choice of a richly endowed dramatist? Why restrict ourselves to the choice between Verrall's nagging anti-Olympian and Murray's monotonously official devotee? We may well believe that as time drew on Euripides became fond of the "rescue-drama",[4] whereby the *deus ex machina* became a figure not of theology at all, but of romance. The most consummate artists have their mannerisms, if we choose to employ a derogatory word. We could well spare a good many lions from the *Iliad*; and the so-called Mona Lisa smile, which we certainly could not spare, is perhaps the most frequent (as the greatest) miracle of Leonardo's brush. Shakespeare, not to mention his passion for disguising heroines as young men, became in his latest phase notably

---

[1] The close of this play is clearly spurious: in the original version Artemis certainly appeared (see Murray's text).

[2] Geffcken, "Der Rhesos" (*Hermes*, vol. LXXI (1936), pp. 394 ff.), denies that this work is Euripidean, contending vigorously for the fourth century and tentatively for the second half thereof; Schmid (*ut sup.*, p. 838) regards Geffcken's articles as making the fourth-century date certain. But Geffcken insists far too much on the difference between *Rhesus* and the other extant plays, forgetting that Euripides had been writing for some fourteen years before *Alcestis*, earliest of the others. Murray, we observe, thinks the play authentic: rightly, it appears to me. I confess to being much swayed by an amusing detail—the passage (264-74) where Hector stupidly refuses to hear the shepherd who brings sensational news: "Stop your quotations from the *Grazier's Gazette!*" or words to the same effect. That is an unusual kind of fun, but very like Euripides in one of his moods (cp. Alcmena in *Heracleidae* 646-59) and like no other Greek (outside comedy) that I can think of. C. B. Sneller in his excellent study *De Rheso Tragoedia* (Amsterdam, 1949) attributes the play to Euripides and dates it in the period 427-424. [3] Pp. 351 f.

[4] Schmid's admirable idea: see below, pp. 28 f. Note that *Charition*, a debased semi-farcical adventure-play, complete with howling savages and a clown, is based on *Iphigenia in Tauris*. (See my *Greek Comedy*, pp. 80 f.)

addicted to dramas of reconciliation; Terence invented a duality of plot-construction that grew steadily more powerful throughout his brief career; Ibsen's retrospective illumination is a recurrent feature of his technique; and Shaw, despite his horror of sentimentality, harboured a weakness for the wise middle-aged woman.

Tragedy made itself as it went along: *solvebatur ambulando*—at times (as will appear) *titubando*. But there was in truth no "problem" to "solve"; poets contented themselves with writing as excellent plays as they could. Nor need we bemuse ourselves with that phantom, "the spirit of the age". There is no spirit of an age apart from the great souls, like theirs, that give the age its meaning and vigour. But three genuine and specific influences (such as they were) the Greek tragedians did in some degree obey: those of the religious festival for which they wrote, of contemporary events and interests, of preceding and contemporary playwrights. How strong were these?

The religious festival: that phrase emphasizes the spirit of worship. As we shall see, the practical conditions of performance were inevitably important for Euripides, often hampering him. But sanctity and the religious mood are at present in view, and for our purpose they meant very little. Tragedy at the Dionysiac festival need not be religious: *Lysistrata* is no religious comedy, though it too graced a Dionysiac celebration. Just as men sacrificing to Apollo did not search for a holy sheep, but were satisfied with a sound animal, so the tragedian made a sound play and had no need to give it a religious tone. Aeschylus, to be sure, composed religious dramas, but only because he happened to be, in the fullest possible sense, a religious genius—even before he became a dramatic genius, as his starveling *Supplices* remains to prove. No other tragic master, so far as our knowledge goes, shared his theological temper: certainly not Sophocles, whose religion was no more (and no less) than a deeply pious mood, which his superb artistic achievements have misled some into investigating with results either self-contradictory or meagre; still less Euripides, a vaguely agnostic soul and a wit who found in the legends material not only for a drama in essence purely human but also for strokes of intellectual fun. A tragedy, then, was not in itself holy at all, and need not deal with religion, the only approach thereto demanded by the festival being the "high seriousness" that Matthew Arnold proclaimed a note of great literature. Even this vanishes at times from the page of Euripides.

The second influence, that of contemporary events and interests, though more important, needs but few words. Aristophanes lives on these concerns; not so the tragedians. Sophocles indeed, though he took a prominent share in his country's business, makes not a single clear allusion to them.[1] But, of Aeschylus' seven extant works, the *Persae* is entirely, and the *Eumenides* largely, dedicated to the most vital concerns of his country. As for Euripides, his allusion in *Electra* (1347–55) to the Athenian armada then on its way to Sicily is only the most arresting among numerous unmistakable reminders of contemporary events and topics. But such things have small interest for the student of dramatic art, making no addition to his enjoyment or understanding of Euripides' work except a faint quiver of the thrill that must have stirred Athenian spectators. An excellent parallel may be seen in one of Sir Sidney Lee's essays.[2] Caliban's defiant ditty "No more dams I'll make for fish" alludes (we read) to the Indians of Virginia, who were specially skilled in building fish-dams, the secret of which they jealously kept from the English settlers, whose food largely depended on these. When the Indians revolted, they broke the dams: this "was a chief cause of the disastrous termination of the sixteenth-century efforts to found an English colony in Virginia". How many of us knew these exciting facts before Lee's essay appeared? Very few, and it matters nothing. It matters hardly more how many knew them among those who watched the first performance of *The Tempest*. No one feels or felt any puzzlement: Caliban's ranting is perfectly clear and good in itself. Shakespeare learned them, and indeed took the whole idea of Caliban, from settlers' reports; but all that (in Aristotle's phrase) is "outside the play"—and so was Alcibiades. The Peloponnesian War is a very different matter. The spiritual and moral degradation, suffering, and wreckage thus brought upon Greece profoundly stirred two great Athenians. One was Thucydides. The other was Euripides. His specific allusions to events, we have just said, need only passing notes in our commentaries. But his pity and indignation, perhaps despair, engendered whole plays. The *Troades* (to mention but the most terrible instance) is of course a magnificent work even if we consider only its ostensible subject; but who can fail to recognize a deadly arraignment brought against the Athens of Euripides' own day? Still, his anguish has in strictness no connexion with his art, unless indeed one can show that his emotion altered his methods or style. We shall not suggest that the fission of *Hecuba* or the *Troades*' lack of structure are thus to be explained.

[1] *Phil.* 410–52 are a conversation perfectly natural in spirit but perhaps rather long if it contains no *arrière-pensée*. It is the likeliest example; yet even here Jebb (pp. xl f. of his edition) will allow no allusion to men of the poet's day, including the recall of Alcibiades from Samos in 411 B.C., two years before *Philoctetes* was produced.

[2] *Elizabethan and Other Essays* (1929), pp. 297–9.

The third influence named above, that of preceding and contemporary playwrights, was at least as strong as either of the others. But modern students usually tend to over-emphasize it, because Darwinism—dominant in literary scholarship only since its prestige in biology has waned—sends them incessantly ferreting for origins. Because Ibsen's art sprang from his studies in Scribe and Sardou, so that pleasure and instruction are gained by comparing *Love's Comedy* with such plays as *Mon Étoile*, therefore we assume that a similar process may be fruitfully applied to Greek tragedy. So it may: if we keep to certainties. But we are not to picture an Attic tragedian, merely because he was a great soul, apprenticing himself to another in the solemn mood of Dante's Virgilian discipleship or the passion of Keats as he studied Spenser, or that dedicated rapture wherewith Milton saturated himself in the Scriptures. Greek poets, for all their adjurations addressed to the Muse, were conscious of no "great Task-Master's eye", still less of any human exemplar. Seldom before the Sophistic age did they work in a mood of deliberate relation to one another like Byron, Coleridge, Southey, and Wordsworth. In that age, as later, they often did: Aristophanes gives abundant proof, for example in the parabasis of his *Knights*. But Aeschylus did not belong to the Sophistic era. Phrynichus was pre-eminently a lyrist, and from him Aeschylus learned a lesson only negative, though momentous, as is clear to anyone who sets the opening of the *Persae* beside what we know of Phrynichus' *Phoenissae*. Nor did Sophocles belong to the Sophistic age,[1] though living in it. He knew and admired Phrynichus' work, as appears from a pleasant anecdote related by Ion of Chios;[2] but it is safe to assert that he learned from him nothing about dramatic art. Aeschylus' introduction of a second actor was vital to Sophocles, for that advance meant no less than the very invention of drama, properly so called. But the whole "feel" and the whole *tempo* of Sophoclean work are un-Aeschylean. Euripides and Sophocles are unmistakably conscious of their mutual differences. In *Hippolytus* and the *Trachiniae* (if nowhere else) they "imitate" one another so as to bring out their own conceptions of dramatic writing. Euripides in effect says: 'Pray let me show you how you should bring gods into the theatre, not as in your *Ajax*' (and, doubtless, in other plays now lost).[3]

[1] Suidas reports that he wrote a prose treatise *On the Chorus*, which (it must be owned) sounds professional indeed. But we hear nothing else about it, and may be forgiven if we pay small attention to an unsupported testimony so late (tenth century), particularly as it asserts that Sophocles "contended" with Thespis: ἔγραψεν ... λόγον καταλογάδην περὶ τοῦ χοροῦ πρὸς Θέσπιν καὶ Χοίριλον ἀγωνιζόμενος.
[2] *Ap.* Müller, *Frr. Hist. Graec.*, vol. II, pp. 46.
[3] Cp. below, pp. 92–94.

Sophocles implies: 'Your *Medea* is ill-conceived and harmful: Deianira will show you the kind of wronged wife whom you should have portrayed.'

So much, then, at present[1] for the three influences under which the dramatists worked. How did they work?

Just as Thucydides was a great writer who nevertheless, because no system of grammar had been promulgated, evolved again and again irregular or defective sentences, so all the four playwrights of whom complete dramas survive were great writers who nevertheless, because they could not study Aristotle or Horace, Boileau or Freytag, composed on occasion irregular or defective dramas. They all possessed genius, two of them cleverness into the bargain, but no models, not to mention rules, of plot-construction. That explains why their forty-four dramas exhibit plots superb, good, weak, and bad: one feels at times that only accident decides which it shall be. They are exploring a new territory without map or compass, and show greater sureness of artistry in characterization than in plot-work because they have Homer at hand, in lyrical composition because they have Stesichorus and Pindar. Compare the gawky manner of the episodes in Aeschylus' *Supplices* with the assured as well as noble style of its odes; the character-drawing of *Philoctetes* with its deplorable "solution"; Menelaus and Hermione with the ramshackle structure of *Andromache*; note the consummate ode that adorns the *Troades*, a play rudimentary in development. Such works are conceived and written on two quite different levels of expertness, much as Shakespeare sets "Fear no more the heat o' the sun" and "Hark, hark!" in the midst of *Cymbeline*, or as Marlowe sheds sudden glory upon *Tamburlaine* with that outburst, lyrical in its quality, beginning "Now walk the angels on the walls of Heaven". A later age would see all smoothed out: probably the younger Astydamas earned his portrait-statue by avoiding the weaknesses as well as missing the sublimities noted in his giant predecessors. 'Longinus', indeed, tells us something of the kind when he writes that Pindar and Sophocles "are often mysteriously quenched and collapse most wretchedly",[2] whereas Bacchylides and Ion of Chios are ever "faultily faultless".[3] This fluctuation appears most notably in Euripides because he was an untiring experimenter[4]—like Mr. Eugene O'Neill, who, although the

---

[1] We shall have more to say below concerning Euripides' own reactions to the first.

[2] περὶ ὕψους XXIII. Aristophanes held a similar opinion about the excellent Crates: ... τοτὲ μὲν πίπτων, τοτὲ δ' οὐχί (*Knights* 537 ff.).

[3] *Ibid.*: ἀδιάπτωτοι καὶ ἐν τῷ γλαφυρῷ πάντη κεκαλλιγραφημένοι.

[4] Professor Kitto (*Greek Tragedy*, 1939) has done all students of our poet a great service by his distinction of the various types (melodrama, romance, etc.) into which the "tragedies" should be divided.

most consummate playwright of his time, has been content to produce such a crude fantasy as *Strange Interlude* or that bad piece *The Iceman Cometh*, because he insists on exploring the possibilities of his art instead of imitating his own magnificent *Mourning Becomes Electra* or writing another *Desire under the Elms*. Euripides' dramas show perhaps an equal variety of merit; and mostly for the same reason: experiments do not always succeed. Had they done so, he would have gained many more than five prizes. Athens by no means condemned the experiments as such. They were presented at the Dionysiac festival and were clearly not comedies or satyric plays: therefore "tragedies" they must be. But in the sense recognized by Aristotle and by us they were not tragedies at all.

Is such talk a mere playing with labels, as when one critic writes of the *Bacchae*: "It seems as if we had before us not a tragedy but a wildly romantic fairy-tale"?[1] A single instance will suffice to show that we need not fear such disabling ineptitude: that (on the contrary) labels, if discreetly used, will save us from it. *Alcestis* contains important elements that make it a bad play—if we insist on judging it as a tragedy. To the tipsy scene of Heracles and the "sordid realism" that marks the conversation between Admetus and Pheres, which of themselves grossly deface the august label, other strange things must be added. Though less shocking, they are even more injurious because they invite the charge that Euripides treats Alcestis' sacrifice itself with a sardonic smile. Admetus' speech of despair and grief, sincere as it is, misses tragedy narrowly indeed but effectually by its hysteria, above all in his talk of the statue. Alcestis' farewell address to him, so icily business-like, destroys for a few moments all our sympathy and admiration. No less odd, though anything but repellent, is the air of all other portions, even the delightful lyric concerning Apollo's sojourn with Admetus and that flawless stanza (995 ff.), the salutation to his wife's grave: we are moved, but nowhere are we shaken; and Alcestis' return from the dead is bereft of awe by Heracles' roguishness. All this cannot be dismissed as a sequence of blunders. If blunders, they are flatly impossible to Euripides: any beginner could have made the last scene more touching. The truth of course is that Euripides has written not a mysteriously bad tragedy, but a superb tragicomedy. We may still object that Alcestis' sacrifice is no fit theme for comedy, however diluted: if so, we are not discussing dramatic art but good taste, the standards whereof notoriously vary even from one generation to the next, still more from ancient Athens to the modern occidental world. On its own presuppositions, this play is thoroughly good. Apollo's

[1] C. Steinweg, *Euripides als Tragiker und Lustspieldichter* (Halle, 1924), p. 165.

prologue and dispute with the Death-goblin establish the serio-comic tone that is to prevail throughout. The altercation between Admetus and Pheres makes excellent comedy, halfway towards that between Strepsiades and Pheidippides, who indeed utters a reminiscence of the Euripidean scene.[1] Heracles and the Butler are admirable: the hero's sudden change when he learns the truth causes us some little amusement, much excitement and pleasure. But it is in the most difficult part of his strange self-appointed task that Euripides has used his surest and most delicate fingering. He has set himself to treat the nobility of Alcestis, the grief of Admetus, in a manner approaching tragedy but always keeping below it. Hence that strained, faintly grotesque tone in Admetus' anguished address to his dying wife. Hence, too, her frigid lecture on her own unselfishness and his duty after she has gone: the other side of her has been fully revealed beforehand with tenderness and power, but in the report of a maid-servant. Later comes a master-stroke subtler still. Admetus returns from the obsequies and gazes at his house: "Ah, my home confronts me. How shall I enter?" But enter it he never does, until his beloved is restored to him. That most awful moment, the return to a home now blank and comfortless, is spared him: for this is no tragedy.

Does Euripides himself give us any evidence about his own conception of his business as a playwright?

In the *Frogs*, it will scarcely be gainsaid, Aristophanes more than once quotes phrases that Euripides had been known to utter. His examination (1124–74) of the *Choephoroe* prologue cannot be an Aristophanic invention: it is too long, and not funny enough, for that. Similarly Euripides' description (959–63) of his own realism, which (if authentic) exactly meets our purpose, contains nothing laughable. Authentic it certainly is: we are convinced by the athletic vigour of thought as of diction, so exactly like that of innumerable passages in the Euripidean dramas and strongly contrasting[2] with the Aristophanic style of what he has been made to say just before.[3] "My subjects were the things of our experience and daily life, about which I could be checked; for the audience could judge my

[1] Cp. *Alc.* 691 and *Clouds* 1415.
[2] The last word, κωδωνοφαλαροπώλους, is, however, Aristophanic enough; and so are the four lines that follow.
[3] Vv. 956–8:

λεπτῶν τε κανόνων ἐσβολὰς ἐπῶν τε γωνιασμούς,
νοεῖν ὁρᾶν συνιέναι στρέφειν ἐρᾶν τεχνάζειν,
κἄχ' ὑποτοπεῖσθαι, περινοεῖν ἅπαντα.

ἐρᾶν has been doubted: Tucker substituted ἔριν (governed by στρέφειν); Fritzsche read στροφῶν ἐρᾶν. *Nil mutandum*: the incongruous word is meant to raise a sudden laugh.

art by their first-hand knowledge. I did not haul them away from common sense with roaring bombast or stagger them with bell-harness-charioteering legendary heroes." That may be fairly summarized thus: 'I reformed the stage, replacing the old Ercles' vein by sound realism'; Sophocles made a similar comment: "I am an idealist, Euripides is a realist."[1] The latter's claim here justifies the frequent assertion that his persons with legendary names are meant to be recognized as types contemporary with the poet's audience, and supports the less customary idea that his epiphanies are not to be taken too seriously. Equally[2] authentic is another passage (907–50), on the crudity of earlier drama and the "treatment", the "diet", whereby Euripides gave it sound health. We must add his claim (971–9) to have educated the audience, though here Aristophanes does play him false by giving his last few lines a damaging comic glibness of wording and metre: the claim itself is entirely just.[3]

So far we have learned less than we might have expected, diverting as it is to hear two great poets speaking at once. More light may be gained from certain features in Euripides' own work. We shall not anticipate a discussion that must be lengthy and (at least in some degree) controversial. At present we must keep to elements that distress everyone. We seek (let it be repeated) his own notion of his business; and must realize what are the characteristics in his work that cannot have shocked him, though they shock his readers. There are certainly two, with a possible third.

Most arresting are the sudden wildly irrelevant lumps of philosophy and science. The despairing Hecuba learns from Menelaus that Helen, the source of Troy's anguish, is to be dragged forth and slain. Her joy finds these words: "O chariot of earth, upon earth enthroned, whosoever thou art, whether Zeus or the law of Nature or human intellect—our knowledge is but doubtful conjecture—, to thee I pray; for treading a soundless path thou guidest mortal life according to justice." Well may Menelaus exclaim: "What is this? You utter very novel prayers!"[4] The queen, however, so far from explaining, instantly returns to normal (or at any rate pertinent) language: "I praise you if you mean to kill your wife, but beware . . ." and so forth. We are at one with Menelaus and

---

[1] Ar. Poet. 1460ᵇ33 f.: Σοφοκλῆς ἔφη αὐτὸς μὲν οἵους δεῖ ποιεῖν, Εὐριπίδην δὲ οἷοι εἰσίν.

[2] Possibly some may question this because "Euripides'" language here, though highly effective, contains a good deal of the Aristophanic quality (τουτί in 913 is no doubt the signal for a πορδή).

[3] See especially pp. 108–10 below.

[4] Tro. 884 f. Euripides was censured by ancient critics for such irrelevant or anachronistic talk: cp. schol. Hipp. 953, Hec. 254, Alc. 780, Phoen. 388.

should be glad to learn, not so much whether she has prophetic knowledge about "the speculations either of Anaxagoras, Anaximenes, or some philosopher of the school of Diagoras",[1] as why she drags in this untimely erudition, by whatever means acquired. A brief acknowledgement of divine justice would certainly be in order: the rest is utterly unsuitable to the speaker, the hearer, and the situation. Can we fairly add therefore "monstrously undramatic"? There's the rub! True, no other playwright, apparently, has ever written so. But Euripides *has* so written, setting these lines in one of his most deeply felt, most piercingly tragic, works. We recognize perforce that he held himself free as a dramatic artist suddenly to voice his own questionings, "in season, out of season", as St. Paul[2] puts it. None of us approves: our feeling at the best is startled amusement, at the worst anger, resulting in cries of "botcher" and the like. But what do we learn about our present theme?[3] He and we argue from different premises. By "relevant" we mean what is appropriate to the *dramatis personae* objectively viewed; he means what is appropriate to them subjectively viewed—that is, viewed as speaking for him as well as for themselves. This unusual subjectivity is not a recurrent blunder, but an element in his unusual conception of dramatic art.

Next come those places where he criticizes—nay, derides—Aeschylus, especially his elaborate censure (*El.* 518-44) of the recognition-scene in the *Choephoroe*, a censure very close in tone and method to that which Aristophanes wrote for (or after) him in the *Frogs* concerning the *Choephoroe* prologue. We shall not rehearse what has been said often and well about this passage and others.[4] But what do we gather from them? That he cherishes a strong artistic conscience at odds with what to us appears his artistic duty. In order to chastise his predecessor's bad art he writes a passage which (like that in the *Troades*) we condemn as art still

---

[1] Paley, *ad loc.*

[2] I name the Apostle in this unlikely context because the comparison helps us to realize that Euripides regarded himself quite definitely as a teacher of his audience. The difference is that he sometimes took a holiday as the fancy caught him.

[3] We need not dwell on other passages like that in the *Troades*, such as the clod dangling by golden chains from Olympus (*Or.* 982 ff.) or the abrupt rejection of a myth just after relating it (*El.* 737 ff.). But note incidentally that *Alc.* 903-10, even if wrongly referred to Anaxagoras, must point at some contemporary of Euripides, since the passage as nothing more than a remark of Pheraean citizens would be worthless because utterly vague. "If the reference is to a fictitious case, why not invent something wholly apposite to the situation, and make the chorus say that they knew or were related to a man who, like Admetos, lost his beloved wife?" (Van Lennep, *ad loc.*; he believes that Anaxagoras is meant.)

[4] E.g., *Phoen.* 751, which Jebb on *Oed. Col.* 1116 mentions as pointing at *Septem* 375-652.

worse. But this complication cannot now perplex us: as we have said, he would not agree that his own critique is still worse, or bad at all. His possession of such a conscience is further attested, in prophetic and direct contradiction of the "botcher" doctrine, by two ancient authorities[1] who could read all his ninety-odd plays. "Suppose next", remarks Socrates in Plato,[2] "someone came to Sophocles or Euripides and told them that he knew how to compose immense speeches on a slight theme and *vice versa*; that he could at will write declamations full of pathos or (just the opposite) terrible and threatening, and other such feats: suppose he imagined that by putting these on the stage he was offering us tragic poetry?" Phaedrus replies: "The two poets you name, Socrates, would no doubt laugh (in their turn) at a man who thought tragedy anything but a combination of the said elements that made them appropriate to one another and to the whole work." Dio Chrysostom[3] writes of "Euripides' sagacity and ever-present care to exclude all unconvincing and negligent detail, handling his material expertly".[4]

The third and last of these revealing personal touches must, as was hinted above, be cited less confidently because not peculiar to him: a licence in handling traditional, if not genuinely historical, data that at times becomes free invention. Minor instances are common in Greek poetry: to alter some less important detail of legend was little or nothing. But fundamental falsifications, like Aeschylus' history of the Delphic oracle at the opening of his *Eumenides*, are rare; when Pindar essays such hardihood, he does not indeed apologize—that would be folly—but gives us to understand that by some means he has found a version more authoritative and better calculated to edify. Euripides equals anyone in the importance of his changes and surpasses all in *sang-froid*. His boldest[5] invention has a magnificent excuse. The last scene of *Heracles* becomes entirely and nobly human. He depicts Theseus as giving his friend asylum and promise of honours and burial in Athens, despite the familiar legend

---

[1] See, however, pp. 42–47 below. Plato himself, for all his eminence, and Dio, for all his deep interest in tragedy, cannot persuade us that Euripides was in this respect to be permanently bracketed with Sophocles.

[2] *Phaedrus* 268c, D.   [3] LII. 11.

[4] So Verrall (*Essays on Four Plays* of *Euripides* (1905), p. 110), after noting that the Chorus of *Helen* cannot have known a certain detail to which the poet nevertheless makes them refer, proceeds: "In some writers this contradiction might pass for an oversight.... But Euripides was, as the nature of his work required, punctilious about such things." A pleasant symptom of this scrupulousness is that messengers frequently explain how they got their facts (e.g., *Heracleidae* 847 f., 856; *Phoen.* 1139 f.).

[5] Moses Chorenensis, however, gave the palm to Euripides' earliest play, the *Peliades*: "in iis quae de Medea refert extremos mentiendi fines attingit", with details of Pelias' destruction. (Nauck², pp. 550 f.)

that Heracles was burnt upon Mt. Oeta and ascended in the flame to Heaven. To Medea's story he added a crowning horror, that she slew her children; in the *Bacchae* Pentheus' death is wrought by his own mother. With genealogies, too, Euripides allows himself freedom in order to suit a momentary purpose,[1] his most remarkable exploit here being alteration of the saga in *Ion*, where his statement concerning the settlement of Ionia contradicts Pherecydes and Hellanicus.[2] These innovations seem to have set a fashion,[3] which naturally produced in time plays that were all invention. Finally we may here note another feature, though in this connexion it deserves little emphasis. Euripides not only writes whole plays, the *Heracleidae* and a *Supplices*, to glorify Athens and perhaps to rebut[4] the common charge that she is a tyrant-city: he also inserts elaborate mention of Athens in dramas but slightly concerned with her, such as the stanzas in *Medea* (824–45) and an aetiological passage about the Athenian Pitcher-Feast addressed to the Argive Iphigenia by her Argive brother (*Iph. Taur.* 947–54); slighter examples are numerous. Clearly, despite the bitter though indirect rebukes that he did not spare his countrymen, he was a zealous patriot, and used tragedy to instruct and brace his hearers.

The few but certain evidences thus collected as to his own conception of his art are valuable because we now see what we must omit from any list of his faults that we may presume to draw up. He meant these things, quite deliberately; they are not slips or concessions to other people's taste: he is evolving a type of "tragedy", and they are part of his results. We must not call Euripides a bad playwright because, in the words of an ancient critic, he mixes physical science into the legends.[5] It is rightly agreed that we should estimate an artist by his best productions, not his worst: he who published *Ellen Irwin* stands nevertheless next to the two greatest among English poets. Euripides also has left some work that we

---

[1] Schol. *Hec.* 3: πολλάκις δὲ ὁ Εὐριπίδης αὐτοσχεδιάζει ἐν ταῖς γενεαλογίαις, ὡς καὶ ἑαυτῷ ἐνίοτε ἐναντία λέγειν.

[2] *Ion* 1581–9: cp. Schmid, *ut sup.*, pp. 539, 541 n. 1 (Pherecydes fr. 155 Jac., Hellanicus fr. 48 Jac.).

[3] Ar. *Poet.* 1451ᵇ19 ff.: οὐ μὴν ἀλλὰ καὶ ἐν ταῖς τραγῳδίαις ἐν ἐνίαις μὲν ἐν ᾗ δύο τῶν γνωρίμων ἐστὶν ὀνομάτων, τὰ δὲ ἄλλα πεποιημένα, ἐν ἐνίαις δὲ οὐδ' ἕν, οἷον ἐν τῷ Ἀγάθωνος Ἀνθεῖ· ὁμοίως γὰρ ἐν τούτῳ τά τε πράγματα καὶ τὰ ὀνόματα πεποίηται, καὶ οὐδὲν ἧττον εὐφραίνει. Aristotle alludes to his own time, with the implication that such writing began with Agathon, Euripides' junior and follower.

[4] So Schmid, p. 417. An Athenian statesman told his countrymen τυραννίδα ἔχετε τὴν ἀρχήν (Cleon *ap.* Thuc. III. 37. 2).

[5] Schol. *Or.* 981: τὰ φυσικὰ τοῖς μυθικοῖς καταμίγνυσιν. A curious parallel occurs in Hardy's *A Pair of Blue Eyes* (chap. XXII), where Henry Knight, while clinging to a precipice in sore peril, experiences a magnificent geological reverie.

shall condemn. But our verdict will not rest upon a doctrinaire objection to this or that type of drama, only upon a demonstration that by writing a given passage he has injured his own play (whatever its type): has belied or forgotten the basic assumptions of the very work that contains it. We shall not object to the drunken Heracles of *Alcestis*, for that play is meant throughout as tragicomedy; we shall object to Medea's dragon-chariot, because her utter lack of help and friends is by the poet himself emphasized again and again as vital to her situation.

By this time it has become clear: first, that to gain the proper standpoint certain Euripidean qualities must be considered, some of which, perhaps, have not hitherto been examined directly and closely enough; secondly, that the stumbling-blocks—things that Euripides was justified in doing but which happen to repel us—must be distinguished from bad work, as described a moment ago.

In the first place, his prologues[1] bore us. They were vivaciously ridiculed in his lifetime by Aristophanes, whose famous "little oil-flask" passage[2] means that they are dull and machine-made; ages later one of his most distinguished successors, Corneille, censured them in his *Discours sur le poème dramatique*. Some few are very good: that of *Medea* was often praised in antiquity, and Ennius translated it. But the charge is on the whole sound. Euripides was content to write (as is often said) a mere play-bill, to tell his hearers baldly what legend he will treat and at what point therein the action of his play opens: he usually declines the trouble of investing this account with charm, depth, or pungency. Aristophanes' distaste was shared, and speedily produced vigorous reaction. Our text of *Iphigenia at Aulis* has two prologues: the first (unfinished) contains sixty-six iambic lines, the second (with no apparent gaps) nearly a hundred anapaestic lines. All agree that the former is Euripides' work, and that the second was written by a later poet, whether Euripides' son,[3] when producing the whole trilogy after his father's death, or some unknown fourth-century writer. The anapaestic prologue is a first-rate piece of work, vastly better than its companion; but, since both survived in the epoch of Alexandrian scholarship, both were admitted to the Euripidean *corpus*. Obviously a change in fashion must be discerned. "We recognize here a development in prologue-technique that begins in the fourth

[1] That is, of course, the explanatory prologues, prologues in the modern sense. His πρόλογοι as Aristotle uses the term—all that precedes the *parodos* of the Chorus (*Poet.* 1452ᵇ19 f.)—are, as wholes, often admirably composed.
[2] *Frogs* 1177–1247. The third Life calls him ἐν τοῖς προλόγοις ὀχληρός.
[3] So Murray, following Bremi (*Philologische Beiträge*, Zürich, 1819): see his *apparatus*.

century at the earliest and in opposition to Euripides aims at a stronger dramatic enlivenment of the prologue; but, not satisfied with restoring the Sophoclean conversation-prologue in iambic trimeters, seeks to heighten still more the dramatic verve by introducing anapaests instead of iambics."[1]

Secondly, "the god from the machine" has long been a byword as a shameless expedient whereby a playwright "cuts the knot" and flounders out of a complication in which his own incompetence has ensnared him. Anyone who forces his plot to conclude "satisfactorily" after all with a violent jerk, unjustified[2] by the preceding action, deserves ruthless condemnation—if he writes tragedy or comedy. His method becomes defensible only if he writes melodrama or farce: such plays, by their very nature, disregard probability and logical development if they can thus create exciting or laughable situations. Genuine tragedies in Greek that employ the vicious *deus ex machina* are hard to find: only *Philoctetes*, in fact—written not by the "botcher" but by Sophocles—provides a perfectly unquestionable instance. That, we must grant, is pressing a definition rigorously; and some Euripidean works may be thought to supply examples no less unmistakable. Deities give a new turn to the action in *Hippolytus*, *Ion*, *Iphigenia in Tauris*, *Helen*, and *Orestes*. Let us consider them.

Hippolytus contains the weakest case. Artemis appears partly for the sake of her beautiful farewell to the hero and her aetiological prophecy. She does indeed affect the action, by revealing to Theseus the machinations of Aphrodite and so causing the reconciliation of father and son. But this could well have been done by the Chorus-Leader or the Nurse; and we may naturally conclude that Euripides gave her this function because in any case he needed her for the other two. *Iphigenia* and *Helen* offer *prima facie* perfect instances of the irrational *deus*, and must be conceded as such to anyone unconvinced by what is to be said later of adventure-melodramas, in which hairbreadth escapes are not merely permissible but almost compulsory. *Ion* will puzzle us if we are the slaves of labels: it has a good many melodramatic touches, but whatever we think of Xuthus and the Paedagogus, the anguish and crime of Creusa are authentically tragic, and Ion's determination to wrest the truth from

---

[1] Schmid, p. 641. He compares the anapaestic prologue of *Rhesus*, which he assigns to the fourth century.

[2] Butcher, *Aristotle's Theory of Poetry and Fine Art* (1895), p. 332, writes: "The weakness of the *Dénouement*, as compared with the complication, of many Greek tragedies is the direct result of the controlling tradition of the plot." This is demonstrably untrue of some plays; in any case it does not excuse the poets for having chosen a subject that they cannot handle.

Apollo himself in his own temple makes tragedy of a noble and most unusual sort. Are we to say that it lasts for but a moment and is then horribly obliterated by the apparition of Athena? Her intervention to save the face of her abject brother, disgusting or laughable according to the spectator's temperament, does (to be sure) most effectually force the action into a new path; and, if that is all, Athena may truly be dubbed an example of the irrational *deus*. But she does far more. The proposed action is averted, but that fiasco makes the tragedy of Ion. His god has utterly failed him: the happy lad who lived for worship and temple-service will henceforth pass his time as a prince of Athens with bitterness in his soul and a dream defiled. But the final play on our list, *Orestes*? Is not this a genuine example of the dramatic collapse labelled "god from the machine"? Verrall's demonstration of its badness[1] stands unanswerable by anyone who takes *Orestes* for a tragedy; those who read it as melodrama can accept Apollo with few qualms or none.

In any case, the importance often attached to this device as an element of tragedy is a crude and careless generalization, due mostly to the Horatian dictum: "Let no god take part, unless a knot arrives that is worthy of his steel."[2] In fifth-century drama, as we have seen, knot-cutting pure and simple is hardly ever his task. We moderns, no doubt, yawn over his aetiological passages, unless they are vital to the action as in the *Eumenides*, or exquisitely written as in *Hippolytus*: Orestes' account of the circumstances in which the Athenian Pitcher-Feast arose, and similar explanations of ritual, seem to us irrelevant oddities. But their first hearers relished these digressions, which shed upon their everyday life a glow from the heroic age. Nor are the gods satisfied with such lore. They reveal the future of those persons whose fortunes we have been watching with tense sympathy, admiration, or alarm: this maimed outcast bears in his hand the key to Troy's overthrow; this heart-broken old hero shall yet meet his glorious son upon a far island in the Euxine Sea. Aristotle points to prophecy as part of their true function in the very sentence that condemns the knot-cutting. "The solution of a plot should spring from the plot itself, not from the machine as in *Medea* . . . the

---

[1] *Four Plays*, pp. 256–64. Murray (*Euripides and his Age*, pp. 159 ff.), despite his subtlety and charm, remains for me unconvincing here. Without arguing the matter, which would be absurd after Verrall's discussion, let us merely note an admirable remark of Schmid (pp. 621 f.), that Orestes ought not to be satisfied by an external, mechanical, discharge after the pangs of conscience to which he confesses earlier (396, etc.).

[2] *Ars Poet.* 191 f.: *Nec deus intersit, nisi dignus vindice nodus inciderit*. Does Horace ever discuss a point of Greek scholarship without—to put it in language softened by affection—sorely puzzling us?

machine should be used for matters outside the play: either past events that a human being cannot know, or future events that need prediction or reporting; for we ascribe all-embracing sight to the gods."[1] This prophetic *deus* more than once undergoes a highly effective transformation, Euripides presenting us with a *homo ex machina*. Medea prophesies at the close exactly as does Athena or Dionysus; Eurystheus in the *Heracleidae*, Polymestor in *Hecuba*, are mysteriously inspired by the horror of their doom and utter stern, even ghastly, bodements.[2] (We should not, however, apply this description to such rescuers as Peleus in *Andromache* and the Pythia in *Ion*: their interventions are steps in the action.) Theseus in *Heracles* is magnificently exceptional. He prophesies concerning the future cult of his comrade in Attica: he also preserves him, not by any mechanical solution but by his noble rescue of a soul that looks upon itself as damned.[3]

A third stumbling-block is Euripides' sardonic piquancy, a feature of his wit that must not be confused with the others. It has no connexion with his great influence on Middle and New Comedy, which manifested itself in romantic themes and plot-devices; or with his own comic[4] or quasi-comic dramaturgy, seen in *Alcestis* and *Helen*; hardly even with his many touches of unsubtle fun. An utterance is sardonic if it voices an aloof and refined gusto for the absurd, spoiling an attitude, pricking the bubble of conceit, pomposity, or self-deception. Euripides is a master here, no less than elsewhere; and anyone unable to share this mood of his, or at least to recognize its presence, cannot truly appreciate him. Never giving his love or hatred unreservedly to any man or woman of his plays, not even to Orestes, not even to Phaedra, he stands always on one side, ready to inflict at the unlikeliest moment a sudden cruel touch, light as a velvet paw felt and withdrawn in a flash. So Poseidon suddenly makes a fool of himself, ruler of the sea or not. When his niece Athena, whom he should know by this time for an inveterate schemer, asks "Will you agree with whatever I desire?" he blandly replies: "Certainly!" then, recovering

---

[1] *Poet.* 1454ᵃ37 ff.

[2] Even the Cyclops pronounces three lines (688 ff.) of prophecy, but they move us little, being a clear "quotation" from the *Odyssey*.

[3] Schmid finely remarks (p. 444): "Es ist ein schöner Gedanke, das Wunder des Deus ex machina durch die rein menschliche Auswirkung von Liebe und Dankbarkeit zu ersetzen."

[4] It must not be forgotten that later ages used "comic" in a quite different sense both from ours and from that familiar in the fifth century B.C. When the hypothesis of *Orestes* says κωμικωτέραν ἔχει τὴν καταστροφήν it means "the play has a happy ending". Dante called his poem *La Divina Commedia* for the same reason, as he explains in a letter to Can Grande della Scala.

his caution, adds: "But of course I cannot know your mind. Have you come to help Greeks or Trojans?" (*Tro.* 62 ff.). A pretty start for a heart-breaking tragedy! That is Euripides' peculiar *espièglerie*: he constantly jars us, and we less nimble readers seem condemned to shut our ears or revile this Puckish sprite as a blunderer; but the dilemma is a delusion. Just so the first audiences of *Arms and the Man* were baffled by the collapse of Sergius Saranoff: before long they learned better. Again, Iphigenia, pining far from Greece and remembering the half-casual farewell that she gave her brother and sister, is made to recall a sentence even more silly than pathetic: 'I won't kiss you good-bye, for you'll see me next year', as we may paraphrase it (*Iph. Taur.* 374 ff.). The brother on reaching man's estate shows the same stiffness. Considering that he has just tried to kill Menelaus' wife (his own aunt) and come within an ace of slaughtering their daughter Hermione, we must call him surprisingly genteel when, commanded by Apollo to marry her, he accepts this *fiat* only if etiquette is maintained: "See, I release Hermione from slaughter and consent to wed her whenever her father gives me her hand", a charming rebuke to the divine matchmaker (*Or.* 1671 f.). A delicious little flick at the audience itself occurs in the conversation between Iphigenia and her dupe, the barbarian Thoas. She asks him to have the Greek captives manacled; he replies that such precaution is needless. She rejoins: πιστὸν Ἑλλὰς οἶδεν οὐδέν, whereupon Thoas exclaims: ἴτ' ἐπὶ δεσμά, πρόσπολοι.[1] The piquancy is hard to translate, as it resides in the briskness wherewith he accepts, in resolved metre, the charge of utter baseness that she brings against her countrymen: perhaps "Never trust a Greek." "Out with the handcuffs, you fellows!" But to labour over such effects is to catch fireflies that turn dull in the fingers. So let us not scrutinize the talk between Electra and her peasant-husband,[2] who so drily reveals his opinion of her trials as a genteel housewife "in reduced circumstances"; or the unsurpassed scene (*Medea* 445–622) where Jason, that insufferable blend of paladin and confidence-man, plunges into fit after fit of suicidal ineptitude; or the many other[3] dexterities of a subtle comic spirit.

[1] *I.T.* 1204 f. Another joke on the audience, not as scoundrels but as connoisseurs of drama, may be found in *I.T.* 660–71. It is very clever but would become tedious if worked out here. (It hinges on the *prima facie* stupidity of τὰ γὰρ ... ἐπιστροφή τις ἦν.)

[2] *El.* 54–81, 355. Not only is he worth fifty times his wife and her family put together: he is a delightfully sardonic character. One resents his dismissal at the close with "a lot of money" (1287).

[3] The quaintnesses of Cadmus and Tiresias, Alcmena's mistake, and Hector's grumbles about *The Sheep-Fold News* have been mentioned earlier. Though less subtle, they belong to the same class. The well-known σὺν παρθένῳ τε καὶ προθυμίᾳ ποδός

Further, these quirks of sardonic imagination at times illumine the action. In the Aulid *Iphigenia* Achilles, despite his preliminary sabre-rattling and his promise to prevent the princess even at the last moment from accepting her death, nevertheless assists at the sacrifice with serviceable agility.[1] *Helen* is steeped in the spirit of burlesque, which may be defined as the sardonic grown frolicsome and accordingly more obvious, so that the play hardly needs our scrutiny at this point. But *Electra* is a very different matter. It was precisely because Schlegel failed to catch the mood in which this whole play was conceived and written that he arrived at his famous verdict "*Electra* is perhaps the very vilest"[2] of Euripides' plays. Of course the poet intended a drama of his own: why copy another? The familiar scene is peopled by figures grown unfamiliar. Electra extols Orestes' courage before they begin their horrible enterprise,[3] but he does not "act up" to her, showing no touch of tragic heroism, slaying Aegisthus by treachery, and collapsing when the two murders are achieved. His sister, too, is a sardonic study, as we have seen, and Clytaemnestra offers the most curious, not to say the most engaging, novelty of all.[4] The interview between mother and daughter is Euripides' best feat of attitude-spoiling. Those who imagine tragedy to consist of attitude-striking will vehemently protest, as did Schlegel: they are lamentably numerous, and include far greater names, among them Dryden and Byron. Orestes' adventure among the Taurians shows him even less dashing at the outset—"let us sail back home again" (*Iph. Taur.* 102 f.)—but by aid of Pylades he rapidly changes to a man valiant and resolute: what is more, a realist like his creator; when all seems lost, he utters a grim epitaph on himself (711 ff.). "The prophet Phoebus has lied to me, fraudulently sending me as far from Greece as he could, in shame of his earlier oracles. To him I entrusted my all, obeyed his word, slew my mother and now myself die in requital." This tone is deepened by many allusions to the image of Artemis that Orestes and Pylades have come to steal. In Orestes' mouth the phrase "goddess' image" becomes a sort of incantation: this object is mentioned twenty-six times in all and grows tiresome, perhaps faintly ridiculous.

Fourth and last of the stumbling-blocks is Euripides' fondness for melodrama. The frequent implication that melodrama is vulgar contains this much truth, that it is difficult for melodrama to be anything else.

(*Phoen.* 1430), though not excised by Murray, is miserably inferior to all these, and must surely be interpolated. [1] *I.A.* 919–74, 1429 ff., 1568 f.
[2] *Ut sup.*, IX (vol. V, p. 162): "Um nicht ungerecht zu sein, muß ich noch bemerken, daß die Elektra vielleicht das allerschlechteste Stück des Euripides ist."
[3] *El.* 274–6, 418 f., 524–6. [4] See my *Greek Tragedy*, pp. 254 f.

Such work not only may, but must, be exciting. Yet it must not sink into unrelieved violence and hysteria, or it ceases to be art. Nor must it ascend into tragedy and thus lose its essence. Tragedy consists of great situations created by strong characters, melodrama of thrilling situations into which violent characters are pushed. In tragedy the situations are rationally and skilfully built up; in melodrama they are thrown up by means insufficient, absurd, or incredible. In *Othello* we admire a superb melodrama, produced by a villain of incredibly perfect wickedness and a woman of incredibly uncharacteristic dishonesty: both Iago and his wife would be impossible in a genuine tragedy. Like Shakespeare, Euripides was a great melodramatist as well as a great tragedian. If we keep this duality in mind without dainty nervousness we shall accept *Orestes*, Apollo and all, no less enthusiastically than *Hippolytus* or the *Bacchae*, just as we place *Othello* on a level with *Macbeth*, though not in the same category. That is, we shall enjoy Euripides' work far more and cure ourselves of some grave errors concerning his art.

Again and again he makes the spectator jump. Sometimes it is a gesture, as when (*Or.* 1068) Orestes draws his sword for suicide,[1] or an abrupt vital intervention, as when (722–8) he espies Pylades running to his aid, and when (in another play) Menelaus' defiance is checked by the messenger who in the middle of a line announces: "Agamemnon, your daughter is here!"[2] Sometimes it is a startling word at the end of a line otherwise simple enough. Clytaemnestra, now aware of her husband's murderous intent, reveals her knowledge to him somewhat thus:

> *Clyt.*: My dear, answer whatever I ask you like a gentleman.
> *Ag.*: No orders are necessary: I am all ears.
> *Clyt.*: Your daughter, my daughter, do you mean to . . . *kill?*

He certainly starts, as his gasp shows.[3] Equally melodramatic is Helen's method of breaking dire news to her own husband. After hearing the tale of his previous tribulations she remarks: "Alas, alas! A long, long time is this you tell of. You have escaped all that and come hither to be *butchered*."[4] She has already given us a good thrill, but a thrill of amusement, in a passage (*Helen* 528–45) that can be not improperly thus summarized. 'What glorious news! Menelaus is alive! Ah, when will you come to me? You would find a loving heart to welcome you. (*Enter Menelaus: she*

---

[1] Note ὡς ὁρᾷς, the absence of a final moralizing line, and Pylades' ἐπίσχες.
[2] *I.A.* 414. The ἀντιλαβή, which would mean little in a modern work, of course doubles the shock.
[3] *Ibid.* 1129 ff. His reply begins with ἔα *extra metrum*.
[4] *Helen* 777 f.; σφαγάς at the end is unsurpassable in its kind.

recoils.) You horrible man, let me alone!' The whole play, indeed, is compact of thrills, usually bogus and therefore amusing. Perhaps the best befalls the soldier who hurries in exclaiming: "Menelaus, your wife has ascended to heaven. . . . Oh, good morning, madam. So you were here all the time! No more of such practical jokes, please: we had quite enough trouble over you at Troy" (605-21). *Iphigenia in Tauris*, too, has many sensational strokes, equally good but nearly all terribly serious. Euripides achieves the finest *coup de théâtre* in Greek drama, perhaps in all drama, when Pylades with such lightning speed fulfils his commission about the letter. We need not proceed to give a list, but one more beautiful little touch (584-7) may be noted, though it is rather a postponed effect, that will strike the hearer as he walks home discussing the play or when he awakes next morning. This same letter . . . why make Iphigenia unable to write? Why not depict her writing it at leisure some time during those years of exile, preparing it "in case" (that melancholy phrase), rewriting it again and again like her father before that frightful dawn at Aulis, with ever dwindling hope? Euripides has brought in this nameless man purely for a microscopic drama in the past: "a certain captive wrote it in pity for me, deeming that not my hand was to slay him, but the law".

That is tragic indeed, not melodramatic. Types of drama are not wooden boxes, and we shall have no misgiving when they shade into one another: all we need is to feel and realize the dominant tone.[1] Here only those elements are in view that produce a momentary, if powerful, effect and lead to nothing further. Such an exciting play as *Medea* lies therefore outside our present discussion. So, almost entirely, does the *Troades*. But it contains an excellent mechanical device that never fails and is therefore much favoured in melodrama. Some definite little occurrence is promised and is later shown, whereupon the audience invariably quivers for a moment with satisfaction. So here: that the trumpet is mentioned beforehand[2] adds something to the awful finale. Again, Euripides (not too neatly, it must be owned) bundles Andromache on board ship half an hour before everyone else so that Hecuba, not she, may utter the outburst over the little body of Astyanax lying in his father's war-stained buckler. The *Phoenissae* has many melodramatic scenes. Notable among

[1] Note the perfect discretion and adroitness wherewith Molière at the climax of *Tartuffe* makes the disillusioned Orgon "enter" on all-fours from beneath the table. Had he walked in, uttering his "un abominable homme" and the rest, he would have become a tragic figure, thus wrecking what is intended, and triumphantly succeeds, as high comedy.
[2] Vv. 1266 f. It is not mentioned later, but of course it sounds, probably at v. 1327.

them is that in which Polynices, unattended and sword in hand, enters his beleaguered native city crowded with foemen.[1]

Another method of heightening suspense is to make the alert auditor fear a sudden incidental[2] twist or "snag" that will frustrate the development he expects—and then spare him, to his amused relief. Here the pre-eminent master is Sophocles.[3] Euripides perhaps learned it from him: certainly he uses it less well. In the Taurian *Iphigenia* Orestes answers his sister's questions about people in Greece, and the sole interest of their talk for us lies in these two features of it: they must not flounder into realization that they are brother and sister; nevertheless they should hover, but hover naturally, around this, keeping the audience on tenterhooks. At one moment Euripides writes clumsily. She asks (535 ff.) whether Achilles still lives: a natural query, for she was lured to her death at Aulis by the pretext of marriage with him.

Iph.: And the son of Thetis the sea-nymph: lives he yet?
Or.: No. *In vain did he marry a wife at Aulis.*
Iph.: Aye, it was a trick, as they know who suffered thereby.
Or.: Who can you be? How accurately you ask of Greek affairs!
Iph.: I am of that country. While yet a child I was undone.

And their talk drifts away from the danger-point. But why does Orestes mention Aulis? He is not playing the game according to the rules. A dozen other facts about Achilles would leap to mind before that: for example 'it availed him nothing that his mother was immortal' would be rhetorically excellent. Orestes has inexpertly let one wheel slip over the edge, and Iphigenia must ignore the blunder. Much better is that passage in the First Messenger's speech, where Pylades is named but (as it

---

[1] Unfortunately we are prepared for it by Iocasta in the prologue (81–83). But her last line about this, the miserably flaccid ἥξειν δ' ὁ πεμφθείς φησιν αὐτὸν ἄγγελος, comes surely from an interpolator. Since, then, these lines are bad verse and bad drama, we may confidently delete them.

[2] An important adjective. The present contrivance must be distinguished from a plot that as a whole gradually assumes a shape and bearing quite other than those for which the spectator looks, because accustomed to certain situations and their traditional developments. The end of *Hecuba* and the end of the *Heracleidae* are good instances; *Heracles* is far more striking, like *A Doll's House*, *The Wild Duck*, *Arms and the Man*, to name but a few modern works. Such plays are revolutionary in technique as in thought; a play containing the expedient now in question may be thoroughly traditional.

[3] In sundry passages of *Oedipus Tyrannus* (for instance) he allows Oedipus and Iocasta to come perilously near saying what must prematurely reveal the truth. At such points he is merely exciting the audience by his virtuosity in driving close to the precipice without disaster; see 361, 558 (the pause), and 717–30 (with Sir John Sheppard's masterly note on 730).

"happens") not Orestes.[1] The latter name, if uttered, would make impossible the great recognition-scene; but of Pylades she knows nothing (915-22).

Sophocles, again, may have been the inventor of another ingenious device: a deliberately engineered hitch or check in the action. He complicates the movement of *Electra* so as to make possible the heroine's address to the supposed funeral urn of Orestes. Already in *Ajax* he handles the same instrument, rather less deftly: the sudden announcement, in a full "messenger's speech", that if Ajax survives this day all may yet be well, has no function beyond increasing the excitement and urgency of the search for him. More adroit and moving is Deianira's discovery, by a trivial accident, that the robe she has sent to Heracles carries poison. Euripides makes fine use of this "hitch-thrill". What power pervades that scene where Ion would slay Creusa but is halted by the priestess with the basket containing his birth-tokens, which we know must reveal that Creusa is his mother! But the poet determines to increase even such tension as this: Ion refuses to open the basket! During five lines we listen in unbearable bafflement ... then he changes his mind. The *Supplices* in its opening scene shows the appeal addressed to Athens and her king by Adrastus that the corpses of the slain champions be rescued for burial, and Theseus' stern refusal to involve his country in a Theban war by doing so. Yet Attic tradition proudly asserted that the rescue was performed; and this tragedy itself portrays that exploit. Then why make the king repel Adrastus? To carve out a place for his mother's magnificent protest. As early as *Rhesus* (161-90) he gave a rudimentary specimen of this method, in Dolon's reluctance to name the reward he seeks. The *Phoenissae* contains a clumsy and inept example (865-959). Tiresias, who cannot forget how he shone in *Oedipus Tyrannus* but has long passed his zenith, tells Creon that to him, not to Eteocles, he will reveal how Thebes may be saved. But having delivered a rigmarole about Oedipodean woes, he declares that after all he will not disclose the secret. Of course he is nevertheless cajoled into doing so, and we learn that Creon's own son must die. The finest thrill is of a quite different type: the superbly told duel between Polynices and Eteocles.

We are dealing here (let it be repeated) not with the normal tension or suspense that must of course mark every play, however simple; but with crisp ingenuities—what may be less politely called tricks. Only one other

[1] V. 321. Notice 248-51 and 499-504. On the last passage Weil writes: "Du même qu'au vers 251, le poëte nous fait croire ici que le nom d'Oreste va être prononcé, et il évite avec esprit cette révélation prématurée."

awaits notice. To intensify the spectator's excitement Euripides at times does not scruple actually to lead him astray in the prologue.[1] In *Hippolytus* Aphrodite, while prophesying the deaths of Phaedra and the prince, drops no hint that the sin to which she impels Phaedra will not be committed. In the *Bacchae* Dionysus implies (50 ff.) that he will lead his Maenads to victorious battle with the Theban army; this comes to nothing. Hermes in *Ion* falsely announces (72 f.) the successful concealment of Apollo's fatherhood.

Passing from this discussion of "tricks" we remark that Euripides is often melodramatic when producing even the normal type of dramatic tension. Schmid has usefully discussed this.[2] "Plot-construction that engenders suspense, surprise, emotion has everywhere more importance for the poet than characterization"; "where the poet by free invention gives novel turns to the traditional legends, this is done with a view to a more telling theatrical effect";[3] "the re-modellings are everywhere adopted not on any grounds of philosophy or views about the world, but in order to heighten theatrical effect". These statements, though here and there too sweeping, are a sound corrective of sundry opinions about Euripidean propagandism. When the poet means to preach or instruct, he makes his intention clear; we should beware of assuming such a purpose anywhere else, in those places especially where modern preoccupations suggest to us an elaborate innuendo. Schmid writes admirably on one frequent[4] melodramatic type, the rescue-play, noting[5] the role of accident (which he calls "a standing requisite"[6] in such work). He observes[7] that in the Taurian *Iphigenia* rescue is the leading interest, Euripides having invented the whole situation to this end, merely tying it on to the Orestes–Apollo story. But the fact most important for the corrective just mentioned is that the rescuer is often a god or goddess. During the Peloponnesian War Athens placed among her cult-gods the "Saviour" Asclepius: "the need of the last war-years has induced a strengthening of piety"; and in his latest plays Euripides depicts people whose plans bring no success and

---

[1] Cp. Wilamowitz, *Griechische Tragoedien übersetzt* (2nd ed.), vol. I, p. 109: "Der Prolog [of *Hipp.*] hat, wie öfter bei Euripides, die Absicht, die Spannung des Beschauers zu erhöhen, indem er ihn auf eine falsche Fährte lockt", etc.

[2] The quotations are from pp. 464, 765, 687.

[3] He points to Medea's child-murder, Heracles slaying his wife, Helen's Egyptian adventure, Agaue killing Pentheus, etc.

[4] He cites *Helen, Iphigenia in Tauris, Alcestis, Medea* (hardly a good example), *Heracles, Andromache* (two separate rescues), *Heracleidae, Supplices, Cyclops*, and lost dramas such as *Andromeda* and *Hypsipyle*.

[5] P. 702, n. 4. [6] P. 496.

[7] Pp. 503, 612.

who are extricated from their plight only by divine aid.[1] All this suggests[2] that Verrall went astray in his discussion of epilogues. His doctrine that Euripides' treatment of religion is a *reductio ad absurdum* involves belief that such divine epiphanies are shams, and meant to be so understood by the intelligent. This doctrine was rejected by nearly all students of our poet, though perhaps none succeeded in offering a satisfactory answer. But now it grows clear that Verrall mistook a skittle-alley for a billiard-table. The deities who disgusted him become acceptable, if not delightful, as glorified rescuers and comforting prophets at the close, not of august tragedies replete with theological significance and moral enlightenment, but of melodramas, tingling with peril, suspense, and headlong adventure, where logic, common sense, and probability may be flouted or forgotten. Apollo is no more open to attack in *Orestes* than he is in *The Winter's Tale*. When he chose, Euripides used deities for the ends of genuine tragedy, and in that sense Aphrodite and Artemis in *Hippolytus* are faultless; in those other works he employs his gods no less well for the purposes of "tragedy" that is so labelled only for an official reason.

In short, he was "a man of the theatre", whatever else he may have been. A man of the theatre, as such, is no more than a highly skilled technician, one who knows all the tricks of the trade. A most delightful trade it is, as the nineteenth-century French "well-made play" and a good many pieces written in our own time, by Mr. Noel Coward, for instance, prove to admiration. Critics who deride Scribe and Sardou prove nothing but their own inadequacy. They are slighting a gem like *Les Pattes de Mouche* because it is unworthy of Marivaux, not to say Molière: they might as well censure a triolet in comparison with an ode. The "man of the theatre" gives us two or three hours' pleasure by exquisite deftness in theatrical manipulation. But he may possess the genius and skill of a great, even a sublime, dramatist in addition to such far humbler skill. Shakespeare offers the most wonderful example of this versatility. Ibsen deliberately apprenticed himself to the French school of *la pièce bien faite*, showed himself in *Love's Comedy* an expert in that manner, and then moved steadily to the summits named *Hedda Gabler* and *Rosmersholm*. And further, a playwright may be magnificent, but no great "man of the theatre": such is Aeschylus, for reasons obvious enough. But Euripides, like Sophocles, is both. Sophocles has much less of the purely theatrical, but no prejudice whatever against it, as he showed in Teucer's altercation with Menelaus and in the scene where Aegisthus is suddenly shown Clytaemnestra's corpse. Euripides in his greater plenty exhibits more variation of

---

[1] P. 758. [2] Schmid himself makes no such comment.

dramatic manner as of dramatic excellence. These facts were recognized by ancient critics[1] and should be held firmly in mind. We must not think Euripides incapable of work artistically superficial or heavy-handed or meretricious; and we shall avoid asserting that "there are no stage villains in Greek tragedy".[2] When we observe[3] that in his later dramas people show their weakness by resorting to conspiracy instead of acting alone, we shall attribute this at least as readily to the desire of poet and spectator for theatrical sensation as to any profound sense of human failings in general or of the Peloponnesian War in particular.

When all has been said about Euripides' right to experiment and his legitimate subjectivity even in this most objective type of literature, there remain features that one condemns without hesitation because it seems impossible to imagine any purpose underlying them: they annoy us every time they confront us, but we never gain a glimmer of enlightenment, never realize what he would be at. We seem compelled to think them flaws in his own artistic being, like the knob in a pane of bottle-glass that distorts a little part of whatever passes in the street. We seem compelled ... but we should seek to diminish the irrational area by finding external causes that he could but partially overcome. Some were inherent in the conditions of the festival.

However magnificent the tragedy, however immense the effort of conception and execution, however varied the task of poetry, music and dance, mounting and rehearsal, the poet could expect but one performance. Some two hours, and *Agamemnon* itself, apparently, must begin to sink towards oblivion. That play met another fate, but Aeschylus had no reason to expect it.[4] Later playwrights did indeed find some prospect opening of a vogue through written copies and repeat-performances up

---

[1] Schol. Soph. *O.T.* 264: αἱ τοιαῦται ἔννοιαι οὐκ ἔχονται μὲν τοῦ σεμνοῦ· κινητικαὶ δέ εἰσι τοῦ θεάτρου· αἷς καὶ πλεονάζει Εὐριπίδης· ὁ δὲ Σοφοκλῆς πρὸς βραχὺ μὲν αὐτῶν ἅπτεται, πρὸς τὸ κινῆσαι τὸ θέατρον. Schol. Eur., for example *Tro.* 1: ὅλος ἐστὶ τοῦ θεάτρου ὁ Εὐριπίδης; *Or.* 128: ἔνιοι δέ φασι ταῖς δμωσὶ ταῦτα λέγειν, οἱ δὲ πρὸς τὸ θέατρον, ὃ καὶ ἄμεινον, ἐφελκυστικὸς γάρ ἐστιν ἀεὶ μᾶλλον τῶν θεατῶν ὁ ποιητής, οὐ φροντίζων τῶν ἀκριβολογούντων. One of the *Lives* (Dindorf, vol. I, p. 10), it must be owned, contradicts all this. It says that his association with Archelaus and Anaxagoras led him to tragedy: ὅθεν καὶ πλέον τι φρονήσας εἰκότως περιίστατο [turned his back on] τῶν πολλῶν οὐδεμίαν φιλοτιμίαν περὶ τὰ θέατρα ποιούμενος. διὸ τοσοῦτον αὐτὸν ἔβλαπτε τοῦτο ὅσον ὠφέλει τὸν Σοφοκλέα. He *was* a "highbrow", but only in certain moods, momentary though frequent.
[2] Murray, *Greek Studies* (1946), p. 14. It is enough to mention Lycus in *Heracles* and Menelaus in *Andromache*.   [3] Cp. Schmid, p. 767, n. 1.
[4] After his death Athens decreed that anyone who wished might revive plays of his for competition with the new tragedies.

and down Attica[1] or even elsewhere: Aeschylus himself brought out his *Persae* a second time, at Syracuse. But normally a dramatist could look for publicity so ephemeral that even in those great days much flashy work[2] must have been written by aspirants not for immortality but for congratulations, a dinner like Agathon's (if they were so lucky), and a few weeks of heads turning in the street. And, more to the purpose, why has but one complete trilogy even of the Three Masters been preserved? The works that so closely accompanied *Oedipus Tyrannus* and *Hippolytus*—where are they? Apparently they were too poor for editors and copyists to trouble with them long. The conclusion is that a tragedian threw all his might into one play and qualified for the Dionysiac festival by dashing off two "fillers" in a week apiece. The prize won, these makeweights gradually sank from sight. Once only did gigantic power defy this suction. The *Eumenides* does not equal *Agammenon*, but none the less has its own glory; and these two have kept their associate permanently afloat: the *Choephoroe*, a much weaker piece. Lack of merit no doubt explains many disappearances; but other causes were at work. Most obvious is the difficulty of Aeschylus' vocabulary even for the next generation. Another is that passion for the Trojan War and the Oedipus story whereby editors and schoolmasters were possessed. A tragedy on one or other of these had thrice the chance of survival open to plays on less familiar themes: hardly otherwise can we understand why *Hecuba* and the *Phoenissae* were preserved and lavishly annotated in preference to *Andromeda* and *Phaethon*. There would also be a tendency to favour works that glorified Athens: the *Eumenides* and *Oedipus Coloneus* (little as they needed such aid), the *Heracleidae, Heracles,* and Euripidean *Supplices*.

A second condition laid upon playwrights by the official presentation was use of a chorus. Aeschylus, so far from being hampered thereby, found in it a magnificent means to deepen, to universalize, his tragedy; Sophocles makes distinguished use of it, but we can believe that had there been no chorus his works would have been equally fine and not essentially different. Euripides (so far as his extant works are concerned) stood in like case only when he composed the *Bacchae*, whose chorus, if not vital to the action, is yet deeply interested, being in this regard on a level with those of *Agamemnon* and *Philoctetes*. Elsewhere his temper and (despite their variety) his methods made the chorus embarrassing. He never fully accommodated himself to it: even in the *Bacchae* its songs offer hard

[1] At the Rural Dionysia. For more on this topic see Haigh and Pickard-Cambridge, *The Attic Theatre* (3rd ed.), pp. 71–77.
[2] Cp. *Frogs* 89–97.

puzzles now and then.[1] His discomfort is visible, occasionally distressing. He often neglects these supernumeraries, merely giving them at intervals songs that have faint relevance or none, and allowing their leader two or three commonplace iambics. When they should intervene, they do so perfunctorily or not at all. Even the *dramatis personae* can find them a nuisance, as when in *Orestes* (140–86) Electra vainly seeks to prevent them from awaking her patient. The poet more than once turns them right out of the *orchestra* to make way for scenes that they must not witness. It should not surprise us that he nevertheless uses two choruses in both *Hippolytus* (61–72) and *Iphigenia at Aulis* (590–7): the huntsmen of the former and the soldiers of the latter[2] would be there in any case, and Euripides pleasantly gives them a little song apiece instead of letting them stand about as mutes. He even makes the huntsmen later join with the official chorus in a lyric: valiant efforts to silence them have been made by scholars who will not condone such behaviour, but the text refutes them.[3]

The third and last limitation imposed by the festival arrangements calls for longer study. Since each trilogy with its satyric companion filled one morning, the trilogy of *A* would be about as long as *B*'s, and all the six tragedies would tend to have much the same bulk. Aristotle implies as much, though vaguely. "The limit of length in relation to dramatic competition and sensuous presentment, is no part of artistic theory. For had it been the rule for a hundred tragedies to compete together, the performance would have been regulated by the water-clock,—as indeed we are told was formerly done."[4] The average length of a Euripidean play is 1370 lines; disregarding *Rhesus* (often thought spurious) and *Cyclops*, 1431 lines.[5] It would be foolish to set up any precise arithmetical standard, because stage-business without words must have varied from play to play, and because a work containing a large amount of lyrics may well have needed more time than a work filling the same number of lines

---

[1] See pp. 67–70 below.

[2] *I.A.* 590 ff. Cp. Murray in his *apparatus*.

[3] *Hipp.* 1102–10, 1120–30. The participles are masculine. Kranz (*Stasimon* (1933), p. 222) will have it that Euripides forgot his chorus was female. Jebb (on *Oed. Col.* 1016 f.) remarks with no sign of dismay that in *Hipp.* 1105 "the masc. sing. is used by the leader of a female chorus".

[4] *Poet.* 1451^{a}6–9 (tr. Butcher). On the first six words Bywater notes: "In actual practice the length of the play is determined by the conditions of the public performances (ἀγῶνες) in which it will be presented on the stage; the time it is to occupy there is fixed by custom and convention rather than theory."

[5] Though *Agamemnon* contains 1673 lines its two companions are so short that the average length of the three is but 1265 lines.

but containing fewer lyrics. Nevertheless dramas that markedly desert the average invite scrutiny. The two longest, at least,[1] need not puzzle us. The *Phoenissae* (1766 lines) is notoriously full of actors' interpolations, added for non-competitive performance, no doubt. *Oedipus Coloneus* (1779 lines) was not presented until after Sophocles' death; and that diffuseness in which it differs from his other works may well mean lack of revision. The other side of this matter holds far more interest. A playwright must often find that his piece when finished proves much shorter than usual. It need be none the worse. Shaw's *Man of Destiny* reveals perfectly his wit, adroitness in construction, knowledge of character; Mr. Coward's sketches are often masterpieces: these are but the most distinguished specimens of a whole class, the one-act play familiar in our time. But it was unknown in Euripides' day. If after working on a tragedy for the Dionysiac theatre he found that he had "finished too soon", what was to be done? Why not show it at a private performance[2] in Aspasia's house or Agathon's or his own, with no rule as to length, no competitors, and (by the Muses!) above all no chorus, to a select audience who would appreciate the novel point of view, the esoteric witticism, the exquisitely inconsistent character? Sooner or later that audience would exclaim: "Why not make this too charming piece suitable for Dionysus? You really *must*!" The poet would shake his head . . . at first. "Suitable" would mean alterations perhaps, certainly additions; and are not substantial additions to a completed play artistically impossible?[3]

Can we gain from this more light upon sundry flaws[4] in his extant work? Certainly *Medea*, so rightly praised and so rightly censured, becomes thus (and only thus) completely intelligible from start to finish.[5]

---

[1] The length of *Orestes* (1693 lines) is harder to explain. Murray says: "nonnulla interpolata videntur ab histrionibus"; but it is unlikely that there is much of that kind. One can but guess, for example that Euripides thought (as well he might): 'I never did better. Not a line goes out!' and supplied two unusually short "fillers" to accompany it.

[2] See below, pp. 118, 162 and *Class. Philol.*, vol. XXV, no. 3, pp. 217 ff. ("'Episodes' in Old Comedy"). For a similar idea about *Macbeth*, and for possible *contaminatio* in that play, see *The Times Literary Supplement*, May 11, 1951, p. 295.

[3] Ar. *Poet.* 1451^{b}37 ff.: ἀγωνίσματα γὰρ ποιοῦντες καὶ παρὰ τὴν δύναμιν παρατείναντες μῦθον πολλάκις διαστρέφειν ἀναγκάζονται τὸ ἐφεξῆς. (See Bywater *ad loc.*, and cp. schol. *Phoen.* 88: τὰ γὰρ τῆς Ἰοκάστης παρελκόμενά εἰσι καὶ ἕνεκα τοῦ θεάτρου ἐκτέταται.) Incidentally, we note that παρὰ τὴν δύναμιν proves Aristotle a sadly mechanical critic of drama: who can say what are the possibilities of a story until it has been treated by a master-playwright?

[4] And upon the reasons for a whole play being what it is: quite excellent, perhaps? Verrall (*Four Plays*, pp. 43–133) uses this idea of a private performance to explain not only certain details of *Helen*, but the light tone that pervades the whole.

[5] Cp. Verrall, *ibid.*, pp. 125–30.

Critics have condemned the Chorus as obtrusive; they have seldom lamented that these superfluous ladies have scarcely anything to say. Amid their twittering of "Lackaday!" and "Who would be a parent?" one brief passage stands out like an orchid among buttercups: the unforgettable Praise of Attica (824–45). Originally there was no chorus at all: how could a group of Corinthian women without protest watch preparations to murder their king and his daughter? When Euripides found himself forced to admit them and dash off lyrics for them, he fetched out and used, to enliven the affair, a few magnificent lines, written perhaps years earlier, that had nothing to do with his play. Nothing, that is, till Aegeus also was admitted to it, ambling in with his very transparent enigma from the Delphic oracle, a king of Athens who does little to maintain that city's renown for cleverness, and is rebuked by Aristotle as useless and irrational.[1] Useless? Does he not save the situation? Medea has declared in set terms (376–94) that her complete triumph can be secured only if some sure refuge is discovered, and discovered promptly. But how is Aegeus needed by her who commands a chariot sent by the Sun-God himself, her grandfather, and drawn (we gather)[2] by winged snakes? Aristotle's objection to this opportune though ostentatious equipage is amusingly mild: that it does not arise out of the action.[3] So momentous a resource clashes ruinously with the repeated assertion of Medea's helpless isolation. Euripides has sorely injured a fine tragedy in his effort to give it the average length.[4] If it be objected that her possession of strange and deadly poison also conflicts with her helplessness, the answer is that poison was traditionally her expedient, a fixed attribute of Medea, and that using it would fail to give her what she seeks: not merely revenge but revenge with impunity. The original version depicted Medea fighting to the end with her own weapons: courage, poison, cleverness, power to handle men so diverse as Creon and Jason.[5] It closed with an utterly unheroic solution: a bargain between her and her husband

---

[1] *Poet.* 1461ᵇ19–21.

[2] From the Hypothesis.

[3] *Poet.* 1454ᵃ37 ff.: φανερὸν οὖν ὅτι καὶ τὰς λύσεις τῶν μύθων ἐξ αὐτοῦ δεῖ τοῦ μύθου συμβαίνειν, καὶ μὴ ὥσπερ ἐν τῇ Μηδείᾳ ἀπὸ μηχανῆς. Grillparzer in his *Medea*, despite a seeming desire to put in everything possible, omits both Aegeus and the magic chariot. A. Rivier stoutly defends the former as "une nécessité *dramatique* simple et indiscutable. Or cette nécessité est impliquée par l'existence du démon [Medea's θυμός] dont nous avons parlé." *Essai sur le tragique d'Euripide* (1944), p. 56.

[4] This need to pad, one may be pardoned for thinking, has produced even more than is required about Medea's agony over the child-murders.

[5] That Aegeus did not appear in the first version is made certain by the fact that immediately after our Aegeus-episode Medea says (798 f.) she has no ἀποστροφὴ κακῶν.

whereby she went off unmolested on surrendering the corpses of their children.[1]

Hecuba has been even more strongly affected. Its glaring lack of unity justifies suspicion that something odd happened before it reached its present shape.[2] Scrutiny brings out inconsistencies implying that the scene is at one time laid in Thrace, at another in the Troad. They cannot be destroyed by excision: nothing will serve but the present theory of a brief play afterwards violently expanded. No one else save Plautus in the *Poenulus* has ever laid the same action in two widely separated districts at the same time; and even he tumbled into this absurdity because he was "contaminating" two Greek comedies.[3] Euripides must have "contaminated" two plays of his own. A *Polyxena*, as we may call it, underlies our existing irrational text: "a drama complete in itself, full of pathos and tragedy, but brief—far too short for public performance, though eminently suitable for private presentation". Later a Polymestor play was added to secure something like the normal length (still only 1295 lines). Euripides himself made the addition: not only the new fiendishness of Hecuba proves this, but also the odd twist whereby Polymestor turns into what we have called Euripides' *homo ex machina*, revealing the horrible future to Hecuba and Agamemnon.

Alcestis, too, though it still has but 1163 lines, must surely have undergone this same procrustean treatment, more gently applied. Euripides padded it by depicting Alcestis' farewell twice: in the maid-servant's description (152–88) and in her own address to Admetus (280–325). Naturally he has made them quite dissimilar: the first conveys her passionate love and grief, the second is a frigid lecture. This difference has no dramatic import. We must not allege that her list of instructions to Admetus implies some heroic but subtle "management" based on profound understanding of his character: this would be quite inappropriate to a drama that (despite its theme) is kept dextrously superficial. That last fact shows us which of the two farewell passages was inserted later. It is the servant's speech, too deeply affecting to be in key with the rest. Concerning the *Heracleidae* it has been convincingly urged that Macaria's self-sacrifice and death were absent from the first version.[4] That they were

---

[1] A hint of this survives in 1375 ff., but in our text comes to nothing. Another occurs in the otherwise curious words of Aristophanes' hypothesis: ἐχωρίσθη δὲ 'Ιάσονος ....

[2] Most of what follows is a summary of J. A. Spranger's able article, "The Problem of the *Hecuba*" (*Class. Quart.*, vol. XXI (1927), pp. 154–8). The quotation is from p. 157.

[3] Cp. p. 180 below.

[4] By Professor J. H. McLean, *Amer. J. Phil.*, vol. LV (1934), pp. 197–224.

"added by a later and weaker hand"[1] may, however, be doubted. The writing strikes one as thoroughly Euripidean: this, considered together with the bad fit of the whole episode, strongly suggests that here again the poet has inflated his own work.[2]

The *Phoenissae* hardly allows a definite statement.[3] Apart altogether from the pretentious forcible-feeble stuff that has been lying at Euripides' door so scandalously all these centuries, there remains a good deal of tawdry writing that must be accepted as his if we would leave him a substantial amount of the whole. Its unwonted length has already been noted, and in view of undoubted interpolation must not be stressed. But the list of characters is comparatively immense: eleven, if we include the two messengers. Some of these, one feels, should be banished. Antigone has been so often chased in and out of the *Phoenissae* that one shrinks from harassing her again. But this is no place for her. The scene where she and the Paedagogus survey the besieging host is a languid attempt to whip up excitement. Her later appearances are certainly due to the enterprising hack who insisted on the finale where her burial of Polynices and departure with Oedipus into exile are impossibly combined. Of Tiresias, too, we should gladly be rid. When he enters with his usual dire oracle we feel like Menelaus (even more of an old stager[4] than the prophet) that "this idea is rather *vieux jeu*".[5] Yet stay he must, if we intend to keep the episode of Menoeceus' patriotic suicide. But when, our cup of woe already brim-full, Oedipus himself totters in, the exclamation "Uncle Tom Cobbleigh and all" rises inevitably to the lips. Oedipus (surely) is pushed forward by the hack aforesaid, who filched his trochaic farewell from Sophocles,[6] and probably the whole idea of Oedipus and Antigone in Attica. How much else is spurious? We can at least so regard the long conversation (696–783) between Creon and Eteocles, most of it stupid. But whatever lumps we tear out, this drama cannot be cured of its feverish falsetto tone, which makes it unfit for the cultivated group we have in mind. Here, as nowhere else, we appreciate a saying in the treatise *On the Sublime*, that Euripides, "being anything but naturally great, nevertheless often does violence to his own nature and forces it up to the

---

[1] Professor J. H. McLean, *ut sup.*, p. 207. McLean deals ably with the whole scene's obtrusiveness, but is less cogent when he attacks its internal qualities. For instance, σοφῶς κελεύεις (588) seems too good for an interpolator.

[2] Despite its present brevity. Murray's final line is numbered 1055; but the known "missing" fragments recorded by Murray suggest that we have lost a good deal.

[3] On the interpolations see J. U. Powell's edition.

[4] He appears in six of our thirty-two tragedies, Tiresias in four.

[5] *Helen* 1056: παλαιότης γὰρ τῷ λόγῳ γ' ἔνεστί τις.

[6] *Phoen.* 1758 ff.; *O.T.* 1524–30 (on which, however, see Pearson's note).

tragic pitch", lashing himself with his tail like Homer's lion.[1] Here for once in Greek we light upon a piece of bad Elizabethanism: it suggests Webster or Marlowe when far beneath their best.

The *Phoenissae*, then, belongs to those portions of Euripides' writing that are bad or at least unsatisfactory, not because of external conditions but through defects in his own artistic character or conscience. We shall set out these flaws in an order of rising importance.

First, then, come what may be termed Little Snags: tiny inconsistencies[2] or puzzles that are trivial enough but must vex both spectator and reader, as when Hamlet's sentence about the "undiscovered country" implies that he has forgotten meeting his father's ghost. Here are a few examples.

Cyclops 611. It is forgotten that the giant wears a one-eyed mask (174, 627, 648).

Ibid. 652. Odysseus invites the Chorus to encourage him, and they do so in a song. This stultifies 624 ff.: "Silence! Don't even breathe!"

Alcestis. How are the obsequies performed? Is Alcestis burned (608, 740)? Is she merely interred (898, τάφρον ἐς κοίλην: θάπτω and τύμβος occur several times)? In either case, how does Heracles secure her body?

Medea 374 f. She promises to slay her husband as well as Creon and his daughter.

Hippolytus 166–9. Why obtrude the fact, crazily incongruous in this play, that Artemis was goddess of childbirth?

Hecuba 571 ff., 604 ff., 671 ff., and 894 ff. muddle the obsequies of Polyxena.

Ibid. 900. After all, the favouring gale purchased by Polyxena's death does not arrive. It waits until 1289 f., after the succeeding affair of Polymestor has been put through.[3]

Supplices. This play is crowded with difficulties, big and little.[4]

Heracles 240 ff. Lycus in Thebes bids his men fetch wood all the way from Phocis.

Ibid. 1386. The unseemly casualness wherewith the Hound of Hell (called merely "an unhappy dog") is mentioned has never been explained away.[5]

Ion 510 ff. Why does Ion enter in excitement, as the trochaic metre

[1] περὶ ὕψους xv. 3: he goes on to quote *Il.* XX. 170 f.
[2] Anachronisms of course are ignored here.
[3] Another item favouring Spranger's idea (see above, p. 35).
[4] See the essay devoted to it, below.
[5] To read ... μοι ... ἀθλίῳ· κυνὸς ... makes things even worse.

proves? Why does he ask for Xuthus? When Xuthus next moment appears, the lad receives him frigidly, a few lines further on threatening to shoot him—with some excuse, but without answering our questions.

Ibid. 1157 ff. The sudden arithmetic about the space enclosed by Ion's marquee is ridiculous.

Ibid. 1364–1438. This recognition-scene abounds in oddities: "Heaven means well, but Fate is hard" (1374 f.); the mysterious[1] πολλὰ καὶ πάροιθεν οἶσθά μοι (1397); σφάζοντες οὐ λήγοιτ' ἄν (1404), which is very odd Greek and should be σ. οὐ φθάνοιτ' ἄν; ῥυσιάζομαι λόγῳ (1406); that notorious crux τόδ' ἔσθ' ὕφασμα, θέσφαθ' ὡς εὑρίσκομεν (1424);[2] ἀρχαῖόν τι παγχρύσῳ γένει δώρημα (1427 f.), which has, however, something of the hangdog look that implies a copyist's error.

Phoenissae. The Chorus are so completely uninteresting that few of us ask whence they come. They themselves seem not to know. If from Tyre (202), all is tolerably well; if from Sicily,[3] as they tell us a little later (211), across the Ionian Sea (208) they must on landing have veered away at the last moment from Delphi, their alleged goal, and journeyed laboriously on to Thebes—because it was founded by Cadmus!

Ibid. 1147. Chariots are to charge the city-gates.

Bacchae 402 ff. The prayer of the Chorus, "Oh that I were in Aphrodite's island", cannot be defended[4] from the charge of absurd carelessness. Their adherents vigorously and wisely insist that Maenads have no concern with that goddess.

Ibid. Why and how is Dionysus at one moment "wine-dark in complexion" (438), at the next "pallid of set purpose" (457)?

Ibid. 823. Dionysus declares that men are not allowed to share in the orgies. Then why do Tiresias and Cadmus attend them? It is useless to reply: "because Euripides insists on their important conflict with Pentheus, which arises from their purpose of joining the orgies". He could at least have let the matter slide when the scene is over; but we are told much later (1223 f.) of their visit.

Rhesus 356 contradicts vv. 304, 617 f. as to the colour of Rhesus' steeds.[5]

---

[1] For the emendations proposed see Owen's edition. But the line does not look wrong, only incomplete. On the other hand, the obvious suggestion of a line accidentally omitted after this becomes unpleasing when we note that οὐκ ἐν σιωπῇ τἀμά should follow σῖγα closely.

[2] See Owen's discussion. None of the emendations that he reports is at all satisfactory.

[3] Or Carthage (see Murray's critical note). The scholiasts are clearly bewildered, one being desperate enough to quote a view that "Sicily" here is "a little island between Chalcis and Aulis".

[4] See p. 68 below.   [5] I owe this point to Sneller (*ut sup.*, p. 86).

Secondly, there is much Feeble Writing. Normally (need it be said?) Euripides shows perfect mastery of that athletic manner, elegant yet unadorned, so frequent in Attic writers. He can turn his hand to other modes, the quasi-Sophoclean in *Hippolytus*,[1] the flamboyant in *Orestes*;[2] but this vivid simplicity is his favoured manner, in which even Aristophanes, even Plato himself and Demosthenes do not excel him. It is all the more astonishing that he can sink into diction spongy, diffuse, woefully flat. His fragments include many a wretched line: πόλλ' ἔστιν ἀνθρώποισιν, ὦ ξένοι, κακά (fr. 204) belongs to a class intolerably large—at first sight: but no one can read long in these remains without feeling certain that many are not his; and the extant plays contain examples enough.

Spongy diction is most plentiful in *Helen*. This we shall not merely condone but enjoy if we read the play as a parody of melodrama, with the Taurian *Iphigenia* especially in view: that is, as intended to be silly. Much of the desired flabbiness is secured by stating the same fact again and again: not merely a repetition of "woes", but details such as Menelaus' absence and the plight of Hermione. Examples are of little use: the whole play must be savoured to get the pervasive effect of stale confectionery. But we may cite πάλιν μ' ἀνάξουσ' ἐς τὸ σῶφρον αὖθις αὖ (932—"again" thrice in one verse!) and the colour scheme in 1501 f., with the tautology οἶδμα, κυμάτων, ῥόθια:

> γλαυκὸν ἔπιτ' οἶδμα κυανόχροά τε κυμάτων
> ῥόθια πολιὰ θαλάσσας.

Above all, note the perverse skill wherewith Euripides anticipates that dismal feat so common in our spy-novels and detective-stories, of being at once sensational and dull: the conspiratorial talk (1035–84) between Helen and Menelaus, which should have been at all costs stichomythic (if not trochaic into the bargain), lounges along at the rate of two lines apiece. Roving to other plays, the eye falls on *Heracleidae* 885 f.,

> οὐ μὴν ἑκόντα γ' αὐτόν, ἀλλὰ πρὸς βίαν
> ἔζευξ' ἀνάγκῃ,

and a mass of *longueurs* in that immense chant (*Iph. Taur.* 123–235) shared by Iphigenia and the Chorus. But the distasteful enumeration may be cut short here.

Sometimes the writing is not spongy, but downright bad, often in explanatory prologues: for though Euripides composes these admirably

---

[1] See pp. 92–94 below.
[2] The Phrygian's monody, 1369 ff.

when in the mood—*Hippolytus* comes to mind with its terrible vigour, and *Orestes* with the insistent coyness of Electra, fiend that she is—more often he is too bored to write well. Even the *Troades* opens with a conference of two deities that is important indeed, but feebly written, and near the close Poseidon declares (91) that the sea-capes "shall have the bodies of many corpses that have died". This shambling stuff is defended from excision by its context. But it is possible to alter a foolish phrase in *Hecuba*: "so long as the boundary-stones of the land *lay upright*".[1] The *Phoenissae* (as we have already noted) must be handled gingerly, and we all hope that our poet did not write (10-13)

> ἐγὼ δὲ παῖς μὲν κλήζομαι Μενοικέως,
> Κρέων τ' ἀδελφὸς μητρὸς ἐκ μιᾶς ἔφυ,
> καλοῦσι δ' Ἰοκάστην με· τοῦτο γὰρ πατὴρ
> ἔθετο, γαμεῖ δὲ Λάιός με . . . .

The wonder is, how anyone could be found to pen such abject verse. A lighter miasma descends fitfully upon other portions than the prologues. Talthybius bids Hecuba "Stand, unhappy one, and raise your side aloft".[2] Stichomythia is responsible for a good many vapid lines, not too severely parodied in Housman's famous skit. Iphigenia tells the Taurian king: "These strangers have come with kindred blood on their hands." He replies: "Which? I have fallen into a yearning for the knowledge" (*Iph. Taur.* 1172). During an excited conversation between two hot-headed young ruffians, who never in their lives gave a thought to politics, one of them remarks that the multitude is to be dreaded when it has unscrupulous leaders. That is already bad characterization enough; and the other insufferably rejoins: "But when they get good leaders, their deliberations are always good."[3] It is the metre that puts this among our specimens of bad writing: trochaics are absurd for such mildewed aphorisms. Clytaemnestra, on the brink of an agonized appeal for her daughter's life, ponders how she had best open it (*Iph. Aul.* 1124 ff.). "Alas! what beginning of my sorrow shall I make? For I can use anything as the first part or as the last or in the middle—anywhere."

We tread less certain ground when criticizing his lyrics; for as he grew older he deliberately subordinated words to music. Again and again

---

[1] *Hec.* 16: ἕως μὲν οὖν γῆς ὀρθ' ἔκειθ' ὁρίσματα, where Murray proposes ὀρθ' ἔτ' εἶχ'. One scholium coolly remarks ἔκειθ'· ἵστατο.

[2] *Hec.* 499 f.:
> ἀνίστασ', ὦ δύστηνε, καὶ μετάρσιον
> πλευρὰν ἔπαιρε.

[3] *Or.* 772 f.

occur passages full of verbiage about suffering, death, and doom tangled in a syntax both vague and harsh; it would be pedantic to study them as poetical literature: one assumes that the audience listened chiefly to the music and noted but one word in three, without time or desire to pursue rambling conditional sentences. The Phrygian's narrative song in *Orestes* is plainly a musical far more than a dramatic or a literary *tour de force*. Yet it would be more absurd to view all the lyrics in that light. Most of them are analogous to the works of Pindar or Bacchylides: they can be appreciated in precisely the same manner, as poems, with no thought of the musical accompaniment, now lost. But in actual merit they are nearly always inferior to Pindaric work, often to that of Bacchylides. Really good odes, beautiful, relevant, and intelligible without patient microscopy, are rare. Such, for the most part, are the lyrics of the *Bacchae*; but how many others can be so described? The Escape and Doom lyric in *Hippolytus*; the Yearning for Hellas in the Taurian *Iphigenia*; and two odes devoted to the same event, Troy's downfall: one casting a golden ray across the gloom of the *Troades*, the other for a moment redeeming *Hecuba* from crude sensationalism. Some few, such as Apollo with Admetus in *Alcestis*, are excellent on the lower plane of sprightly charm; and we can add certain stanzas extracted from other lyrics: the quiet loveliness of the Salute to Alcestis (995 ff.), the Praise of Attica in *Medea* (824–45), and Euripides' own noble proclamation in *Heracles* of his undying loyalty to Graces and Muses for ever at one. To him these hours come but seldom. Pindar, like his own eagle, is at home in the empyrean; Shelley's natural voice is song; Hugo bears the immense bulk of *La Légende des siècles* through sunshine and murk unfalteringly. Euripides, one cannot but feel, more often than not produces his odes by bracing himself to a professional duty; and it is significant that in *Helen*, which he wrote largely for his own amusement, he keeps us waiting (not impatiently) for over four hundred lines[1] between one lyric and the next.

No lover of Euripides will dwell on specimens of bad writing in the songs that he hammered out unaided by the Muse. It is enough to glance at the astonishingly flat lines (*El.* 112–24) wherewith Electra introduces herself; the hideous ἐξάρξω 'γώ in *Troades* 147; five words in *Ion* knotted up by three different genitives, συρίγγων ὑπ' αἰόλας ἰαχᾶς ὕμνων;[2] and an utterance[3] by Apollo (of all singers) that contains a huddle of ten datives in nine short lines. Finally, though we pass here from bad writing to bad

---

[1] Vv. 698–1106. Note too the extreme brevity of the lyric passage 515–27.
[2] Vv. 499 ff. See Owen's note for this and other troubles.
[3] *Or.* 1682 ff. (in anapaests, not lyrics: but that matters nothing here).

structure, we must echo the frequent complaint that Euripidean lyrics often have small relevance to the action. Extreme cases are *Electra* 432 ff., where, after husband and wife have discussed a difficulty about luncheon, the Chorus offer a pleasant trivial ode on the Shield of Achilles; the astonishing though delightful satire on Apollo's infringed monopoly, which (after all) is not so much irrelevant in theme as both damaging and utterly out of key;[1] and Demeter's Search for Persephone (*Helen* 1301 ff.), composed in a metre too airy for its grave theme and having no discoverable relation to its context. These poems, in themselves not unsatisfactory, impair the effectiveness of the plays that contain them: it appears that Euripides wrote them *in vacuo* on his good days and thrust them in where they now stand when he found himself needing an ode but deserted by the lyric mood.

Thirdly, we must face his Faulty Construction, to which the remarks just offered about irrelevant lyrics form a bridge. Here we may seem to contravene (and, in fact, do contravene) certain evidences already adduced about Euripides' care and precision.[2] But he was no more consistent in this respect than in others.[3] He could write superbly constructed drama, but very often did not. At the outset we are confronted by Professor Kitto's doctrine.[4] He asserts that in the "great tragic period" (containing *Medea, Hippolytus, Heracleidae, Heracles, Andromache, Hecuba, Supplices, Troades*) Euripides wrote plays that are "all but the *Hippolytus* badly constructed by Aristotelian standards"; and, explaining this badness as anything rather than incompetence, sees in it a deliberate and excellent kind of dramaturgy, the poet being concerned not with elegant structure but with some tragic idea: "If conflict arises between the development of the idea and the smooth conduct of the action, it is the action that has to give way".[5] But a good playwright, like all other good

---

[1] *I.T.* 1234 ff. It recalls the most gamesome passages in the *Iliad* and the pretty account of Eros and Ganymede in Apollonius Rhodius (III. 111–53). See further Verrall, "Euripides in a Hymn" (*Euripides the Rationalist*, pp. 217–30).

[2] See p. 16 above.

[3] This sounds dangerously light-hearted, and may provoke the rejoinder: "Is there nothing that we can depend on? What, then, becomes of criticism?" The truth is, a description of Euripides' work at once precisely worded, complete, and fully true cannot be devised. Fluidity is of its essence, and we can hope only to determine which parts or aspects of it are the least fluid.

[4] *Greek Tragedy*, p. 185; see also pp. 187, 200, 208, 211, 238, 360. Despite one's admiration for the skill wherewith this theory is developed and for many brilliant *obiter dicta*, one can hardly acquit the author of implying that Euripides made bad dramas because he was an unusually fine dramatist.

[5] *Ibid.*, p. 226.

TOWARDS UNDERSTANDING EURIPIDES 43

artists, invariably does two things at once, often three or more; such dexterity is vital to the artistic process: the clumsiest of us can juggle with a single orange. Euripides had no sound reason for not displaying his tragic ideas in perfectly constructed dramas.

Even in *Hippolytus* Theseus contradicts himself, unmistakably and with emphatic repetition, about the punishment he meditates for his son.[1] More objectionable is Menelaus' absurdly fumbling excuse (*Androm.* 732 ff.) for the sudden withdrawal whereby he abandons Hermione to a wretched plight caused by his own encouragement. Verrall's theory that both the incitement and the withdrawal are parts of a plot to throw Hermione into Orestes' arms receives no justification from the play itself.[2] In *Ion*, the audience hears Creusa's sad history, at greater or less length, actually four times.[3] (But when Ion, stepping forward to challenge Apollo, forgets his own warning against such rashness, that is a natural and most engaging inconsistency.) We have already remarked that Andromache is improbably hurried away (*Troades* 1126–35) before everyone else so that Hecuba also may lament over Astyanax.[4] In the *Heracleidae*, where the destitution of these fugitives (unless Athens consents to protect them) is a basic fact, Hyllus returns in time for the battle with a positive army from elsewhere. Euripides is coolly "having it both ways": glory of Athens in succouring the helpless, glory of Heracles' son in fighting his father's oppressor. To secure this, Iolaus has three lines (45 ff.) in the prologue that disingenuously create a loophole: Hyllus and his older brothers have gone—to seek some refuge (not an army), though we have heard (15–25) that all hope of refuge has already been tried in vain.

Similar items, of less importance, can be added. Xuthus in *Ion* naturally plans to attend the "birthday" feast of his newly found son (651 ff.); but he is never seen again, because his presence would have been embarrassing at the dinner as eventually mismanaged by the loyal old poisoner. *Andromache* has two time-schemes.[5] That is perhaps trifling: the spectators would not notice this: how many detect it in *Othello* or the first act of *Cyrano de Bergerac*? Schlegel censures the *Troades* as "a series of situations and events with no other connexion than a common source in the capture

---

[1] See, however, pp. 87 f. below.
[2] *Four Plays*, pp. 9 f., 20 f., etc. Verrall has to postulate an earlier play making the situation clear.
[3] Vv. 336–58, 859–922, 934–65, 1470–1500.
[4] See p. 25 above.
[5] Wilamowitz, *Hermes*, vol. LX (1925), p. 288: "Mit der Zeit springt das Drama besonders gewaltsam um." Cp. Verrall, *Four Plays*, pp. 15–20.

of Troy; but in no respect have they a joint aim".[1] That is a misleading half-truth. Euripides has given far more than "Scenes from the Fall of Troy". Had he not, the *Troades* could be called "episodic": that is, a succession of scenes each complete in itself, but having no vital connexion with those preceding and following, so that no artistic whole is produced.[2] But Euripides has done more. He intends to show not merely the fall of Troy, but a picture of war itself in its full horror, to startle and admonish his own contemporaries. This purpose the *Troades* fulfils: there we see the "joint aim" of its scenes. Moreover, they depict a crescendo of anguish. But it must be allowed that the play's structure is rudimentary: it has no *peripeteia*, or recoil of the action upon itself: only what the French call *péripéties*, a series of exciting moments, such as Cassandra's outbreak. Aristotle would have described it as "simple", not "complex".[3] Episodic *plays* are not to be found among the extant tragedies.[4] But "episodic" *scenes* are naturally possible: that is, single scenes that could be omitted without structural damage to the remainder. Euripides has left us a few.[5] The suttee of Euadne in the *Supplices* is impressive,[6] but has received frequent censure as being thus intrusive. The charmingly foolish talk in *Helen* between Teucer and the heroine leads nowhere, as does that of Menelaus and the portress (to which, however, we owe perhaps the finest of all Aristophanes' parodies, in his *Thesmophoriazusae*). The *Phoenissae*, one feels now and again, is wellnigh built of insertions. For example, the interview between Iocasta and her horrible sons is structurally useless.[7] (But the trochaic altercation makes splendid reading, and at such things as μολὼν ἐς Ἄργος ἀνακάλει Λέρνης ὕδωρ the reader thumps his desk, especially if those three lines remind him of another brilliantly rhetorical scoundrel, Richard III: "Now by my George, my garter, and my crown", etc., with those stinging retorts.) In *Iphigenia at Aulis* imagine the wrangle between Menelaus and Agamemnon expunged. We should lose two capital declamations and two good thrills at the opening and near the end; but the whole action would receive no injury. If it is objected: "But

[1] *Ut sup.*, X (vol. V, p. 166).
[2] Ar. *Poet.* 1451ᵇ33–35: τῶν δὲ ἄλλων μύθων καὶ πράξεων αἱ ἐπεισοδιώδεις εἰσὶν χείρισται. λέγω δ' ἐπεισοδιώδη μῦθον ἐν ᾧ τὰ ἐπεισόδια μετ' ἄλληλα οὔτ' εἰκὸς οὔτ' ἀνάγκη εἶναι. [3] *Ibid.* 1452ᵃ12.
[4] At the moment of writing I see in *The Times Literary Supplement* of January 29, 1949 (p. 76) *Oedipus Coloneus* described as "this episodic play". No: the whole drama is slow, indeed, but assuredly not casual or sprawling, in development.
[5] Including the scene of Athena and Paris in *Rhesus*, if that drama is Euripides' work.
[6] Kitto (p. 226) defends it as vital to the poet's purpose. See, however, the *Supplices* essay, below, pp. 124 f., 125 f., 159 f.
[7] It is among the passages condemned as padding in the longer Hypothesis.

then Agamemnon's letter would have been delivered to his wife", the reply is obvious: she was only a mile away at the moment supposed, and she certainly would not have turned back on the instant, taking Iphigenia with her all the long way home—though (to be sure) they needed no luncheon, having picnicked already (420–3). Far more open to question, of course, are such wantonings as the attack on Aeschylus' recognition-tokens in *Electra* and the unreal bickering in *Heracles* about the bow as a gentleman's weapon.

But much graver faults of construction remain. The Messenger, after briefly announcing some dread event or danger, will insist on the canonical long and picturesque narrative, even though the person addressed ought instantly to deal with the crisis. Astonishing instances occur in *Ion*, *Iphigenia in Tauris*, *Helen*, and the *Phoenissae*.[1] These are undeniably big faults: to make opportunity for a purple patch, Euripides sacrifices the necessary minimum of verisimilitude.

Again, the plot itself occasionally slips through his fingers. This terrible blunder has received small attention, partly because the poet's brilliance in other features of his work dazzles us, partly because we unconsciously assume that such a thing cannot happen. But happen it did. We must recognize that Athenian playwrights were more capable of this lapse than their modern successors: they realized, it seems, that they could "get away with it" because the play would have but one performance.[2] Even Sophocles is not unquestionably free from this imputation: long before the end of *Oedipus Tyrannus* everyone in Thebes has forgotten the plague that started the action. This (one gladly owns) is no grave blemish: we forget it too, which many will think a perfect defence. The close of *Philoctetes* must not be cited:[3] Heracles' intervention is immensely worse, but a quite different mistake. Aristophanes in *Plutus*, written after his

[1] Sophocles has a milder example in *Ajax*, with a much stronger excuse (see p. 27 above). The ῥῆσις in *Medea* is different: urgent as the crisis looks, she has no reason for haste, as we find.

[2] This may seem to contradict Aristotle in *Poet*. 1455ᵃ22–29: δεῖ δὲ τοὺς μύθους συνιστάναι καὶ τῇ λέξει συναπεργάζεσθαι ὅτι μάλιστα πρὸ ὀμμάτων τιθέμενον· οὕτω γὰρ ἂν ἐνεργέστατα ὁρῶν ὥσπερ παρ' αὐτοῖς γιγνόμενος τοῖς πραττομένοις εὑρίσκοι τὸ πρέπον καὶ ἥκιστα ἂν λανθάνοι τὰ ὑπεναντία. σημεῖον δὲ τούτου ὃ ἐπετιμᾶτο Καρκίνῳ. ὁ γὰρ Ἀμφιάραος ἐξ ἱεροῦ ἀνῄει, ὃ μὴ ὁρῶντ' ἂν τὸν θεατὴν ἐλάνθανεν, ἐπὶ δὲ τῆς σκηνῆς ἐξέπεσεν δυσχερανάντων τοῦτο τῶν θεατῶν. Aristotle's advice is perfectly sound. His instance, however, refers to physical contradiction. We know nothing more about it than he tells us; but the mistake clearly was that, in face of preceding events, Amphiaraus could not have been "coming up from the temple" because, for example, he must have started from the palace. The faults quoted above are not physical.

[3] Still less, and least of all, that change in the *Eumenides* where Orestes fades away in presence of a dispute that shakes the Universe.

genius had been killed by the fall of Athens, completely forgets throughout one important scene the whole point of his play.[1] The mighty Cratinus, we read,[2] made a practice of throwing his plots overboard. As for Euripides, it has already been noted that Medea's miraculous escape stultifies earlier statements about her helplessness, so vital to the tragic tone. No less badly does the *Heracleidae* go to pieces. Difficulties connected with Macaria's sacrifice and Eurystheus' doom are here irrelevant. But the play's very theme, Athens' glory as champion of the oppressed, is first dimmed by the arrival of Hyllus with a foreign army, later eclipsed when the father of these suppliants himself takes the field in divine majesty and power. Even the *Bacchae* shows a tinge of this weakness. Dionysus' opening speech suggests a battle between Theban troops and his followers.[3] Tiresias plainly foretells (306 ff.) that Pentheus will live to see Dionysus established mightily in Hellas. Neither statement is fulfilled.

And, finally, in more than one extant[4] play he has taken a course that to some will appear only less blamable and must at best be called ramshackle work. The action falls into halves, visibly separate though tied together. In each instance a champion of the poet, if ingenious and resolute enough, can devise some statement that will force unity of action upon his recalcitrant material;[5] but the mere fact that he must so labour refutes him. In *Andromache* the division into two brief dramas is clear: the plight and rescue of Andromache, the plight and rescue of Hermione. In both, preliminary statement, complication, *peripeteia*, and *dénouement* stand clearly forth; though Andromache gives her name to the whole, she disappears early from the action and from our minds, until at the final moment Thetis tells what is to become of her. Hermione, no doubt, has great importance in both sections but sections they remain. *Heracles* is still more disconcerting. The peril and rescue of Megara and the rest are a complete drama, however rudimentary. Then the action begins anew, the fact being as it were defiantly proclaimed by what amounts to a second prologue,[6] the scene of Iris and Frenzy; and a second play follows,

---

[1] Cp. my *Greek Comedy*, pp. 275 f.

[2] Platonius (Kaibel, *Com. Graec. Frag.*, p. 6): εὔστοχος δὲ ὢν ἐν ταῖς ἐπιβολαῖς τῶν δραμάτων καὶ διασκευαῖς, εἶτα προϊὼν καὶ διασπῶν τὰς ὑποθέσεις οὐκ ἀκολούθως πληροῖ τὰ δράματα.

[3] This can, however, be defended as a deliberate trick: cp. Wilamowitz's remark quoted on p. 28, above.

[4] We may surmise that some of the lost plays were similar. As regards *Hypsipyle* we stand on firmer ground since reading the Oxyrhynchus fragments; the two parts were Eurydice's loss of her infant and the recognition of Hypsipyle by her sons.

[5] See Verrall's essay on *Andromache* (*Four Plays*, pp. 1–42).

[6] Mahaffy, *History of Classical Greek Literature*, vol. I, p. 346.

no less rudimentary than the first in structure, though a masterpiece of tragic force, pathos, and beauty. Heracles is far less engaged in the early part than Hermione in the first half of *Andromache*: he corresponds technically not to her but to Neoptolemus. A great Hellenist, who is the last man to hunt for blemishes in Euripides, has rightly called *Heracles* "broken-backed".[1] In *Hecuba*, finally, the division into the Polyxena-tragedy and the vengeance taken for Polydorus must be held hardly, if at all, less obvious, though Hecuba dominates both: the pins that join these two halves prick the reader's finger.[2] It has been asserted that real unity is given by "one overriding idea, the suffering which the human race inflicts upon itself through its follies and wickednesses."[3] But such an idea creates (at best) moral unity; the present objection concerns dramatic unity.

Such are the puzzles, weaknesses, or sins, some trivial, some grave, that (whether by his fault or not) have for many readers made Euripides' work less profoundly delightful and artistically satisfying than, they feel, it might so easily have proved. Goethe's famous protest cannot be ignored, that if a modern critic is to pick holes in this great ancient he should do so on his knees; but, having assumed the required posture, we must certainly pick the holes. Only thus can we appreciate Euripides' vast merits also. And only thus can we explain the fact with which this essay began, that eminently competent readers have held so diverse opinions concerning

[1] Murray, *Greek Studies*, p. 112: "I do not mean that I consider the *Heracles* of Euripides to be a very great work of art. I do not. It is broken-backed; it has too much conventional rhetoric; but for sheer loftiness of tragic tone the last act, after Heracles awakes . . . , will stand beside anything in ancient drama."
On the merits of this last act Kitto writes admirably, above all in his comparison (pp. 246 f.) of Theseus and Heracles. On the first section he is less convincing (p. 242): "the scenes are flat because, we may say, Euripides is really dramatizing a negative, the absence of the great man". But a good playwright will not depict emptiness by being empty himself. Shakespeare shows Justice Shallow as an ass, but does not write like an ass for the purpose; Euripides shows Achilles as an utter fool, but does it brilliantly. The first part of the *Trachiniae*, too, passes in the absence of the great man (the same man, as it happens) with how much greater force!

[2] Spranger's view (see p. 35 above) of the play's composition, by so well accounting for the fission, strongly emphasizes it.

[3] Kitto, *Greek Tragedy*, p. 219. Professor G. M. Kirkwood, "Hecuba and Nomos" (*Trans. Amer. Philol. Assoc.*, vol. LXXVIII (1947), pp. 61–68) finds unity in "a reconciliation of the two personalities of Hecuba" or the picture of her degeneration: her "great speech of appeal (786–845) . . . provides the link that gives the play a logical unity": she first extols Nomos, but finding this of no avail turns to Peitho, basely working on Agamemnon's passion for Cassandra, her own daughter. This cannot satisfy: the change is devised so as to secure her triumph over Polymestor, and is thus relevant to only one of the parts.

his plays. But we have now completed our grim catalogue and may proceed to our final task. That is not a corresponding survey of their splendours: critics beyond number have dilated on these; and there is less need for such a disquisition here because succeeding essays will bear witness direct or indirect to Euripides' greatness. Let us rather seek now the deepest cause of those "puzzles, weaknesses, or sins" that have disappointed, perhaps alienated, us.

One fact accounts for these lapses: with him intellectual control of imagination was apt to fail abruptly. Hence the sudden inconsistencies, big or little, that we have noted; the fits of inopportune, if not unseemly, open-mindedness; the changes of mood; the ramshackle or even self-contradictory plots. Euripides—can it be denied?—more than once began a play with no clear notion of how it was to develop. This frame of mind is bad enough in a novelist, as when Dickens suddenly dispatched his hero to America and a gallery of new grotesques because the sales of *Martin Chuzzlewit* were falling off; and when Scott, having wisely killed off Athelstane, was persuaded by "his friend and printer" to resuscitate him in a later page of *Ivanhoe*. More recent novelists have reported that "once started, my characters take charge: I have no further control over them". When this irresponsible mood lays hold on Euripides he chases every hare that shows its scut. Often it is as handsome and nimble a beast as ever was coursed in March, but it means equivocal reputation for the man who promised his guests a leopard. Lucretius once acted no less oddly, when he set his great invocation to Venus at the opening of a poem that gives it the lie; but we have it on a saint's authority that Lucretius wrote in the intervals of madness. Euripides was certainly not mad, but no less certainly he was seized at times by a wantonness that he did not control. Just as Wouverman instinctively put a white horse in every picture, so Euripides created some big or little muddle or perplexity in each play: his "signature" as it were, like the phrases whereby Phocylides and Theognis claimed their own verses.

Athenian "tragedy", we have said, was what each poet made it. No rules of composition existed: only the tradition of "high seriousness", the state's insistence on a chorus, and the Greek instinct for balance, beauty, and chaste outline. Enter Euripides, endowed with the instinct for dramatic method: that is, for depicting life and ideas by the clash of personalities; endowed too with immense poetical and rhetorical skill. So far he goes with other fine playwrights, but no farther. His "high seriousness" was strong but intermittent; his sense of balance, beauty, and chaste outline, no less strong, was equally apt to take flight before a sudden impulse to instruct or shock or amuse. Though loyal to Athens, he found no sanctity in the ideas of Pericles or Cleon, being not so much a mouthpiece of the sophistic age as the citizen of a future commonwealth,[1] with strange ideas and an art not hieratic but social and at bottom thoroughly secular. Secular. . . . When people throw their religion overboard they find themselves on the morrow bereft of much that they never dreamed of losing. Like the Sophists, Euripides indeed taught men to think, but also dispelled their hitherto instinctive awe. Aeschylus had warned them against that loss;[2] and if we but compare the *Septem* with the *Phoenissae* we observe a revolution both artistic and moral in the treatment of the curse that Oedipus laid upon his undutiful sons. Euripides is clever, Aeschylus shakes our soul. The *Phoenissae*, we remarked earlier, makes a reader thump his desk with rapture at sinister rhetoric. The *Septem* is like to make him cross himself. There we watch the creeping curse slowly entangle two men in damnation. The *Phoenissae* thrills us with a magnificent brawl between two repulsive careerists.

In short, Euripides was not a classical writer at all, but a romantic, who entered the theatre still groping. He did not conceive, write, and present his drama as an expression of his whole nature, completely articulated and organized, but was content to admit his doubts and fumblings into the "finished" work: like so many lyrists of our day, he permits us to watch his soul and intellect yet struggling. Our dramatists, and nearly all dramatists, are not so minded; even in "problem" plays they are quite sure not only what the problem is but also what is the solution. Euripides was always sure of his problem: the solution perhaps always eluded him, for his genius was rarely in harmony with itself. This inconclusiveness may disappoint our intellect, but it bestows on our spirit and imagination the thrill of a wider horizon, the stimulus to adventures that we may ourselves carry through. Shaw and Hervieu settle something: you hear the key click, and all is over. Euripides settles nothing: that is one reason why he cannot become obsolete.

There is another reason, which should be too obvious for mention; but critics have strangely ignored it. Euripides is magnificently readable. He belongs to that priceless and rarest class of writers whose work is both

---

[1] Nestle closes his *Euripides, der Dichter der griechischen Aufklärung* (1901) with a quotation from Schiller's *Don Carlos*:
>Das Jahrhundert
>Ist meinem Ideal nicht reif. Ich lebe
>Ein Bürger derer, welche kommen werden.

[2] Especially in the *Eumenides*: ἔσθ' ὅπου τὸ δεινὸν εὖ (517), etc.

genuinely great and genuinely attractive in the commonplace sense,[1] who can reward the study of half a lifetime or entertain the last hour before sleep. Rich as Greek is in first-rate authors, perhaps only four of them can be placed hopefully on the bed-table: Homer, Herodotus, Euripides, and Plutarch. With many students that aspect of literature counts for nothing. The vastly expanding trade in research has engendered a debased fashion of valuing writers in proportion as they abound in "problems" and "questions". During these last two or three generations the basic truth uttered by Schiller has wellnigh vanished from the mind of critics: "All art is dedicated to joy, and there is no higher, no more serious enterprise than to make people happy: the only genuine art is that which gives the highest pleasure."[2] What does technique matter, be it never so adroit, complex, and novel, if it results in a dull, even repellent, drama?

Some great authors, nevertheless, among whom Euripides is conspicuous, confront us with problems that cannot be neglected. We should err if we lamented that he does so, for they arise from his very nature. It is no accident that he challenges us to use our wits: like his friend Socrates, he thought an unexamined life a contradiction in terms. Such inquiries as the present need no apology: without them we are sure to miss a good deal of the enjoyment and edification that Euripides' great but elusive genius can impart.

Still, let us not lose our sense of perspective. These inquiries, however justifiable, must be kept in their place: they are evil if they lessen, instead of increasing, our relish for an author who (whatever his failings) saw deeply into the human spirit and displayed what he saw with piercing beauty and wit. His very faults in the end arouse the exhilaration that springs from suddenly more intimate understanding. And with it all he carries us along like a cunning story-teller. *Andromache* is ill constructed: so be it. But who has ever read that play without zest for each brisk scene, without eagerness to know what comes next? A distinguished scholar[3] thinks it "easy to suppose that Euripides was not very proud of the *Andromache* and preferred to disguise his authorship". If Euripides did not realize that Andromache's tirade against Sparta bears his indelible

---

[1] Such pretty embellishments as the temple-reliefs and tapestries in *Ion*, the lullaby in *Hypsipyle*, and the echo in *Andromeda* are a minor outcome of this quality.

[2] In his preface to *Die Braut von Messina*: "Alle Kunst ist der Freude gewidmet, und es gibt keine höhere und keine ernsthaftere Aufgabe, als die Menschen zu beglücken. Die rechte Kunst ist nur diese, welche den höchsten Genuß verschafft."

[3] D. S. Robertson (*Class. Rev.*, vol. XXXVII (1923), pp. 58–60). The "disguise" (p. 59) is the ascription of this play to Democrates.

signature he was a feebler judge of literature than we thought; and if he blushed for this drama he suddenly displayed the pedantry, so often flouted by him, of preferring iron regularity to free imagination. When all is said, what gives us our greatest pleasure in reading him, and probably gave him the greatest satisfaction as he wrote? Wit, not only in word but in action. He rejoices to eavesdrop on gods and heroes in their dressing-gowns;[1] by a flick of the wrist to exhibit the lowly and rejected as heroes or sages when their hour strikes; to show us that disillusionment can be a heartening or an amusing instead of a dismal surprise. These dexterities are not that dull stuff, stage moralizing, but human nature caught in the act by what we name today the candid camera. Euripides, like Shakespeare, can turn his hand to Polonius-twaddle when (as we might surmise) he wishes to do anthologists a good turn. Both understand their audience thoroughly and provide something for everyone: lucid banalities for the dullards, infinitesimal dramas in half a dozen lines for those who prefer to crack their own nuts. That is constructive wit indeed. Scholiasts may grumble that "all the persons are bad except Menelaus"; but in this mood, his most characteristic and illuminating mood, he cares nothing whether they are good or bad so long as they are pungently alive, radiant from every facet. Though rarely a great dramatist in the official sense, he is always a master of the miniature: his characters are better than his plays.

[1] Schlegel (*ut sup.*, VIII, vol. V, p. 136): "Er bemüht sich . . . die Kluft zwischen seinen Zeitgenossen und jener wunderbaren Vorwelt auszufüllen oder zu überbauen, und die Götter und Helden jenseits im Nachtkleide zu belauschen."

II

THE *BACCHAE* AND ITS RIDDLE

SINCE the year 1908 students of this play have been perturbed, more or less deeply according to their own temperaments and those of the commentators whom they have read, by a discussion published that year in *The Riddle of the Bacchae*. Whether it is true or not that this book's contentions "lie outside the main current of thought about the play",[1] it has occasioned a good deal of talk and writing; therefore its author, having conceived new ideas on certain features of the *Bacchae*, cannot but think a restatement desirable, with whatever apologies for egotism may seem needed.

The whole book arose from one fact, and one only. That fact remains unshaken.

When, after a scene of excitement, fear, and hubbub, Dionysus[2] emerges from the palace to reassure his followers the Asiatic bacchants who form the Chorus, his description of what has occurred includes this (632–4):

πρὸς δὲ τοῖσδ' αὐτῷ τάδ' ἄλλα Βάκχιος λυμαίνεται·
δώματ' ἔρρηξεν χαμᾶζε· συντεθράνωται δ' ἅπαν. . . .

"And in addition Bacchus works these further outrages upon him [King Pentheus]: he broke the house to the ground, and all is utter ruin . . .."[3]

---

[1] E. R. Dodds, edition of the *Bacchae* (Oxford, 1944), p. xliv. Though unable to accept all Professor Dodds's views, I gladly record the admiration and gratitude with which I have studied his work.

[2] The *Riddle* usually calls him "the Stranger". As will be seen, I now discard the belief that he is a human prophet.

[3] My translation has been made as literal as possible. I have even avoided using "palace" for δώματα, though Euripides assuredly would not have written it had he not meant the king's house in general (cp. ἅπαν). Had he intended "the stable", as is often maintained, would he not have used a word or phrase (as in 509 f. he says ἱππικαῖς φάτναισιν) that meant as much and no more?

For συντεθράνωται see Dodds's note, where he translates it by "is shattered". He rightly rejects Verrall's contention (*The Bacchants of Euripides* (1910), pp. 79 ff.) that the line means "'Bacchus dashed the building to the ground,—though it is all put together', or more exactly still, '—though its beams have been all put together'"; and "the story of the adept, rightly understood, demands that, when he has used his earthquake . . . he should *get rid of it again*." (V.'s italics.) It is perhaps worth adding that

Language could not be plainer: the overthrow of Pentheus' palace, to the beginning of which the Chorus have borne frenzied witness, was in fact accomplished. That is the sole meaning the words can bear, the sole meaning that anyone[1] (so far as appears) attached to them before the *Riddle* was published. Only then did scholars, shocked by the conclusions there drawn from this passage, seek to explain it otherwise; only then were heard those suggestions that "complete ruin" means "noises off" or a collapse merely of the stables. The apocalypse of an offended and triumphant god may be terrible, even fiendish: but at all costs it must not be shabby.[2] The best defence of that desperate position has been made by Professor Grube:

> First they [the Chorus] call upon the god to appear; then there is some reference to an earthquake..., and we must evidently suppose this to be shown..., perhaps by a sudden lurching movement of the chorus, accompanied by a shaking of the palace walls. The next voice says that the palace... will soon be shaken to the ground.... The future tense seems important, so far at least nothing is said definitely to happen to the palace.... Then come the words: "Did you see the entablature parting asunder?" Here something does happen to the palace, namely a fissure in the wall, by a metope or the top of a column, which may possibly fall to the ground. But the phrase would be strange if the whole palace were falling in ruins. It is not necessary for any great destruction to be seen on the stage.... What takes place are great crashing noises within.... The palace is still standing.[3]

Anecd. Bekk., p. 352. 15: ἀθράνευτον· ἄστρωτον tells against Verrall. It implies that θρανεύω (and so θρανόω?) means στορέννυμι and that συνθρανόω should therefore mean "spread completely" or "evenly": as it were "lay a floor".

[1] Beginning with the Hypothesis: ὁ δὲ σεισμὸν ποιήσας κατέστρεψε τὰ βασίλεια. Horace (*Odes* II. xix. 14 f.) is no less uncompromising: *tecta Penthei disiecta non leni ruina*, where *non leni* sounds like a prophetic rejection of the petty damage favoured by later students. The sweeping assertion above is true so far as I can recall; but it is many years since I made as thorough an examination as I could of the "literature". Pater, indeed, writes (*Greek Studies*, Library ed., p. 70): "Dionysus is seen stepping out from among the tottering masses of the mimic palace." That (as usual with him) is exquisitely written—also (as too often with him) evasive: "from among" suggests that the palace is down; "tottering" suggests that it is not, as yet.

[2] For the idea that the poet "plays down" this whole passage see below, pp. 58 f.

[3] *The Drama of Euripides* (1941), pp. 409 f. In a footnote he discusses the corresponding scene in *Heracles*: see below, p. 56. Kitto quotes with approval an earlier article by Grube, adding a wise remark of his own (*Greek Tragedy* (1939), p. 380): "But though a calm study of the text reduces the miracle to these dimensions a difficulty remains, namely, to explain why the difficulty arises. Why did Euripides so contrive matters that we have to look into the text so carefully before we can decide whether it is sense or raving nonsense?" His answer is a statement of the "playing-down" idea (see preceding note).

M. Pohlenz was content to write thus, without further comment: "Bald dürfen die Bakchen jubelnd ihren Führer begrüßen. Hohnlachend erzählt er ihnen, wie er

So far, well. But does not Dionysus in a moment unequivocally report that the whole palace lies in ruin? Professor Grube accordingly goes on:[1]

> Dionysus says the god deceived Pentheus with a phantom, and then finally Bacchus "wrecked the place[2] to the ground. All fell together around Pentheus who thus found my imprisonment a source of woe." This seems very definite, and so it is. But Dionysus is now describing what happened *inside* the palace, or more exactly inside the stables. We may if we wish suppose that these are wrecked, but there is no reason to suppose that they were visible on the stage. Even if they were, the characters for the rest of the play have other things on their minds than the state of Pentheus' outhouses.

But δώματα naturally means the king's house, and would be used by no writer, understood by no reader, to mean stables or outhouses unless ambiguity were (for whatever reason) deliberately sought. ἅπαν, naturally again, means the whole house. The wild cries uttered by the Chorus and their proclamation that the god "will shake Pentheus' *halls* [μέλαθρα, 587 f.] to pieces", though they prove nothing, would be a gross clumsiness on Euripides' part if no worse disaster were afoot than the destruction of outbuildings. Such a disturbance makes a silly anticlimax to that formidable outcry,

ἅπτε κεραύνιον αἴθοπα λαμπάδα·
σύμφλεγε σύμφλεγε δώματα Πενθέως.

"Light the thunderbolt's blazing torch! Consume utterly, consume with fire, the house of Pentheus!"[3]

We are thus confronted by two facts. Dionysus proclaims that the palace lies in complete overthrow. That statement is untrue. First, it is of course physically false: no one will allege that the stage-building itself collapsed.[4] Further, it is false dramatically: the palace does not "really" fall in the sense that Desdemona or Banquo "really" dies. That is proved by the silence of Pentheus (who was inside it when it "fell"), of the First

---

drinnen Pentheus genarrt habe, so daß der statt seiner einen Stier fesselte, wie Dionysos dann das Innere des Palastes einstürzen ließ." *Die griechische Tragödie* (1930), p. 488.

[1] I have used inverted commas to show quotation, which Grube indicates by pacing.

[2] Not a misprint for "palace", as one may think at first sight: "place" is repeated in the first line of p. 411. It is surely an odd translation of δώματα.

[3] Vv. 594 f. Grube (p. 409) assigns these verses to the Chorus. Our two manuscripts give no speaker's name, and Murray assigns them to Dionysus, "following Tyrwhitt, Bruhn and others".

[4] Except G. H. Meyer (see *Riddle*, p. 40).

Messenger, of the Second Messenger, of Agaue (both when delirious[1] and later when sane), of Cadmus, and indeed of the Chorus[2] as soon as Dionysus returns to them. Had only one of these six parties said nothing, we should have been puzzled: their unanimous blindness may strike us as another miracle.[3] But the king's silence has significance far beyond the rest. Not only does he re-enter his palace and summon Dionysus to accompany him (843): the poet invites our attention to his silence at the very moment when he should be most appalled by the collapse of his house. Dionysus ends his address to the Maenads by saying that he hears Pentheus at the door. "What will he say after this?" The king duly appears, full of wrath, but giving no sign that he has just witnessed a blasting epiphany of godhead. "This is an outrage! The stranger, but lately held fast in bonds, has escaped me. Ha! There he stands! What does this mean? How did you come out to show yourself before the portals of my house?" And again: "How did you escape your bonds and pass outside?" Verrall puts the case admirably.[4]

We have here no casual discrepancy, no separable pictures, seen to disagree only if we bring them together.... We might conceivably so explain ... the neglect of the earthquake and its effects, though visible (according to the women) in the palace-front, by those who come to the palace afterwards from without.... We might ... say that the escape of the prisoner, with all its incidents, is then no longer in view, but done with and dismissed. But it is not done with, it is not dismissed, when Pentheus comes out. On the contrary, we are still expecting, and are expressly told to expect, the most important part of it, that is to say, the effect of it all upon the King. And this effect, the full effect of all that has really happened, we see: the escape of his prisoner is the whole subject of his discourse. Only the alleged circumstances of it, such trifling accompaniments as a fire and an earthquake, are unnoticed, forgotten, ignored. And the audience, in spite of this, are to imagine that he has seen and felt them!

Attempts have been made to rebut the *argumentum ex silentio*—apparently as stated in the *Riddle*,[5] for they are powerless against Verrall's handling of Pentheus' own silence. Professor Dodds writes: "There is,

[1] Euripides even lets her mention (1212-15) the triglyphs, up to which she would have Pentheus (supposed still living) ascend by a ladder.

[2] Moreover, their question (613), "how did you escape from your encounter with the wicked man?", normally quite natural, is inept if they remember the terrific events, including the god's own triumphant arrival, that have allegedly occurred.

[3] "But neither the poet nor we can trouble ourselves with repeated exclamations of the kind that you appear to wish; the play must go on." (So, e.g., Grube as above, and Kitto, p. 381.) That is sound, in theory. But no dramatist, however eccentric, has a right to get himself, his characters, and his audience into such a muddle.

[4] Pp. 67 f.; cp. pp. 66 f. Verrall was the first to observe and expound the importance of the king's silence: the *Riddle* (p. 43) barely mentions it.   [5] Pp. 43-48.

however, one way, and one way only, to show a thing not-happening on the stage—you must introduce a character to point out that it has not happened. This could easily have been done: Pentheus was at hand to do it. But Pentheus denies nothing."[1] Surely no one, whatever his view of these events, can expect Pentheus to contradict an assertion that he has not heard. Professor Grube points to the silence of Theseus in *Heracles*,[2] who arrives to find the hero's house ruined but says nothing of it: this argument was met by anticipation in the *Riddle*.[3] A third suggestion has been made by Dr. Gilbert Murray[4] and others. "The Greek habit was to let each scene stand very much by itself, producing its own effect uninterrupted by references to other parts of the play. An incident or a character which has done its work is simply allowed to drop." To explain thus the silences now in question—at any rate the king's—is to assail the very basis of drama.

And so, when the Maenads ask "You saw how yonder stone lintels upon the columns gaped apart?"[5] the alert spectator[6] will answer: "I did not. You are well named Madwomen: your eyes deceive you." He will give a nod of recognition later when he watches Agaue brandishing her

---

[1] P. 141, quoting the *Riddle* (p. 48): "He [Euripides] has shown us the thing *not happening*."

[2] P. 409. Dodds also refers to *Heracles*, adding other supposed parallels. For answers to most of these see the *Riddle*, pp. 40, 134–7. As regards *Prometheus*, we should remember that its stage-management is a recognized difficulty, and that nothing whatever happens after the collapse.

Professor Winnington-Ingram remarks that in *Heracles* "not only do the characters make no subsequent reference to a general collapse of the palace, but Amphitryon at 1056 is afraid that Heracles, if he wakes, will destroy it!" (*Euripides and Dionysus* (1948), p. 184, n. 1.) But the account in that play is spoiled for our purpose by the poet's "deliberate vagueness", as Winnington-Ingram rightly calls it.

[3] Pp. 135–7.

[4] In his review of the *Riddle* (the London *Nation*, May 16, 1908). Schmid says: "Der Dichter hat von dem alten homerischen Recht Gebrauch gemacht, ein nebensächliches Motiv fallen zu lassen, nachdem es seinen Dienst getan hatte." (Müller's *Handbuch der klassischen Altertumswissenschaft*, Abt. VII, Teil 1, vol. 3 (Munich, 1940), p. 674, n. 4.) Kitto (p. 381) and Dodds (p. 141) also maintain this view.

Incidentally it brings to mind an oddity that seems to have passed unremarked. Why are Ino and Autonoe not "allowed to drop" at the close? Of course they are concerned therewith, but we are not in the least concerned with them: at the most, a brief phrase or two might have been let fall by Cadmus and Agaue. But they are directly or indirectly mentioned no less than thirteen times in the last scene: I can suggest no reason.

[5] Vv. 591 f. (Dodds's translation).

[6] That such shrewd and watchful persons were numerous in the Athenian theatre at this date is proved beyond question, not only by well-known passages in the *Frogs*, but also by the fact that Aristophanes thought fit to offer such a play—and won the first prize with it.

son's head and calling it the head of a lion. This delusion of the Chorus was ascribed in the *Riddle* to hypnotism,[1] but is better ascribed to glamour, as we shall see in a moment.

So much for the palace-miracle in itself: but we must by no means forget that it belongs to the whole scene of excitement (576–656). It has just as much, and just as little, reality as the phantom and the rest that Pentheus saw or experienced indoors.[2] As the Chorus believe that they see the house-front reeling, precisely so the king believes that he sees fire assailing his house.[3] This whole passage describes a scene created by glamour, in the full and original sense of that word: an enchantment cast over people, objects, or places, causing the onlooker to see them as quite other than they are. So Odysseus in Homer,[4] treading at last the soil of his longed-for island home, fails to recognize it because of glamour cast by Athena and breaks yet again into lamentation; so Horace[5] tells of an "Argive personage" who sat in the empty theatre applauding tragedies that were hallucinations. But one need scarcely dwell on the frequency of such tales, in Spenser and so many others. Perhaps the nearest parallel to Euripides' picture occurs in *The Tempest*.[6] That boisterous and terrifying first scene is pure delusion: Ariel's speech later shows that all was the

---

[1] Pp. 84, etc. Allusions to *human* magic, γοητεία, etc., of course become frequent later. The only clear mention of similar trickery in Euripides is *Orestes* 1497 f., where the Phrygian attributes Helen's disappearance to φάρμακα or μάγων τέχναι or θεῶν κλοπαί: note the distinction between magicians and gods. Other possible examples of *glamour* are the bull in *Hippolytus* (see below, pp. 91 f.) and Athena in *Heracles* 1002 ff.

[2] Cp. Verrall, pp. 73–75. But he rejects (p. 73) what is said in the *Riddle* (p. 105) and above: that Pentheus here as later is cast under a spell and does "see" the phantom, etc., subjectively. Verrall says "All lies"; I suggest "All lies, supported by glamour". Pentheus thinks a bull Dionysus, just as he later mistakes Dionysus for a bull (920 ff.). His sight of the fire is described by δώματ' αἴθεσθαι δοκῶν (624), which is very like 605 f., ᾔσθησθ', ὡς ἔοικε, Βακχίου κτέ., a strong hint at hallucination. Dionysus' release is no kind of marvel: he tells us himself (615 f.) that Pentheus never even laid a finger on him (evidently, therefore, καθεῖρξ' in 618 should be καθείργ') and he simply walked out, leaving the king to his own devices (636 f.).

[3] Verrall (*loc. cit.*) asks why we should believe the prophet concerning what passes within, any more than we believe him about the downfall of the palace. He remarks that Pentheus is said to have collapsed (κόπου δ' ὕπο διαμεθεὶς ξίφος παρεῖται) and yet in a moment rushes forth full of excitement and energy. To the first point we may reply, not indeed logically but in accordance with what seems natural to our imagination, that such a *detailed* account convinces us of its reality, though reality as an imposture: Pentheus did think what we are told that he thought. The second point is weak: why should not the victim, in these strange circumstances, be supposed to recover with strange promptness?

[4] *Od.* XIII. 187–216. [5] *Ep.* II. ii. 128 ff.

[6] The resemblance would have been still closer had Shakespeare assigned "We split, we split!" not to "a confused noise, within" but to "Ariel, within". No doubt he would have done so, had Ariel been already known to us.

work of his own magical activity. No one drowns, the ship rides "safely in harbour", even the passengers' garments are "fresher than before"; and on reading that

> Not a soul
> But felt a fever of the mad, and play'd
> Some tricks of desperation

we recall Pentheus' behaviour within his palace.[1]

Why substitute glamour for that hypnotism whereof the *Riddle* made so much? Hypnotism is a human influence, and in that book Dionysus was mistaken for a human prophet, whose feats could have been performed only by such skill.[2] But if he is a god, as we now find, he must use its divine analogue, glamour. The essay on *Hippolytus* will note[3] that Aphrodite (who of course does not use glamour) could have instantly destroyed the prince; but Euripides has undertaken a play, which means development, so that an intermediary, Phaedra, becomes involved—illogically, from a theoretical, non-dramatic, point of view. Dionysus, equally divine, has a purpose more complex than Aphrodite's. To slay Pentheus he needs no intermediary; but, if he is to punish Agaue as he does, her mediation becomes inevitable. The death-scene is thus perfectly consonant with the idea that Dionysus is a god omnipotent in the situation as depicted, who works his purpose merely by putting forth his will in the form of glamour cast upon Agaue. His success is complete. Her rejection of his worship at the end is a personal attitude for which he cares nothing: she acknowledges his power, and Thebes accepts his religion. What happens to Pentheus' house is merely incidental, exciting as Euripides chooses to make it. No one in the play is in the least affected or impressed by it save the Chorus, who need no converting. But this scene too is worked by glamour, though with no intermediary. All these feats prove Dionysus divine just as well as physically real miracles could have done.

On the whole turbulent scene Professor Winnington-Ingram has a striking passage.[4]

> The story which he [Dionysus] has to tell . . . has an atmosphere of its own, . . . lighter and less impressive than the unseen voice and the lyrical responses of the Chorus. . . . Pentheus . . . organised a fire-brigade. . . . The Bacchic god, for further measure, razed the buildings to the ground! And now the footsteps of Pentheus are heard. What will he say? The Stranger is ready for him. The tone

---

[1] Cp. *Riddle*, p. 105.   [2] See p. 106.
[3] P. 104 below.
[4] Pp. 83–85, partly anticipated by Kitto (p. 381) and Dodds (p. 144); see also the *Riddle*, p. 84, n. 3.

is light as the detail is vague, not merely because of the condition of the Greek theatre or the current role of the god, but for a more fundamental reason of dramatic construction. . . . If the miracles at this stage were too overwhelming, they would make what follows an anti-climax; they would anticipate the complete epiphany of Dionysus. . . . The dramatic interest of the play largely turns upon the struggle of wills between Dionysus and Pentheus. . . . to this defeat the palace-miracle is but a prelude . . . foreshadowing indeed the ultimate catastrophe, but itself impalpable and phantasmagoric.[1]

That is skilful and attractive; but, excepting the last clause, it must be rejected. To "play down" the marvellous events so as to secure an unbroken rise of tension would, we may readily agree, have been an excellent device. But of what use is our agreement if Euripides himself disagrees? He has refused this method: so far from playing the scene down, he plays it up. He could easily have omitted the most exciting passages. Not to mention the words, so often adduced already, about complete downfall of the palace, why, if he means to dilute the scene, does he go out of his way to make Dionysus bid the thunderbolt's blazing torch consume the house of Pentheus utterly with fire?

Dionysus alleges that the palace collapsed. That it did not is proved by the silence of Pentheus (to mention no one else) and by his re-entry with Dionysus. What can have induced the poet to manage things so astonishingly?

At this point the *Riddle* went deplorably astray. Its author, assuming (safely enough) that Euripides was a consummate dramatist, proceeded naïvely to argue as if such a dramatist was always consummate. All now seemed crystal-clear, however amazing. Euripides must intend—there was no alternative— to depict Dionysus as a shameless impostor. Despite its immense power and beauty (which the *Riddle* of course nowhere denied) the whole tragedy was an exposure of sham religion, counterfeit miracles, and a human prophet brilliantly able, completely unprincipled, horribly cruel. As a result, the *Riddle* was committed to proving that all those marvels reported earlier or later—the escape of the imprisoned Theban votaries, the strange feats described in the First Messenger's narrative, and whatever may appear supernatural in the magnificent presentation of Pentheus' setting-forth and death—that all these were false, based on nothing more divine than ignorance, trickery, superstition, or crass partisanship.

[1] I have picked out what suits my own topic. To the author's views my extracts do less than justice. For instance, he finds impressive symbolism in the incident of Pentheus and the bull, remarking (p. 84) that "it is the symbolism which counts and is of lasting effect"; the suggestion has much interest, but lies outside the scope of this essay.

That is far too high a ransom for Euripides' reputation (supposing it ever existed) as not only a great but also a faultless playwright. If anything ever written sounded as though it should be accepted at face value it is the passages that we have named; and, indeed, nearly all the play. The author of the *Riddle* was not indeed perverse, but pedantic, in shouldering his way across those wonderful scenes and trampling over those noble blossoms in pursuit of a will-o'-the-wisp, Euripides as a blend of Ibsen and Voltaire. Not perverse, for he held what seemed an infallible clue: the poet's treatment of the one miracle that happens in presence of his audience. Pedantic, nevertheless, for his exposure of the other miracles was both feeble and captious; moreover, he failed to ask himself why Euripides had not continued his dire work and ruined those other miracles himself instead of waiting twenty-three centuries for so clumsy an accomplice. At length a sense of perspective returned, and the critic's eye rested long on that club of Heracles, the palace-miracle. He had described it aright: that remained certain; but was there perhaps some better view of it? Gradually another explanation assumed clear form in his mind, the first to give due weight to all the elements of this distracting shadow-show.

Euripides, we found in the first essay, was capable of astonishing freakishness and wanton gambols, perhaps unparalleled in dramatic history; and of sad blunders too, that must be condemned not because they infringe standards ancient or modern, but because they damage, confuse, even contradict the very plays in which they occur. Is this bogus miracle an irresponsible frolic or a destructive blunder? Or is it something that looks now like the one, now like the other, but must be understood as different from either?

Before we attempt to answer, is it not well to ask whether our dismay at these questions should be tempered, perhaps banished, by recollection that the *Bacchae* belongs to his last trilogy? One of its companions, *Iphigenia at Aulis*, was left by him unfinished and was completed by the son who bore his name. Shall we suppose that the *Bacchae* also was not indeed unfinished but incompletely revised:[1] that our disconcerting scene would have received a different shape had the poet lived long enough? But all we can offer in support of this without begging the question is that here and there the writing shows little smudges.[2] It would be absurd to

---

[1] Cp. Murray (p. 172 of his translation): "This scene in longer metre always strikes me as a little unlike the style of Euripides, and inferior. It may mark one of the parts left unfinished by the poet, and written in by his son." See also the *Riddle*, p. 84, n. 3.

[2] Vv. 606, 614, 647. These obviously must not be pressed.

THE *BACCHAE* AND ITS RIDDLE 61

regard the passage as a rough sketch and thus not open to critical scrutiny. We can no longer postpone the questions raised a moment ago. They should be answered as follows.

Euripides resolves to place at this point a miracle proving Dionysus' divine nature, might, and purpose. So far it exactly resembles all the others. But for obvious and excellent reasons he will make it happen before the audience. In this sensational quality it is paralleled only by the scene where Dionysus completes[1] his subjugation of Pentheus. But that involves no difficulty whatever of stage-management, whereas the earlier scene treats the overthrow of a building. If it is to succeed in arousing the spectators' excited awe based on complete if temporary acceptance, then a furore on the stage and thunder without are indispensable. But the fifth-century theatre was poor in such devices. Then will this serve? Dionysus has been taken as a prisoner to the stables. Shall he release himself amid loud crashes "off" and come forth to tell his votaries uncanny details of Pentheus' discomfiture? Would that not be a somewhat cheap epiphany, especially for so dashing a god? But it might be used as groundwork. We could add *éclat* by . . . ? Yes! We can shout from within that the deity has arrived in person, and the Chorus shall give support to the affair by ecstatic cries of welcome; while they are about it, let them or Dionysus raise a scream of "earthquake"! That is the presentation as imagined by opponents of the *Riddle*. Had Euripides contented himself with it, there would have been nothing to explain, as they have so often told us.

But he was not content[2] with this simple statement which, so far as one can judge, would have been adequate. Suddenly his audacious wanton mood lays hold upon him. "Adequate? What a word! Nicomachus and Xenocles are 'adequate'. Mark me now; now will I raise the waters. Did I not once say ἐρρέτω πρόπας δόμος? I say it again. The whole house of this tedious monarch shall fall into utter ruin, and serve him right! 'Impossible', you exclaim? I would have you know that more wizards than one have a hand in this tragedy."

He intends to fulfil his promise, but theatrically; and theatrically in an unusual sense. The normal stage-illusion occurs when the actor

---

[1] The earlier phase is conducted within the palace. On this division see below, p. 66.
[2] We cannot allege that he was swayed at all by Aeschylus' *Edoni*. Pseudo-Longinus (XV. 6) writes: καὶ παρὰ μὲν Αἰσχύλῳ παραδόξως τὰ τοῦ Λυκούργου βασίλεια κατὰ τὴν ἐπιφάνειαν τοῦ Διονύσου θεοφορεῖται· ἐνθουσίᾳ δὴ δῶμα, βακχεύει στέγη. But he goes on to find an Euripidean parallel in v. 726, πᾶν δὲ συνεβάκχευ' ὄρος, not in the scene before us.

personating Agaue pretends to be mad, the abnormal when he pretends to think that the head he carries is a lion's. By what Coleridge called "that willing suspension of disbelief, which constitutes poetic faith", the spectator believes that the actor is Agaue and that she is mad; there his belief halts: he does not take the head for a lion's. In precisely the same way the Athenian choristers pretend to be mastered by glamour, and so to believe that the house falls; the spectator believes them thus possessed, but does not believe that it falls. He cannot, for he sees that it is unchanged, just as he sees that the head is in fact the king's. The miracle, in short, is effected, but it is not the downfall: it is the divinely induced belief in the downfall; and Euripides shows the method by which glamour may be created—that and nothing more. Through Dionysus he casts on his Maenads the spell that every competent playwright casts on his audience. But it is immensely harder to cast. He asserts that the palace collapses; and his method of doing so is an unsurpassed achievement in dramatic illusion. He deftly mingles what is both false and incredible, downfall of the palace,[1] with what is false but credible enough because untested by the eye: namely, the apparition, the bull, and so forth behind the scenes.[2] This dovetailing should be watched carefully. First, Dionysus shouts from *within* that the god is present, and summons Earthquake to heave the ground. (Here, perhaps, rumbles are heard.) Then the Chorus, on whom the divine potency is falling, just as it falls later on the Theban votaries in the forest, excitedly describe what "will" happen to the *palace-front*: "Soon he will shatter the house in collapse"; they add: "Dionysus is afoot *in* the halls";[3] and "*Saw* ye those stone *architraves* gaping apart on the columns?" This is at once followed by "Bromius yonder cries his triumph *inside* the dwelling". Now the tension rises anew. Dionysus (still unseen) shouts: "Kindle the thunderbolt's blazing torch! Consume utterly, consume with fire the *house* of Pentheus!" Instantly the possessed women seize their cue: "Ah! Ah! Fire! *Seest* thou not, meets it not thy gaze, round the holy tomb of Semele? . . . Hurl, hurl your trembling bodies to the ground, ye Maenads! For our king, the seed of

---

[1] The words translated below as "house", "halls", etc. are μέλαθρα, μέλαθρα, στέγα, δώματα, μέλαθρα; later δῶμα (or δώματα). Who can believe that all these mean "stables"?

[2] It has already been said (p. 57 above) that these events are no more, and no less, real than the allegedly visible events. But the spectators can accept them by the usual dramatic convention for the time being; they cannot so accept the palace downfall. Whether miniature crashes are used to help in the stables affair, may be left to the reader's taste and fancy.

[3] ὁ Διόνυσος ἀνὰ μέλαθρα is cunning. ἀνά suggests that he now ranges at large: if we care to think so, passing from the stables to wreck all the premises.

Zeus, *cometh*[1] upon these *halls*, setting them *upside down*." Then, while the spectator, agitated as perhaps never before by a theatrical scene, sits in a daze as to what has happened, is happening, or may be about to happen, and almost as to where he is himself, Dionysus enters.

He comes to calm his votaries, so he says; in reality, to drive home the illusion. Here the poet's cunning itself borders on the miraculous. Mark first the change of metre, from lyrics to trochaics. These latter are regularly employed by Euripides to show a tension less than the lyrical but greater than that of the most excited iambics. We are thus caused to feel that we have left hysteria for calmness and reason, whereas we are still bemused: else, why not iambics? That metrical change puts Dionysus' conversation with his Maenads, and his ensuing narrative, on a deceptively reassuring plane. He employs the method already noted, with a masterly development. His first two words give us, as the phrase goes, "a salutary shock", completely bogus, but almost everyone thinks rudeness a by-product of sincerity. The form of address, literally translated, is "barbarian women", and cannot justly be made more courteous than "ladies of Asia", if anyone prefers that. He proceeds:[2] "Are ye so distracted by terror that ye have fallen to the earth? Ye perceived, it appears, Bacchus shaking asunder the *house* of Pentheus; but rise, be of good cheer and quit this trembling of the flesh." The destruction of the house is cleverly brought in as a detail. "It appears": is that Dionysus' sardonic little gibe at credulous barbarians, or the poet's eye-twinkle at his audience? After a moment or two Dionysus relates the sensational events that have passed *indoors* (hitherto indicated by nothing[3] more than cries about earthquake and the god's presence), inserting, as if it were but another item, the collapse of the whole *palace*, now and only now described[4] as having actually occurred and with completeness beyond all denial. That overwhelming miracle is thus firmly established, not indeed as a genuine occurrence but as a thoroughly successful delusion, the theatrical credit for which goes to the god and the artistic to Euripides. The latter genius proceeds forthwith to dissipate it like vapour, because (as the modern slogan has it) "the show must go on"; in other words, because it did not happen and we shall soon need a habitable palace again. He acts at once, before the spectator has time to reflect. Dionysus exclaims (in brief): 'I hear Pentheus coming. What will he say? Now

---

[1] ἔπεισι (602) is present, not future, or τιθείς would be θήσων.
[2] The reading of v. 606 is doubtful, the meaning clear.
[3] Unless we assume the crashes aforesaid, of which there is no trace in the text.
[4] Vv. 632 f.: the vital passage on which the *Riddle* was based.

comes the tussle!' The king rushes forth, crying: "Outrage has been done upon me!" What outrage? "My palace is a ruin"? Nothing of the kind. "My prisoner has escaped me, despite his chains.... Ah! There he stands. How came you here to the front of my house?" The great miracle is unknown to its victim. In a flash we have moved from grim illusion to far grimmer realities.

That astounding scene surely has never been approached as a masterpiece of dramatic sleight-of-hand. Euripides shows both the eye-defeating dexterity of a conjuror who forces a card and that iridescence whereby Pindar's fancies or themes pass into one another. No wonder our greatest Hellenist has written of the *Bacchae*: "Like a live thing it seems to move and show new faces every time that, with imagination fully working, one reads the play"![1] Nevertheless, we are no longer hoodwinked by this truly phantasmagoric scene, and discover that both sides in the controversy were right and both were wrong: a conclusion happily frequent in open-minded disputes, chastening self-complacency while unearthing facts all the more welcome for their long seclusion.

This new idea obviously renders most of the *Riddle* untenable. Nevertheless, the discussion must proceed: a few additional notes on that work may interest some students; more important are certain pages, not yet considered, of Verrall's essay; and we have still to face another problem that cannot be termed a mare's-nest.

We naturally begin with the remaining miracles. The escape of those Theban devotees whom Pentheus has imprisoned (443–50) should be accepted as the marvel that its narrator thinks it. Still, the male Theban sympathizers improperly mentioned[2] in that connexion do exist: one of them addresses Pentheus.[3] The First Messenger certainly damages his own story. Having interrupted his account of the miraculous feats done by the bacchanals with an enthusiastic appeal to Pentheus—"Had you been present, the sight would have made you approach with prayers the god whom now you blame"—he at once tells how the herdsmen who did see all these marvels began to dispute about them and how both he and the rest soon agreed to capture Agaue and thus please the king.[4] Here is a

---

[1] Murray, *Euripides and his Age*, p. 196.   [2] Verrall, p. 63.

[3] I cannot give up my belief (*Class. Rev.*, vol. XIX (1905), pp. 434 f.) that vv. 775–7 are spoken by a man of Thebes: their tone is utterly unsuited to the Chorus-Leader, who exclaims "Heresy!" and other bold rebukes at the close of Pentheus' first speech (264–6). See *Riddle*, p. 67, and Verrall, p. 93.

[4] Vv. 712–21. Cp. Verrall, pp. 86–88; *Riddle*, pp. 70–73, where the parallel scene in *Iphigenia in Tauris* is adduced.

sudden oddity that cannot be blinked. But to suppose that Euripides intended to ruin evidence about Dionysus' godhead is a mistake. To mention only one argument, the narrative is too beautiful, too convincing,[1] above all too long, to be damned for a single incident, however strange. Euripides here delivers one of those sardonic strokes discussed in the preceding essay: that is all, though to some it will appear much. He insists on writing these, and if we do not relish them we must swallow them as best we may.

The only[2] other scene, rightly or wrongly believed supernatural, that we shall examine is the horrible though superbly written degradation[3] of Pentheus. The *Riddle* was content to explain it as yet another exhibition of hypnotic power.[4] Verrall, however, insists that for this "the prophet" has no need to take his victim indoors[5] and that nevertheless he manœuvres Pentheus into suggesting withdrawal:[6] this cannot be gainsaid. He proceeds to argue that Pentheus' collapse is caused by a potion; for the king on emerging gives a familiar sign of drunkenness, the double sun and double city; and his tormentor's first words allude to wine-libations:[7] "Pentheus and the stranger, having now made an alliance or truce, have pledged each other, as usual, *in drink*."[8] So far, convincingly put: what of the further assertion,[9] that Pentheus' cup holds a poison?

[1] R. Nihard justly condemns the attempts of Verrall and myself to discredit these wonders. *Le Problème des Bacchantes d'Euripide* (Louvain, 1912), pp. 73 f.

[2] The story of Pentheus' death no longer needs examination. It is wrought by glamour: Dionysus casts illusion and hysteria upon Agaue and the rest just as he casts them upon the Asiatic women earlier.

[3] Vv. 912–76. Winnington-Ingram has much to say of the king's prurience (pp. 45 ff., 52, etc.), and rightly. But he would have been less severe had he pondered Verrall's remarks on this scene (where Pentheus obviously should not be judged by normal standards), e.g., p. 126: "The mind of the victim is not only enfeebled, but fouled. He becomes beastly. . . . He pictures the worst discoveries with chuckling anticipation." Cp. M. R. Glover, "*The Bacchae*", *J.H.S.*, vol. XLIX, p. 86, n. 15.

[4] P. 106. Cp. Murray, *History of Ancient Greek Literature*, p. 271: "In a scene of weird power and audacity he slowly controls—one would fain say 'hypnotises'—Pentheus."

[5] Pp. 101–3.

[6] Vv. 810–61. Verrall, p. 105: "From the triumph of the stranger upon this move (which he first suggests [827]), we learn that he has manœuvred for it,—and therefore that his project, needing the move, is something quite different from mesmeric influence."

[7] Vv. 912 f.:

σὲ τὸν πρόθυμον ὄνθ' ἃ μὴ χρεὼν ὁρᾶν
σπεύδοντα τ' ἀσπούδαστα, Πενθέα λέγω . . ..

Verrall rejects Musurus' reading σπεύδοντα and retains that of our one manuscript. Murray prints σπεύδοντα.

[8] Verrall, p. 109 (his italics): he notes (p. 111) vv. 923 f.: ὁ θεὸς ὁμαρτεῖ . . . ἔνσπονδος ἡμῖν.

[9] Pp. 109–25. It is based on words that, to be sure, we all think odd: νάρθηκά τε,

It is ingenious, but plausible only if we can think the chief actor no god but a human prophet. How else could he thus enslave his victim? We have just heard Verrall destroy the notion of hypnotism: *a fortiori* his argument would destroy that of glamour. But closer inspection shows that after all only one detail of it makes any obstacle to belief in Dionysus' godhead. The talk about wine proves nothing. He assaults Pentheus' sanity without external aid, for the dionysiac power of itself produces intoxication, just as Aphrodite compels love without administering a philtre. As Tiresias says[1] (if we may without qualms paraphrase that dubious theologian), Dionysus not only gives wine: he *is* wine. But the withdrawal, which (as Verrall remarks) is first proposed by him? The reason offered by Dionysus is the need to disguise Pentheus. Could that not have been done without withdrawal? A good deal of valeting is bestowed on the king after they return. This, the real foundation of Verrall's case, disappears if we consider the adjacent passages. Suppose that they do not retire, expunge the ode sung in their absence, and mend the gap by a little rewriting of their earlier conversation and by omitting Dionysus' speech of triumph (848–61). What is the result? An impossible scene, containing the palace-miracle, a short altercation, the First Messenger's narrative, the conversation between Dionysus and Pentheus, finally the king's disguising and degradation: an intolerably long and heterogeneous mass. Euripides of course breaks it up by an ode, during which they would have nothing to do; and retire they must, wine or no wine. Dionysus throughout acts as a god, of however repellent a kind; his treatment of Pentheus here resembles his treatment when he threw mad confusion upon him in the stables.

Of non-supernatural elements discussed in the *Riddle*, that alleged conspiracy[2] between Tiresias and Bacchus deserves least attention. Everyone (it seems) rejects it; and rightly. It does indeed explain Tiresias' language in 326 f.:

μαίνῃ γὰρ ὡς ἄλγιστα, κοὔτε φαρμάκοις
ἄκη λάβοις ἂν οὔτ' ἄνευ τούτων νοσεῖς.

πιστὸν Ἄιδαν, ἔλαβεν εὔθυρσον (1157 f.). He will have it that "faithful death" or "trusted death" is "an expression barely conceivable": that "*pistos Hades* signifies poison taken in a draught, and could hardly signify anything else"; moreover, νάρθηξ, he says, can mean "capsule". This latter point, though dubious, may pass: see L. and S., *s.v.* But his explanation of πιστός is too bizarre: for, though of course πιστὸς Ἄιδης can mean "potable death", no discreet poet would use the words in that sense when every hearer, the context not plainly forbidding, would be sure to give πιστός its vastly more frequent sense. We are forced to accept "reliable death", meaning "certain death", strange phrase as it is, in Greek as in English. See also Dodds *ad loc.*

[1] Vv. 278–85: οὗτος θεοῖσι σπένδεται θεὸς γεγώς κτέ. [2] *Riddle*, pp. 95–100.

"For mad you are, most grievously: neither in drugs can you find a cure, nor is your malady uncaused by them."[1] The last words must mean that Tiresias "knows something", or believes he does, which is almost the same thing in the circumstances. If the conspiracy-idea is wrong—no other support for it exists[2]— we must be content to leave this passage in its darkness.[3]

The character of Pentheus may be almost ignored here: opinions are various, since they depend so largely on the reader's temperament. No commentator has agreed with the Chorus, who look on him as what a later age would call "Antichrist"; none has seen in him a martyr to *sophrosyne*, which Greeks so highly extolled but so rarely followed. The *Riddle*[4] comes nearest, perhaps, to maintaining this latter opinion; its author admits that he failed to emphasize Pentheus' tyrannical language and conduct, which forbid us to make him the "hero".

The lyrics glow and vibrate with a beauty unparalleled in Attic literature: on that we are all agreed.[5] But they contain inconsistencies of statement and of spirit, disconcertingly complete: one almost said, grossly obtruded. "There is a double paradox in these Maenad preachers of *sophrosyne*, these Asiatic Hellenists."[6] At one moment they rapturously hymn the beauty of holiness and the serene bliss of worship amid Nature's peace;[7] at another their fevered outcry demands the rending of animals, hysterical music and dance, or gloats over the bloody destruction of the human monster who spurns and persecutes their religion.[8] Again, though the play as a whole depicts this religion as novel, indeed as an upheaval of Greek life, they loudly praise traditional belief and amazingly proclaim themselves upholders of the time-honoured natural faith cherished by simple-hearted folk.[9] These two contradictions, of tone and of fact respectively, have often been noted but seem to need a more searching

---

[1] Dodds *ad loc.* rightly decides that the text is sound, but seems mistaken when he implies that the φάρμακα are metaphorical, as in Aesch. *Ag.* 1407 ff.; ἄνευ τούτων, though we cannot (as it happens) explain the phrase, is too definite for that.

[2] Vv. 360 ff., ἐξαιτώμεθα κτέ., need not imply, as the *Riddle* (p. 100) suggests, "that the prophet is on friendly terms with Dionysus". Any Theban subject might so intercede, even had he never spoken to the Stranger before.

[3] Sandys ("Pentheus is under a spell") and Tyrrell ("the supernatural infatuation"), *ad loc.*, fail to deal with the downright word φάρμακα.

[4] Pp. 66 f.

[5] Among so many praises must be noted Dodds's penetrating words on vv. 873–6.

[6] Winnington-Ingram, p. 59.

[7] Vv. 72–88, 370–86, 416–23, 902–11.

[8] Vv. 135–67, 877–81, 976–96, 1153–64.

[9] Vv. 427–32, 882–96, 1006–10. Cp. Cadmus' appeal (331) to his grandson: οἴκει μεθ' ἡμῶν, μὴ θύραζε τῶν νόμων.

examination,[1] even after Professor Winnington-Ingram's recent discussion.[2]

First, however, a smaller puzzle, that may be thought similar to these, should be considered. In vv. 402 ff. the Chorus sing: "Oh that I might repair to Cyprus, island of Aphrodite, where dwell the Loves that cast a spell on mortal hearts, and to Paphos," another famed haunt of Aphrodite. This sudden prayer surprises us, not so much because unparalleled in these odes as because the charge of unchastity brought by Pentheus repeatedly against the female adherents of Dionysus is repeatedly denied by their friends.[3] Attempts have been made to alter the text: Verrall would emend so as to give what may be thus summarized: 'Oh to seek ... not the Nile Delta or Paphos, but Macedonia, home of beauty and passion.'[4] (Macedonia appears in the next lines: it was there that Euripides wrote this tragedy.) Two objections must be made. Such a change throws the elaboration (whether enthusiastic or not) "where the Loves" etc. sadly out of focus. Still worse, the whole passage becomes very awkward in structure. The summary above is clearer than Verrall's Greek: what auditor would not be baffled for a moment by "Oh to come —why to the island"? Professor Dodds justly rejects it, with an attractive note on the connexion between Aphrodite and Dionysus; but he does not meet the obvious rejoinder that in the circumstances of this particular drama the Maenads would have been well advised to say no word of the goddess. Certainly we should follow him in accepting Dr. Murray's text,[5] and should be content to remark that Euripides is fond of startling us like this.

Of the two unmistakable contradictions, that between tranquil piety

[1] The *Riddle* (pp. 51 f., 114 ff.) makes little of them. Verrall (pp. 147–52) does less well than usual, and shuts us out from one way of escape by asserting (pp. 148 f.) that the Chorus do not speak for Euripides. Nihard (pp. 359–67) fumbles. Steinweg takes the opposite view to Verrall's: "Der Chor also befeuert und zügelt zugleich. So wird er für den Dichter ein tönendes Instrument, sowohl für das Fortissimo seiner Stimmung, als auch für das Moderato seiner Überlegung." *Euripides als Tragiker und Lustspieldichter* (Halle, 1924), p. 178.
[2] Pp. 38 f., 162 f., 172 f. See below, p. 69.
[3] One of them makes a *gaffe* in v. 773, however.
[4] Pp. 152–7. He suggests

$$\dot{\iota}\kappa o\acute{\iota}\mu\alpha\nu\text{---}\tau\acute{\iota}\ \pi o\tau'\ \ddot{\alpha}\nu\ \tau\grave{\alpha}\nu$$
$$\nu\hat{\alpha}\sigma o\nu\ldots$$
$$\text{\"E}\rho\omega\tau\epsilon\varsigma$$
$$\Pi\acute{\alpha}\phi o\nu,\ \ddot{\alpha}\nu\ \theta'\ \kappa\tau\acute{\epsilon}.$$

Otherwise as Murray. The two places rejected are Paphos and "the Delta(?)", Κύπρον being explained as a gloss.

[5] Not entirely that of the manuscripts, but the differences do not concern our problem.

and bloodthirstiness will seem less abrupt if Professor Grube's comment is accepted: ". . . the chorus reflect and amplify the Dionysus theme as they usually reflect the feelings of a main character, and they change from joy to fury with the changing mood of the god."[1] He has described what normally happens. Here we find not only one ode differing sensationally from another ode, but sensational differences between adjacent passages of the same ode. Though Dionysus has his widely different moods, he does not jerk in a moment from one to the other, whereas the Chorus pass straight from their picture of the Fawn set free, and from musings on traditional religious faith, to the cry "Triumph over one's foe, that is wisdom, that is glory!" (862–901); the praise of serene holiness is instantly followed by "Let Justice advance in manifest power, with bloody sword slashing him right through the neck, that earth-born son of Echion, enemy of God, of law, of justice" (1005–16). He who would explain such a medley must look deeper and more widely. Professor Winnington-Ingram does so.

. . . the poetry has almost throughout two aspects. One is towards the singers . . . an adequate and beautiful expression of what is immediately in their minds. Of the other aspect they are entirely unconscious; not so the poet and the audience. . . . the poetry is so written as to involve wider relationships than the singers have in mind, to invoke standards, emotional, moral or intellectual, which are not their standards. So it may happen that the song contains a comment upon or criticism of the singers themselves. . . . the poet has so written their song as deliberately to leave certain elements in it unintegrated and inharmonious.[2]

This recalls Goethe's comment on a chorus of his own.[3] "In the dirge the chorus passes completely out of its role. Hitherto it has remained thoroughly antique, or at least has never belied its girlish nature; but here it suddenly becomes grave and loftily contemplative and expresses things that it has never thought and indeed never could have thought." But the German scenes are imagined fantastically throughout: the Chorus begin as Trojan captives before the palace of Menelaus, later visit a medieval castle, and end by becoming dryads, naiads, oreads, and vine-nymphs. It is passing strange that a fifth-century Athenian should anticipate Goethe in dealing thus with his barbarian women. Still, he has undeniably done so; nor, in fact, is this the first time that unexpected thoughts come to us concerning Euripides' idea of a dramatist's business and the mental

---

[1] P. 399. [2] Pp. 38 f.
[3] Eckermann's *Gespräche mit Goethe*, July 5, 1827. He is discussing *Helena* (*Faust*, Part II, Act III).

agility supposable in his audience. We shall, then, explain the contradiction between serenity and murderous hate as Euripides' own reminder of the perils inseparable from a religion that is all emotion and no brains.[1]

And the other contradiction? Does this too reveal his own views: may we believe that he, of all men, cherished this enthusiasm for vulgar[2] tradition? We cannot evade the difficulty by pointing out that all the descriptions of Bacchism as novel are spoken by Thebans, who could truly utter them; for the Chorus too imply novelty when they allude to Semele as mother of their god: she was Cadmus' daughter, and Cadmus takes a notable part in the action. Their religion cannot be more than forty years old at the utmost. Our choice lies between two explanations. The first is that Euripides in his latest years has gone over to the unphilosophic multitude and (with an intolerably violent jerk) foists this reverence for ancient unquestioning faith upon the Maenads who are promulgators of a religion founded yesterday. The other is to believe that from time to time—not only in his lyrics but also in the dispute between Pentheus and the old men—he throws drama to the winds and (still with a terrible jolt) speaks of Bacchism as it exists in his own day upon the Macedonian uplands.[3] We must accept the second proposition, disagreeable as it may be, for it is at least credible, unlike the first.

What does Euripides think of Dionysus himself? He is as truly a "god" as other Olympians: a very real fact of our world and life, but not a genuine person with emotions, will, and aims. Nevertheless, since Euripides is not only a philosopher but a dramatist also, Dionysus becomes in this play, like Artemis in *Hippolytus*, an authentic *dramatis persona*, no less genuine than Tiresias.[4] This deity utters every word, performs every act, attributed by our text to Dionysus; but for nearly all the time he pretends to be his own prophet. Euripides deals with him quite straightforwardly until the very close, indeed until the god has finally disappeared. Then by a sardonic twist he makes Cadmus contradict (1360 ff.) the promise of Elysium uttered by his astonishing grandson.

---

[1] Winnington-Ingram is extremely good on this: see, for example, his chapter XII. "When Aristotle said that the solitary man must be either a beast or a god, he forgot perhaps that there were social groups which could make a man both at once" (p. 176). See further pp. 72 f. below.

[2] Not too severe a translation of φαυλότερον (431). The view here rejected is accepted by Murray (*Essays and Addresses* (1922), p. 84), by Schmid (p. 685), and the *Riddle* (pp. 117-25).

[3] See further Dodds on 201-3.

[4] This topic is treated more fully in pp. 102-6 below. The sardonic twist mentioned above, brief as it is, corresponds to the satire that Euripides blends with his glorification of Artemis (see pp. 96-100).

We thus arrive at the last question of all: can we discern Euripides' own opinion[1] about the Dionysiac religion? Whatever may be thought of its founder, everyone sees that it rises from the depths of human nature, surviving not only until the day of our poet and the Sophists, but (with whatever shifts of mood and emphasis) until our own, and destined to continue in one form or another so long as recognizably human beings exist. But, since (when all is said) even he normally uses the familiar methods of drama, his opinion is naturally, and notoriously, hard to detect. Dr. Murray has written that "for all his lucidity of language, Euripides is not lucid about religion".[2] Verrall confesses it imaginable that he would have quarrelled with no one on the benches who accepted the story of the *Bacchae* at its face value.[3] His last pages[4] deal with the "balance" therein maintained: Euripides' witness, despite the cruelty and horror, to whatever attractiveness or edification may be found in "the prophet's" demeanour and the utterances of his adherents. Nor is the old "palinode" idea quite dead:[5] that, closing a long career during which (to employ the most tentative phrasing) he has taken up an equivocal attitude towards the gods, Euripides here recants and proclaims himself vigorously orthodox, whatever that word might imply at the close of the fifth century. On the whole, however, opinion has now long, and rightly, denied such recantation, asserting that Euripides' fundamental quality and temper have not changed, though his manner has grown gentler under the impact of a worship met and studied in Macedonia during his last years. Our question has nevertheless received divergent or opposed answers, of which a few shall be quoted.

Dr. Murray tells us: "We have in the *Bacchae*—it seems to me impossible to deny it—a heartfelt glorification of 'Dionysus'". Definite enough! But, like the sensitive critic that he invariably shows himself, he proceeds to speak of a "Dionysus in some private sense of the poet's own. . . . The

[1] Of the religion itself nothing more need be said here. Dodds's Introduction gives an excellent account; his remarks (pp. xx ff.) on Sabazius are especially interesting (cp. my *Greek Comedy*, pp. 293 f.).

[2] *Euripides and his Age*, p. 190. Cp. M. R. Glover, *ut sup.*, p. 83: "He could entertain if not simultaneously, then alternately, different points of view, and would write a play to put forward and explore a possible interpretation of human life and destiny."

[3] Pp. 17, 62.

[4] Pp. 144 ff. Three points there may be specially noted: the lyrics treat the Bacchic religion from outside (cp. Nihard, p. 361); they criticize not only Pentheus but Tiresias also; the discussion of the Cyprus passage (see above, p. 68).

[5] As recently as 1924 Steinweg wrote (*ut sup.*, p. 170): "Er hatte nun einen Gott gefunden, dem er huldigen konnte, und hatte Frieden mit den Olympiern geschlossen" (cp. p. 171). But this contradicts what he has just said (p. 169): "Euripides denkt über die Götter auch hier noch genau so wie früher."

presentation is not consistent. . . . [Euripides might say] 'The vision you see there, as it is the most beautiful of things, is likely also to be the most destructive.' . . . He will clasp it even though it slay him."[1] Verrall disclaims any insight here.[2] "How far Euripides . . . was ready to go with such religion, we have no means to determine. . . . He saw . . . its beauties. . . . He saw also its moral and intellectual dangers. . . . He saw these things and excellently painted them; and as a dramatist he is committed no further." Mr. W. H. Salter holds yet a third position. "We do not feel that he had any use for religion of any kind at all. There is a human type in which the ethical passions attain to the fervour and take the place of religious conviction, and to this type Euripides, with his unbounded pity, his flaming hatred of cruelty, fraud, and injustice in every form, seems to have belonged."[3]

Professor Winnington-Ingram remarks that "if Euripides has portrayed the mythological Dionysus as a fiend or even explained him away as a young Asiatic, the religion of Dionysus remains",[4] and thus summarizes what he thinks to be the poet's own feeling about the Bacchic evangel:

> Euripides saw Dionysus clearly and whole, both in his beauty and in his great danger, and presented him as he saw him. The entire play is concentrated . . . upon this single, if various, subject. Though we are shown the effects of Dionysus upon certain individuals, there is no conflict except the contradiction in the nature of the god, no tragedy except the tragic condition of humanity exposed to this contradiction. For, if Euripides . . . showed Dionysus first as beautiful and then as cruel, this was not mere subservience to a given plot or to obvious dramatic effect, but he so shaped the play as to focus attention upon the cruelty and to demonstrate the inexorable interdependence of the cruelty and the beauty. Euripides recognised Dionysus for the danger that he was, publicly in the societies of men . . . and privately in the lives of individuals. The worship of such a god he could not commend. . . .[5]

That perhaps identifies the Euripidean Dionysus too closely with his religion. But as a comment on the religion itself it is admirable, embracing all the elements and effects thereof as here presented, explaining contradictions in the odes that else must baffle us and accounting for the

---

[1] *Euripides and his Age*, pp. 188 f. Cp. M. R. Glover, pp. 87 f., e.g.: "Part of the tragedy of the play lies just here—the evil thing looked so fair, it was the hope and even the taste of exceeding joy that brought men into woe. . . . We must sometimes forgo happiness, say no to the intolerable promise of joy. So too the beauty of the Dionysiac religion must not mislead. . . . 'Beauty is good', we cry, with passionate insistence. And as in the old tale of the sirens, 'there lie close at hand the rotting bones of men' (*Od.* 12. 45)." [2] P. 152.
[3] *Essays on Two Moderns* (London, 1911), pp. 66 f. [4] P. 5.
[5] Pp. 178 f. See also his Index, *s.v.* "Dionysiac religion".

varied reactions of the human characters to this new worship. It should be accepted as probably the nearest approach that modern students can make to the poet's emotional experience, intellectual judgement, and spiritual conviction.

Anyone who chances to be interested will have now learned what portions of *The Riddle of the Bacchae* its author wishes to reaffirm, restate, or disown. What does and should interest every student of this play is, however, not one man's vagaries but the fact that we all from time to time realize some alteration, great or trifling, not perhaps in our "verdicts" but in our feelings, the response of our whole nature. The *Bacchae* gleams with shifting lights and hues like an enchanting landscape seen under alternate sunshine and tempest by travellers preoccupied each with his own concerns: botany, painting, geology, the defects of his horse, vehicle, or climbing-boots, perhaps his own folly in forgetting to pack field-glasses in addition to a microscope. Still, no explorer of Euripides, however wayward, need accuse himself of involving this glorious work in excessive controversy. That is the poet's fault, if we unwisely choose to talk of faults.

III

GOD AND MAN IN *HIPPOLYTUS*

THIS play is not only the most beautiful, the most pathetic and penetrating, among Euripides' extant works: it is also the most finely wrought and many-sided, therefore the most difficult for modern readers, who are almost compelled to discover in it puzzles non-existent for the Athenians who awarded it the first prize in the festival of 428 B.C. Above all, we are uncertain what the deities of the play really mean: does or does not the poet offer them as equally authentic with his human personages? Aphrodite in the prologue, Artemis in the epilogue, agree in perfectly definite language that to Aphrodite's anger is due all the woe here depicted; nevertheless, whereas some of us accept this, others deny it. Let us, then, attempt to secure clarity of thought and poise in appreciation by postponing theology and studying what the chief human *dramatis personae* actually say, do, and suffer. All three—Phaedra, Hippolytus, and Theseus—engage our affection, respect, sympathy, and compassion undeniably though in varying degrees. But all are far from blameless, and seem at least in virtue of their own characters to account for all the pain and misunderstanding.

Let us begin with Hippolytus. Such a man—not perhaps he himself, for the notion of the chaste Hippolytus was familiar, and most opinions are nothing more than acceptance of the established—such a man would have been censured by nearly all fifth-century Greeks for his outlook in general, not (of course) for his horror at the Nurse's disclosure. Theseus' attack,[1] in a novel case, would have found the support of nearly everyone in the theatre. "*Thou* consort with gods as a man set apart? *Thou* chaste and innocent? Those boasts I disallow: gods are not foolish, nor am I. Now vaunt thyself, thou fleshless dietarian; and, loyal to St. Orpheus, play the devotee awed by the reek of copious scriptures! For thou art caught, ha!" It is all here, every gibe that the "plain blunt man" has always flung at the "superior person": the taking religion so seriously, the sanctimonious air, the niggling about special food and fussy little "devotional" books, the lofty language that cloaks grossness of life. So might a master of fox-hounds, when stung to the extreme, taunt a son given over

---

[1] Vv. 948–55 (I accept Weil's τροφάς in place of σίτοις).

to "the millinery of ritualism". But it is the very worst that can be said of Hippolytus, for perversely enough he follows the hounds himself. Save for one thing, he is the Athenian ideal of an aristocrat. The difference lies in his vivid personal religion.

How much truth the sneers of Theseus contain it is hard to determine.[1] Nothing else in the play suggests that Hippolytus was an Orphic adept, still less that he took part in Bacchic "orgies", though he had been initiated at Eleusis,[2] as was for such a youth a matter of course in Euripides' own time. Artemis claims his whole worship, his life is inspired by her purity. Passionate absorption in this allegiance, joined to a natural exuberance of imagination, has produced in him a sense of personal companionship with the goddess. Whatever Hippolytus becomes when confronted with the sordidness and pain that lie in ambush for all the sons of men, this secret garden of his life remains inviolate.

> For thee, my Queen, this garland have I twined
> Of blossoms from that meadow virginal
> Where neither shepherd dares his flock to graze
> Nor has the scythe come thither; yet the bee
> In spring-time haunts that grassy sanctuary
> Watered by hermit-piety and awe.
> No evil man, but he alone whose heart,
> Unlearnèd else, is lit by purity
> In all his ways, the flowers there may cull.
> Ah, Queen belovèd, for thy shining hair
> Accept this crown from dedicated hands!
> To me alone of all mankind is given
> Converse to hold and company with thee,
> Hearing thy voice, although the face be hid:
> So may I close my life as it began.

Small wonder that the scholiasts ponder his meaning at great length! The prince has brought back from some grassy nook a garland for his Queen. The only creature, save himself, to venture thither is the bee. By the brook and amid woods and blossoms he has felt the besetting Power that we vaguely call 'Nature', and for which he uses the untranslatable word *aidós*. It is the coyness of natural beauty that has laid hold upon his imagination, the Presence descried but never observed in all its lineaments as it glides beneath flower-petals or vanishes into the silvery mist of olive-branches, seductive yet not responding to the gesture of the soul.

---

[1] His language contains at any rate one word customary on his son's lips, ἀκήρατος: it occurs twice in Hippolytus' salutation to Artemis.
[2] Vv. 24 ff.

And at the thought of the flitting bee, purest of creatures,[1] at the sound of his own word *aidôs*,[2] he passes to the soul's virginity, his own rapture of maiden communion with the chaste goddess. He is not announcing frigid allegory, but musing at once on two dear influences that make the music of his existence: his spiritual comradeship with Artemis, and the secluded peace suffusing forest and meadow; for these two are one, since the Queen of virgin life is the divine Huntress herself.

Upon this youth, lofty in rank, sundered from others by his religious ardour and by the unique favour of his goddess, in whom the narrowness of sympathy natural to his years is terribly reinforced by spiritual pride, descends a cloud of horror. His stepmother's nurse, in a disgusting yet pathetic interview at which we are left to guess, tells him that her mistress passionately desires him. We learn from Phaedra's tortured gasps that he is reviling the temptress, and in a moment, as she sinks down beside the door, he bursts forth, appealing to Earth and Sun against the iniquity, while the wretched attendant endeavours to secure his silence. After his first exclamations of fury, we observe that he is at point to deliver what we have been dreading, the connected statement or invective usual in Greek tragedy at such moments of crisis. Each man in the audience, aware that he could not handle it well, feels wretchedly certain that he could handle it better than Hippolytus. Unversed in such emotions as these, by no means fully accustomed even to intercourse with the world in general,[3] capable of intolerance at the best of times,[4] is this lad to hold forth on the shortcomings of Phaedra?

The speech more than answers our expectation. It exhibits the vulgarity of imagination that so often startles us in over-refined and fastidious natures when confronted by an emotional crisis. As Hippolytus' prayer to Artemis showed him at his best, in an ecstasy of religion, so does this preachment reveal of what he is capable in an ecstasy of self-righteousness. He begins, and continues, with a random sprawling tirade against female depravity. Here is no distinction between women like Phaedra and women like the Nurse: how, indeed, is he capable of knowing any? His only distinctions are rhetorical antitheses, which do for a moment compel him incidentally to mention good wives, who however spoil the blessing they confer by their "useless relatives".[5] At last he reaches the point of

---

[1] καθαρώτατον γάρ τι ζῷον ἡ μέλισσα (schol.). Cp. Gow's note on Theoc. I. 106 f.

[2] Ἄρτεμις Αἰδώς appears on an Attic vase (P. Kretschmer, *Die griechischen Vaseninschriften* (1894), p. 197).   [3] Vv. 986 f.

[4] See his conversation with the old Huntsman (88–113).

[5] Vv. 634–7. These lines are rejected by Willems and Murray. But they are not bad Greek, nor is their style un-Euripidean. True, they are irrelevant and silly; but

his denunciation:[1] "So didst thou too, base creature, come to me making traffic of my father's sacred bed! Thy speech will I cleanse away in streams of water, sluicing my ears." There he should have ceased. What he has said up to now might have been forgiven: this last thought reminds us simply and rather beautifully of his excuse, the shock that he has suffered. But, true to his type, he knows not when to stop. "How then could I be vile, who feel myself debauched by the mere words? . . ." At this point we feel that he has begun to listen to his own voice, and our pain becomes disgust. On that note he continues: "I tell thee, woman, 'tis my piety that saves thee: for, had I not been caught off my guard by a solemn oath, I should not have refrained from revealing this to my father." That is how, were he free,[2] he would deal with a dreadful family secret, crying it recklessly in the ears of the last person to whom it should be revealed, whose knowledge would do nothing but double the agony and make even more difficult of attainment the slow half-oblivion that is the only peace Phaedra can hope for. He continues: "But, as it is, I shall leave the house for so long as Theseus is abroad, and hold my peace." This, at any rate, is a satisfactory close, however late; his speech would have been infinitely better had it consisted of these two lines alone. But . . . this is *not* the close. Will he never cease? "With my father I shall return to watch how both thou and thy mistress face him, and shall know the savour of thy daring."[3] This, surely, more than any other sentence of his, decides Phaedra not to die alone; and if ever vile taste deserved death, it is now. Hippolytus deliberately proposes to gloat. The piquancy of the contrast between Phaedra's passion, baffled but enduring, and his own stainlessness, of the complicated and unavowed intimacies wherein he is to revel blamelessly under the eyes of his unconscious father and tortured stepmother—all this he relishes delicately in prospect. If ever a man was damned by his virtues, that man was the son of Theseus.

Such is the provocation. The woman to whom it is offered has precisely the qualities, and finds herself in precisely the situation, that

---

the poet is plainly not concerned here to depict the prince as logical or wise. Elsewhere (fr. 657) he voices our feeling: "Whoever generalizes about women to revile them individually is a blundering fool." Cp. *Hec.* 1183 f.   [1] Vv. 651 ff.

[2] Cp. Miss L. E. Matthaei: "Had the inner or spiritual control been perfect in Hippolytos' nature, the question of the oath would have been almost indifferent. He could not, by nature, have taken part in spreading a moral evil over a wider area than was necessary." *Studies in Greek Tragedy* (1918), p. 94.

[3] Contrast Racine, *Phèdre* II. vi. 6 f., where the prince, on the point of revealing the secret to Théramène, breaks off:

> Phèdre... Mais non, grands dieux! qu'en un profond oubli
> Cet horrible secret demeure enseveli.

guarantee her answering the challenge with fatal promptness. Phaedra is the most subtly and beautifully drawn character in Euripides, and we may congratulate ourselves, thanks to the structure and tone of our society, on thoroughly understanding Phaedra,[1] or at the worst understanding her better than did Aristophanes.[2] It was clear to Euripides, if to no one else in his day, that mere horror or mere disgust, even mere compassion, are of little help in understanding women like his heroine. His was perhaps the first European voice to insist that people must be blamed, if at all, for their conduct, not for their instincts. Instinct is the raw material of ethical existence, whether virtuous or depraved. To make war on it is self-damaging blindness in the society that undertakes the struggle. Passion, instead of shining forth as a fire, at the worst dangerous only to those who know not what fire is, will by the very force of its repression act as an explosive, destroying widely and indiscriminately.[3] Euripides, without prejudice to his ultimate verdict on Phaedra's conduct (supposing he intends to give any verdict at all), is determined to study this painful old story and try to discover what kind of woman it can have been who did these things: what instincts prompted her, what means she took to control or use them, and what we may thus learn for the conduct of our own lives.

Asking, then, what known facts of human nature can have produced Phaedra, this good[4] woman who despite her goodness commits suicide

[1] See Dodds's study of her psychological state (and that of Hippolytus) in *Class. Rev.* vol. XXXIX (1925), pp. 102–4.

[2] The celebrated scene in *Frogs* 1006–98 contains his most elaborate strictures on the women of Euripides. (Phaedra is cited by name, probably on the strength of the lost *Hippolytus Veiled*, as an example of Euripides' scandalous women, in *Thesm.* 153, 497, 546 ff., *Frogs* 1043 f., 1052 ff., and apparently in *Polyidus*, fr. 453.) These seem to us superficial and slightly vulgar, but there may perhaps be something on the other side. *Frogs* 1079 ff. do seem to reveal that Euripides' work was at times marked by morbid imagination and lubricity. But Aristophanes' known methods in caricature, together with our ignorance of *Stheneboea* and the earlier *Hippolytus*, forbid us to accept the suggestion unreservedly: Aristophanes' censure is no harsher than the first English criticisms of Ibsen. Still, it should be added that vv. 1050 f., concerning respectable women who had been driven to suicide by "your Bellerophons", read like an allusion to contemporary fact, however distorted.

[3] Cp. Dodds (*ut sup.*, pp. 103 f.): "As Phaedra does violence to αἰδώς in the name of αἰδώς [see below, p. 81], so does Hippolytus to σωφροσύνη in the name of σωφροσύνη: each is the victim of his own and the other's submerged desires masquerading as morality. Complementary and interdependent, these are the two determining moments on which all the rest of the action hangs.... In the formal aspect, it [*Hipp.*] is a representation of the interplay of two personalities, both of them 'nobler than we, but marred by some ἁμαρτία'; in conception, it is a study of the effects of conflict and repression in the sphere of sex."

[4] Good, but more complex than any other character of ancient drama. Naturally,

and by a lying message murders an innnocent man, Euripides finds one cause in the legend. Lawless sexual passion is in the woman's veins. She knows and remembers only too well the history of her house. Early in the play she agonizes over the predisposition towards unchastity whereto these examples point: her confession to the Nurse begins in this key: "Ah, wretched mother, what strange love was thine!" (the bull-legend); "And thou, unhappy sister, wife of Dionysus!" (Ariadne in Naxos). To which the other replies, more to the purpose even than she imagines: "Child, what ails thee? Thou revilest kinswomen."[1] Phaedra unheedingly goes on: "And I, the third—ill-starred, undone!" where "third", though by no means implying an inherited curse, does point to the dreadful appropriateness of the speaker's situation. She comes from Crete, "the Isle of awful Love",[2] and this sinister name occurs repeatedly.[3] Phaedra, then, inherits an abnormal tendency to sexual passion: it is her tragedy that, whatever she may do, her mind is not free from it: "my hands are pure, my heart not undefiled".[4] Hippolytus, also, seems to utter the poet's own thought much later.[5]

We are not, of course, to credit the dramatist with the common and mischievous error of supposing that construction of quasi-scientific phrases, like the "abnormal tendency" just mentioned, offers escape from theories of supernatural causation. We can still ask whence came this tendency. But we must distinguish the investigation that traces human feelings and acts to human history and excludes theology save as an

---

therefore, readers have differed in their judgements of her. Grube hints distaste (*The Drama of Euripides* (1941), p. 185, n. 2). Pohlenz condemns her for weak conventionality (*Die griechische Tragödie* (1930), pp. 279, 281). Wilamowitz is bitter and contemptuous (*Griechische Tragoedien übersetzt* (2nd ed.), vol. I, pp. 101–4); nevertheless he atones by an acute remark (p. 101) on her delirium: "Bilder, wie sie Ophelias Phantasie beherrschen, bringt in Phaidra der Wahnsinn nicht an die Oberfläche.'

Few have noted her instinctive outcry (672) after Hippolytus' tirade: "I am rightly served!" (ἐτύχομεν δίκας).

[1] V. 340: τέκνον, τί πάσχεις; συγγόνους κακορροθεῖς. It seems less good to punctuate (as do Weil, Murray, etc.) with a question-mark at the end.

[2] Murray's phrase. Cp. Seneca, *Phaedra* 127:

Nulla Minois levi
Defuncta amore est: iungitur semper nefas.

D'Annunzio in his *Fedra* constantly calls the queen "la Cretese", and alludes often with horrible vigour to the crime of Pasiphae (especially Act I, 829 ff.).

[3] Vv. 155, 372 (very emphatic), 719, 752–75. This last is a vital passage: note especially ἀνθ' ὧν, οὐχ ὁσίων ἐρώτων δεινᾷ φρένας Ἀφροδίτας νόσῳ κατεκλάσθη. Aphrodite in the prologue calls Phaedra εὐγενής (26). It is significant that the deity to whom on one view—that life's vicissitudes are caused by sudden irruptions of gods—Phaedra's misery is to be attributed, obliterates the other view (about heredity).

[4] V. 317.   [5] V. 1034. See below, p. 89.

ultimate and mysterious foundation, from the superstition that introduces "Heaven" at the first moment through intellectual sloth. Whether Phaedra's inherited trait is ultimately derived from a personal Aphrodite or not, it makes sudden *interference* by her unnecessary. We can therefore reasonably refer the queen's passion to "natural" causes.

Tragedy not seldom arises when great emotional energies, already in existence, are unleashed into clashing activity by the touch of accident. Phaedra's instinct is aided by this unpredictable but potent ally. It was no doing of hers or of the prince's that Theseus left Athens and brought Phaedra with him to Trozen, where she was again thrown into Hippolytus' society. In that retired little town occurred—they could not naturally be avoided—the long talks in which the queen took a trembling delight.[1] And again the force of accident[2] withdraws Theseus to a distance. This and other causes produce the weakening that involves her, not in offence against her husband, but in the Nurse's fatal revelation to Hippolytus. She is conscious that sin has been born with her; the thought arouses fascination as well as horror. She allowed herself in the past to toy with her passion, when she founded a shrine of the Love-Goddess at Athens for Hippolytus' sake,[3] and even now she delicately feels the thrill stirring through her reluctance. The intensity of her struggle with desire has brought exhaustion. For two days she has tasted no food,[4] and is now in a physical state that painfully increases her sensitiveness while undermining her will. This fact, that Phaedra is at the end of her bodily if not of her spiritual resources, should be borne steadily in mind throughout.[5]

---

[1] V. 384.   [2] V. 281.

[3] Vv. 29–33. On this difficult passage see Verrall, *Class. Rev.*, vol. XV, p. 149 and Murray's note to his translation (pp. 77 f.). Racine (*Phèdre* I. iii. 125 ff.) has adroitly given this action a wholly different meaning:

> Je reconnus Vénus et ses feux redoutables,
> D'un sang qu'elle poursuit torments inévitables.
> Par des vœux assidus je crus les détourner.
> Je lui bâtis un temple...

[4] Vv. 135 ff.

[5] Patin (*Études sur les tragiques grecs: Euripide* (7th ed. (1894), vol. II, p. 317), Wilamowitz (*Analecta Euripidea*, p. 214) and A. Kalkmann (*De Hippolytis Euripideis* (1882), pp. 20 f.) forgot this, and far too severely judged her weakest moment (507–24). Kalkmann writes: "Servat speciem pudicitiae, attamen ab omni culpa liberari nequit, cum omnino ad nutricis simulationes descendat; quod ut palam fiat ... poeta fingit Phaedram tam levicula et inutilia interrogantem. Aptum praeterea sibi parat hoc modo transitum ad ea, quae sequuntur; quibus dilucidius etiam vetit aspes, qua mulier amans furtim nititur, aperitur. Nam cur illa anum ambigue semper respondentem et ad extremum per Venerem iurantem non retinet?" That is not completely untrue but misleading, a harshly masculine condemnation: no one can appreciate Euripides who has no feminine sympathy. (Vv. 515 f. are a rebuke to Phaedra as a little girl quarrelling with her medicine.) Moreover the whole censure can be refuted

Such, then, is Phaedra and such her plight when temptation finds lineaments and stands pleading before her eyes. The amiable vulgar old attendant, passionately fond of her young mistress, but coarse-grained in feeling, narrow in mind and sympathy, is a familiar type, useful to dramatists as comic relief and as a foil to the refinement of her youthful charge: Juliet's nurse is only the most celebrated of such comfortably corrupt old women. Euripides has taken over[1] this character and given her far greater pungency: she utters words that sting and affright; she is capable of gross good-humour and abject cajolery, but capable too of voicing the wish of one tortured soul and the half-unconscious yearnings of all humanity.[2] Read her earlier speeches and note the moods of this amazing woman. First comes a banal lamentation about the troubles of sick-nursing. "Now", she tells her patient, "you are beneath the open sky as you insisted. No doubt you will soon change your mind and wish to return within. Such is the way with invalids. I would rather be the patient than the nurse. Double annoyance! . . . But all human life is wretched: no cessation of troubles." And then suddenly bursts forth the melancholy enchantment of a cry that might have been uttered by Hamlet or Prospero: "But whatever else there may be, sweeter than life, darkness hides in its misty veil; we set our pining hearts openly on the mirage of this world, because other life is beyond our ken: of subterranean things we have no revelation, but float astray upon legends." Before she enters into conversation with the Chorus we read another utterance of hers,[3] about the pains of a too passionate friendship reaching into "the soul's marrow", where the same depth of feeling is combined with mental banality. "Therefore I praise immoderation less than 'Nothing too much'; and the wise will agree with me." This masterpiece of triviality completes her descent to the plane on which she is to converse with the visitors about Phaedra's illness. Next follows the scene showing how her affectionate importunity forces the queen's secret into the light,[4] whereupon dismay

from the text: see Phaedra's words throughout vv. 565–600, which give no hint of baffled lust.

[1] A woman to whom part of the above description applies had been heard already in the Athenian theatre, bringing a moment of artless charm into the *Choephoroe*.

[2] Shaw's *Getting Married* contains a parallel in Mrs. George, whose vision or trance recalls the lyrical side of the Nurse.   [3] Vv. 250–66.

[4] Dodds (*ut sup.*) connects this passage with vv. 385 ff. about the two kinds of αἰδώς, which he explains convincingly. "At v. 244 αἰδώς saves Phaedra; at v. 335 it destroys her. . . . She appeals in vain for release from that [the Nurse's] compulsion, and then her resolution breaks: δώσω· σέβας γὰρ χειρὸς αἰδοῦμαι τὸ σόν. . . . Small wonder if in her succeeding agony of remorse and fear she recognises that αἰδώς can be an ἄχθος οἴκων. . . . she means . . . that the αἰδώς of v. 335 was ἄκαιρος: she has sacrificed to the conventional claim of the suppliant the deeper claim of her own spiritual integrity."

startles her into an exhibition of that pathetic absurdity with which Euripides, in his passion for depicting real people, often relieves a tragic situation. "Alas, my child, what wilt thou say? How hast thou destroyed me!" This would have been dignified, but she must needs dilate upon her virtuous distress: "Ladies, it is unbearable! I will not endure to live. Hateful is the day, hateful the sunshine, to my sight. I will fling, I will throw away my body, quit of life by dying. Farewell! I am no more", and so forth.[1]

After this unseemly foolishness, she sits recovering herself until Phaedra has finished her confession to the Trozenian ladies. Then she rises to her height in the terrible and magnificent appeal wherewith she almost overbears her mistress. Her chief argument is drawn, with extraordinary art and vigour, from theology itself.

> Thy love—why marvel thereat? 'Tis the tale
> Of many. Wouldst thou slay thyself for love?
> Good sooth! A guerdon strange, if lovers now
> And evermore must meet such penalty!
> Who shall withstand the Cyprian's rising flood?
> Yield to her might, she comes with quietness:
> Exalt thy pride and stand on niceties,
> She hurls thee pell-mell into ignominy.
> Amid the heaven she walks, amid the spray
> Of yon sea-billows: all life flows from her.
> The seed is hers, and hers the passionate throe
> Whence spring we all that walk the ways of earth.
> Ask them that con the half-forgotten lore
> Of elder time, and serve the Muse themselves.
> They know how Zeus once pined for Semele,
> How for love's sake the Goddess of the Dawn
> Stooped from her radiant sphere to Cephalus
> And stole him to the sky. Yet these abide
> In Heaven, nor shun the converse of the gods,
> Bowing, belike, to conquering circumstance.
> And wilt not thou? Nay, if this law thou spurnest,
> Thy sire, when he begat thee, should have writ
> Some compact countersigned by gods unknown.

Next, she would have Phaedra contemplate the ways of mankind. How many agree to ignore, or even aid, irregular conduct! It is hopeless to aim

[1] It is true, as Miss Matthaei (*ut sup.*, p. 80) points out, that in her last sentence the Nurse "well describes the real meaning of Aphrodite when she says: 'Kypris, then, it seems, is no goddess, but whate'er there may be greater than a god.'" That hardly redeems the whole speech.

GOD AND MAN IN *HIPPOLYTUS* 83

too curiously at perfection: would we have tilers work with the deft nicety of mosaic artists? If one's life shows more good than bad acts, a mortal woman should be well satisfied. The sum is: "Nay, dear child, quit thy evil mood and cease this insolence: for insolence it is, to seek mastery over gods." Such is the moral deadlock to which we are reduced by belief in the personal Olympians.[1] She ends with vague talk of incantations, charms, and woman's cunning.

A marvellous speech! The attentive reader will observe how her language rises and falls in dignity with the phases of her theme.[2] Later we hear again the note of bustling good-natured coarseness,[3] and the gross misunderstanding that must have galled Phaedra unendurably: "If your life had not been so entangled in distress, and *you had happened to be a chaste woman* . . . ." After the revelation to Hippolytus, she is swept away, first by his scorn, then by the bitter invective of her mistress, and we hear no more of her.[4]

To this appeal what reply or defiance can Phaedra offer? She herself at once recognizes its dreadful eloquence (486–9) and owns its effect:

> Nay, in God's name forbear! Thy words are fine,
> Yet base withal. Love in my soul too well
> Hath mined his way. Preach shame thus winningly,
> And, foothold lost, the fate I shun engulfs me.[5]

[1] The position is to be found stated, more definitely than anywhere in Euripides, by Terence, whose "hero" is encouraged to detestable conduct by seeing a picture of Jupiter and Danae (*Eun.* 586 ff.). St. Augustine's comment on this (*Confessions* I. xvi) is the most effective passage in his attack on the *flumen tartareum* of pagan education. For other parallels to our passage see Eur. *Tro.* 933–50 (cp. 988), Ar. *Clouds* 1079 ff., and Menander *Eun.* fr. 187 (Kock).

[2] Note the plain style of vv. 433–45, which reaches downright colloquialism in πῶς δοκεῖς καθύβρισεν, followed by the majestic description of the World-Goddess in vv. 447–50. Then at the change of argument come the two unadorned lines 451 f., with the half-casual expression αὐτοί τ' εἰσὶν ἐν μούσαις ἀεί. Next, when she mentions the romantic legends of the gods, we find charm and artifice, the *anaphora* ἴσασι μὲν . . . ἴσασι δὲ . . ., and the *epitheton ornans* καλλιφεγγής. So one might proceed to the end.

[3] Vv. 490 f. are wellnigh indecently direct.

[4] At v. 776, where a voice from within cries the news of Phaedra's suicide, the scholiast writes: τινὲς βούλονται τὴν τροφὸν ἔσωθεν ταῦτα λέγειν, ἔνιοι δὲ ἐξάγγελόν φασιν. It cannot have been an *exangelos*. Such speakers come forth with their news: here the speaker goes on (786 f.) to say "lay out the corpse", etc.; but that is done within, for only at v. 810 is the *eccyclema* used. Whether the unseen person is a nameless attendant or the Nurse it is impossible to determine; nor does it matter.

[5] Vv. 503–5:

καὶ μή σε πρὸς θεῶν—εὖ λέγεις γάρ, αἰσχρὰ δέ—
πέρα προβῇς τῶνδ'· ὡς ὑπείργασμαι μὲν εὖ
ψυχὴν ἔρωτι, τᾀσχρὰ δ' ἢν λέγῃς καλῶς,
ἐς τοῦθ' ὃ φεύγω νῦν ἀναλωθήσομαι.

The metaphor in these lines seems to have been missed. (ὑπείργασται in *Med.* 871 is a

There is only one reply conceivable, and she has already given it: "Whatever gods may do, or men think, I must and will act so as still to respect myself."[1] It is significant that, in a play which on the face of it recognizes "the gods" as ruling human conduct, Phaedra's great speech (373–430) should so plainly belie this view. "Cypris" is mentioned once or twice,[2] but the whole passage makes it clear that she feels and faces her calamity as purely human. Socrates was said[3] to have brought philosophy down from Heaven to earth when he concentrated his interest upon ethics; his friend carries the same development forward by insisting that the centre of ethics is to be found in Man himself. The endless question, whether divine *fiat* or human conscience is the foundation of righteousness, has been settled by Euripides for himself in the latter sense. Phaedra finds no soul on which she can rely save her own: "I will tell thee also of my spirit's journey". The whole speech deserves minute study for its precision both of thought[4] and of language. But what specially concerns us now is this "journey" of her mind.

The diction is frigidly clear, almost bald. "When love stabbed me, I took thought how to bear it most honourably. My first plan, then, was to keep silent and conceal the malady, for the tongue is treacherous.... My second thought was to bear folly well, conquering it with a chaste heart. Thirdly, when I saw that by these means I was not attaining mastery over Cypris, death seemed to me—and none shall gainsay it—the best counsel." We who so often understand by "virtue" nothing nobler than absence of sin, and are ever at a loss to translate that word *sophrosyne* (corresponding to the "chaste heart" in the version just offered), may here learn from this ancient sinner. *Sophrosyne* is no mere "temperance", the refusal of self-indulgence: why else should Phaedra mention it as the

different and much simpler use of the verb.) ὑπείργασμαι means that Love has gained power over her by working under the surface, as engineers undermine a town; ἀναλωθήσομαι expresses the helpless horror of the victim who sees first the apparently solid earth and then her own feet slipping and sinking into the pit.

[1] Cp. vv. 415 ff. and her whole attitude, which accounts (as we shall see) for her denunciation of Hippolytus.

[2] In v. 401, Κύπριν is surely a mere synonym for ἔρωτα (cp. 392) or ἄνοιαν (398). ὦ δέσποινα ποντία Κύπρι (v. 415) is of course more striking: but the most independent thinkers slip back easily now and then into traditional language. Sometimes they at once correct themselves: Hecuba (*Tro.* 469 ff.) sardonically says:

ὦ θεοί ... κακοὺς μὲν ἀνακαλῶ τοὺς συμμάχους.
ὅμως δ' ἔχει τι σχῆμα κικλήσκειν θεούς,
ὅταν τις ἡμῶν δυστυχῇ λάβῃ τύχην.

[3] Cicero, *Tusc. Disp.* V. 4.

[4] For instance, she carefully refutes (375–83) the Socratic identification of virtue with knowledge.

second of her expedients, different from repression?[1] That first resource is negative virtue, confined to a refusal of sin. But the second is chastity sword in hand, the cherishing of instincts, emotions, and thoughts that not only restrain but fortify: a vibrant loyalty to husband and children,[2] but also, and even more, to one's own personality as utterly intimate and precious, whose annulment is damnation. Therefore, when these defences fail, there is, there can be, for such a woman as Phaedra no escape but death.

Hearing those chill words, we realize how empty of comfort life can at some hours show itself to those who reject formulas[3] and face their own souls. Here is no thought of a saviour from without: the human spirit must struggle alone with an uncomprehended universe. Aeschylus had found a saviour in Zeus,[4] as recreated by his own spiritual energy; Euripides finds no comfort in gods attested by legends that dim their splendour with weakness or ill deeds. In this speech, moreover, we find for the first time a really vivid portrayal of temptation at work, and a clear realization of conscience. In Medea's bosom the struggle is waged by two conflicting emotions. The sense of abstract Right, as a conception of the individual spirit and a guide of individual conduct, takes no part in her agonized perplexity. Here it dominates Phaedra. Sophocles understands well how duty can brace the soul to heroic life or death, but for him the sanction of duty lies in the will of external deities; for Euripides, conscience is sufficient as a moral law.

Yet this speech reveals fully but one side of Phaedra's nature.[5] Pure

---

[1] Euripides is so determined to make the distinction clear that he actually numbers the methods: ἠρξάμην, δεύτερον, τρίτον. Nevertheless, students of this play have often been blind to it. Murray's translation renders it plainly. But Pohlenz, acute as he usually is, ignores it (p. 276). Wilamowitz is content to say (Griechische Tragoedien übersetzt, vol. I, p. 101): "Sie liebt die Tugend, wenigstens redet sie sehr viel davon." But Artemis (of all people) understands clearly, being in some sense a Greek: γνώμῃ δὲ νικᾶν τὴν Κύπριν πειρωμένη (1304).

[2] Wilamowitz writes (ibid., p. 102): "Ihr Ruf ist tadellos. Aber ein innerliches Verhältnis hat sie zu Kindern und Mann nicht, geschweige zu etwas anderem." But see vv. 420–5, 720 f.—surely quite enough: however strong her feelings for Theseus and their children, a very natural αἰδώς would make her, situated as she is, reluctant to speak at length about them.

[3] Pohlenz (p. 279), contrasting Phaedra with Medea, says: "Phaidras Natur ist Schwachheit, Abhängigkeit von fremdem Einfluß, von konventioneller Sittlichkeit, vom Urteil der Gesellschaft." That is unfair. She values her repute, and why not? But she prizes highest her own soul. Again, he says (p. 281): ". . . dieselbe Rücksicht auf das Urteil der Mitmenschen, die sie vorher auf der Bahn der Tugend erhielt, macht sie nachher zur Verbrecherin." It is enough to reply (though one could say more) that she is determined to guard her children's happiness (421–5).   [4] Ag. 160–83.

[5] Obviously it is complex, as was remarked earlier. But Pohlenz writes too pedantically (pt. II, p. 78): "Den Gegensatz der beiden Phaidren kann man mit Termini der

reason, as she says (375 ff.), is not the only factor in life: "Often ere this, in other moods, have I pondered, during the long night-time, how man's life comes to ruin. I believe that unworthy conduct springs not from intellectual fault—sound sense is common enough—but that this is the way to look at it: we see and accept the right, but do not practise it, some from indolence, others through giving the first place, not to honour, but to some one of the many pleasures found in life. . . ."[1] So she herself harbours strong instincts and passions. The whole action centres upon the fact that Hippolytus at his worst comes upon her when in complete despair and therefore at her deadliest. However incredible we may have thought the story, baldly told, of the destruction she works in her last hour, no sympathetic reader can fail to understand her behaviour when portrayed by this master of psychological drama. We can share her dread that the prince will reveal everything: "But come! I need to change the story. For yon man with anger-whetted heart will speak against me to his father of thy misdoing, will speak this sorrow to aged Pittheus and fill the whole land with shameful talk." Such is her plain reason for destroying Hippolytus in whatever way seems certain, however terrible.[2] She is mistaken in him, but his known character, his recent words, her own circumstances and emotions, all combine to persuade her that one course alone will save her good name and the happiness of her family. Revenge? She has little thought of that; but how humanly she relishes the reflection[3] that Hippolytus will hereby learn a bitter lesson in *sophrosyne*!

Theseus, although Euripides has given him two of the loveliest lines[4] that he ever wrote—

ὄρνις γὰρ ὥς τις ἐκ χερῶν ἄφαντος εἶ,
πήδημ' ἐς Ἀιδου κραιπνὸν ὁρμήσασά μοι—

späteren Philosophie (vgl. z. B. Plut. de virt. morali 445d ff.) dahin zusammenfassen, das die erste ἀκόλαστος war, d. h. mit Denken und Fühlen dem einen Ziele zustrebte, die zweite ἀκρατής, in innerem Zwiespalt lebte." There are more than two parts in this woman, as in all of us.

[1] I do not apologize for offering these flat sentences instead of Murray's beautiful translation, because Euripides here writes in the most unadorned style possible to verse.

[2] Vv. 688–92. Racine (*Phèdre* IV. i), however, refuses to follow Euripides and assigns the slander against Hippolytus to the nurse Oenone, not to her mistress. But this makes Theseus more hasty and credulous than in Euripides, where he reads Phaedra's own testimony.

[3] Vv. 728 ff. Miss Matthaei (p. 103) makes a further point: ". . . he will realise her: she will impress herself on him for ever".

[4] Vv. 828 f.: "Like a strange bird hast thou vanished out of my hands, swooping from me into the abode of Death." But one cannot hope to render the quiet pathos of lines which recall Sophocles at his most magical: it "vanishes" indeed from under the

is far less subtly studied and portrayed than the other characters, even the Nurse. That shows perfect control: the play would not bear, nor could we, a fully elaborated Theseus towards the close. But he contributes as much as anyone to the disastrous story,[1] despite the pathetic blindness wherewith he imputes his misery to some ancestor's sin (831 ff.). Hippolytus is the offspring of his youthful incontinence, as the king's own utterance reminds us,[2] if we are capable of forgetting it. Thus, when in later life he becomes a pillar of morality, his very marriage brings down upon his head the consequences of the past, in that his son and his wife are of nearly the same age. Theseus dimly knows this. During his altercation with Hippolytus he commands himself until the prince in despair cries out: "Ah, my unhappy mother! Ah, woeful birth! Never be any friend of mine a bastard!" Instantly he loses self-control: "Henchmen, drag him away!"

Responsible for Hippolytus' existence, is he responsible for his death also? If Poseidon's Gift of Prayers is genuine, and if Theseus believes in it, then he is fully responsible. If the Gift is a delusion, but if Theseus nevertheless believes in it, he cannot be responsible for his son's death, although he has the guilt of murderous intention. Most readers appear to think him practically his son's executioner, and the dying Hippolytus implies as much.[3] But does he believe in the Gift?

At the first onset of horror he seems determined on taking Hippolytus' life. "Come, sire Poseidon, who didst long ago promise me three prayers: with one of these destroy my son; and may he not outlive this day, if thou hast granted me true prayers!"[4] For the moment, of course, we take the last clause not as expressing doubt, only as a kind of ejaculation: "Keep thy promise!" But when the Chorus-Leader protests, he at once goes on: "No! Moreover I will drive him out of this land: he shall be smitten by one of two fates: either Poseidon will respect my prayers and send him in

clumsy pen. Perhaps τις touches one most, hinting that Theseus has never really known his wife.

[1] It cannot, however, fairly be maintained that he does so by undue haste in believing Hippolytus guilty. Grube remarks (p. 189): "It is no accident that the king here [1059] uses the same words—πόλλ' ἐγὼ χαίρειν λέγω— which Hippolytus used against Aphrodite in the earlier dialogue with his slave (113). They are hubristic here also. For this is Theseus' sin, that he trusts his dead wife's words too implicitly, and does not try to seek any proof." But Phaedra's suicide, and the letter, coupled with the fact (see below) that father and son have never been affectionate or even particularly friendly, makes the king's attitude (though not all his words) pardonable. Hippolytus urges delay, but that is because he knows himself innocent of the alleged crime. Artemis (1320 ff.) agrees with Grube; her claim to be heard shall be considered later.

[2] Vv. 967–9, where note the emphatic ἐγώ.
[3] Vv. 1411–13.
[4] Vv. 887 ff.

death to the house of Hades; or, cast out of this country and wandering in a foreign land, he shall drain life's bitterness." This, surely, pulls us up: Theseus feels unmistakable doubt.[1] Later he breaks off the terrible wrangle and pronounces his sentence: "Avaunt from this ground with all speed into exile and come no more to God-established Athens or the frontier of the land ruled by my sword." Not a hint of death to be met this very day! Later again, Hippolytus roundly tells him that, had their roles been interchanged, he would have slain his son Theseus and not been content with banishment. To this the king astonishingly replies: "How cheap a sentence! No such end shall be thine, for speedy death is easiest to a ruined man": he proceeds to dilate upon the woes of banishment. Even that does not suffice: no less than four times during the remainder of the scene he mentions exile, that being literally his last word. Later, when he learns from the Messenger that Hippolytus is at the point of death, his state of mind becomes (if possible) still more patent.[2] He does not cry: "Ha! Poseidon has heard my prayer!" but "By whose hand died he? Can he have quarrelled with some man whose wife he outraged as he outraged his father's?" The Messenger must tell him. "His own chariot-team was his death, and the prayers of thy lips, which thou utteredst against thy son to the Sea-God thy father."[3] Thereupon he at last exclaims: "Ye gods, and Poseidon! How truly art thou my father, after all:[4] for thou didst hear my imprecation."[5]

Theseus must be acquitted of intending his son's death. We have been astonished that throughout he utters no word of outraged fatherly love: "Didst *thou*, my son . . . ?" The whole play shows that between these two men there has never been strong affection. But he really intended no

---

[1] Mainly because he has never before tested the Gift. The scholiasts, to be sure, assert thrice (on vv. 46, 888, 1349) that the Prayers were used to secure escape from Hades, escape from the labyrinth, and Hippolytus' death; and in two of these places say that Hippolytus' death is the third wish. Cicero, *De Off.* I. x, writes: *Ex tribus enim optatis, ut scribitur, hoc erat tertium, quod de Hippolyti interitu iratus optavit*. So Wilamowitz (*Griechische Tragoedien übersetzt*, vol. I, p. 100) and Schmid (Müller's *Handbuch der Altertumswissenschaft*, Abt. VII, Teil 1, vol. 3 (Munich, 1940), p. 387). Nevertheless the three most distinguished successors of Euripides have made this prayer the first. In Seneca (*Phaedra* III. 115 ff.) Theseus absurdly says that even in Hell he did not use the Gift to obtain his deliverance, but waited for a serious occasion! Racine (*Phèdre* IV. ii. 35 ff.) was unwise enough to imitate him. D'Annunzio (*Fedra* II. 2665 f.) merely says "il primo". That they have Euripides with them is certain. Theseus' word μιᾷ (888) strongly implies it. Later Artemis says (1316) ὧν τὴν μίαν παρεῖλες, where the verb must mean that one or two, and μίαν that two, of the three remain unused.

[2] Vv. 1153–70.

[3] Note the emphatic "thy" in v. 1167: ἀραί τε τοῦ σοῦ στόματος, ἃς σὺ σῷ πατρὶ . . . .

[4] The familiar idiom of ἄρα with the imperfect.

[5] The belief thus attained endures of course throughout the finale.

more than a severity natural and (as it seems) quite justified. In his first dazed horror he breaks forth into the curse, but at once begins to forget it, because it was a cry of agony, not a judicial sentence. He has never believed seriously in the Gift; and at last, when it is apparently proved authentic, he lets fall words of astonishment as well as awe.

His quarrel with his son, their later reconciliation, and Artemis' converse with the dying man give us deeper insight into Hippolytus' soul.

Under his father's onslaught he makes a very poor impression: that we cannot deny. It is scarcely an exaggeration to say that his "eager self-glorification, for it can hardly be called a defence, manages, through sheer blind lack of tact and sympathy, to insult both the dead woman and his furious father".[1] And we can agree to lament the contrast between his speeches to Theseus and "such beautiful lines as he knows so well how to utter *when alone*".[2] His awkward argumentation, his cumbrous affected rhetoric, repel us as they repel the king. But he has a perfect excuse: it should be needless to dwell upon his horror of Phaedra's passion, of her suicide, and of his father's affliction, coupled with his own inability to blurt out the truth so far as he knows it, and the distress awakened in him by a dawning sense of Phaedra's true character and the phases of her anguish. Moreover, as we have already noted, there has never been any strong affection between the two men. Hippolytus feels this, and clearly attributes it to his own illegitimacy. At the close of all they are reconciled, and most affectingly; but the poet's faultless skill has avoided lyric metre.

To another also is Hippolytus reconciled. His heart now understands Phaedra, whom his intellect and temper had so arrogantly rejected. Her last utterance was the promise "he will learn sobriety of soul",[3] which she meant in bitterness though it is fulfilled in sweetness. Hippolytus' newfound wisdom puts forth a few words[4] of spiritual insight and beauty, flowers equal to those he offered his goddess earlier in this tragic day.

ἐσωφρόνησεν οὐκ ἔχουσα σωφρονεῖν,
ἡμεῖς δ' ἔχοντες οὐ καλῶς ἐχρώμεθα.

Though chaste she could not live, yet chaste she died:
And I lived chaste, yet wrought amiss thereby.

[1] Grube, p. 189 (on vv. 983-1035). But where is the insult to his father, unless we mean that the point-making style is an insult? For that matter, Theseus has already (948 ff.) grossly insulted Hippolytus, though he may well be forgiven. By the insult to Phaedra, Grube means vv. 1034 f. (ἐσωφρόνησεν κτέ.), as to which see below.

[2] Grube, p. 190 (his italics).

[3] Yet another attempt to translate σωφρονεῖν (731).

[4] Vv. 1034 f. The aorist tense of ἐσωφρόνησεν is to be taken as ingressive; cp. Dem. XXX. 33: ἐκείνῳ συνῴκησε.

He sees that Phaedra has saved her soul perforce: a true heroine, by destroying her life she has destroyed her passion. He sees[1] too that his puritanical arrogance has persuaded her to discredit him utterly as she dies, lest it destroy her good repute, the loss of which would half-ruin her victory.

But to the gods he is not reconciled. When he knows that these disasters have been caused by Aphrodite, the grotesque but not surprising blasphemy springs from his lips: "Oh that humankind could lay a curse upon the gods!" At once he is silenced by Artemis' "Let be!" and her promise of vengeance on another mortal and of worship paid to Hippolytus by the maidens of Trozen. The communion of Artemis and her devoted follower is beautiful, but though he loves her, she loves not him.[2] If we listen closely we can hear her quiet yet firm repulse of his desire to be not only her follower but loved by her as a woman loves. When she explains that Aphrodite has destroyed him in malice he answers: "Us three hath Cypris destroyed: I see it all." And he means, with the audacity of utter and innocent love, Phaedra, himself—and Artemis. This wild thought she sees and corrects: "Thy father, aye, and thee and his wife, all three." He answers, with sad submission to the rebuff: "Aye, also my father's woes I lament."[3] This strange anguish appears again for an instant in his last words to her, Sophoclean in their poignant simplicity:

> χαίρουσα καὶ σὺ στεῖχε, παρθέν' ὀλβία·
> μακρὰν δὲ λείπεις ῥᾳδίως ὁμιλίαν.
>
> Farewell thou too, blest Maid, and go thy way,
> Thus lightly quitting long companionship.

An age ago (as it seems) the Nurse used a poignant word of mankind: δυσέρωτες, "pining", yearning only to our sorrow. Aspiration towards complete understanding and fruition, wedded ever to disappointment, is the tale of Phaedra's heart and of every heart that would seize and hold elusive joy or beauty. Thus do she and Hippolytus share at last the same sad knowledge. For as she lost the beloved sight by stretching out vain

---

[1] We must not be misled by his later boasts when carried in at the point of death. He is protesting against Heaven's injustice; he cannot be expected to show discretion in his agony; and such recognition of one's own virtue is common form in Greek tragedy.

[2] The feeling meant by v. 1333 is of course quite different. W. F. Otto (*Die Götter Griechenlands* (1929), p. 104) rightly calls her "die Reine, die zum Entzücken hinreißt und doch nicht lieben kann".

[3] Vv. 1401–5. That he includes Artemis, astonishing as the thought may seem, is proved by καί in v. 1405.

hands to the unapproachable, so does he in his dying hour find himself sundered from the Spirit that has given meaning and beauty to his life: what he has been to Phaedra, that is Artemis to him.

The last sentence hints that we have completed our examination of the purely human drama, as we may perhaps call it, and must now ask what meaning, relevance, and value should be allowed to the divine elements of this tragedy.

Let us consider Poseidon first, as probably the easiest to appraise: for he does not appear in person, and is concerned with but one moment of the action. His Gift of Prayers has already been discussed, but only from Theseus' point of view: the king, we saw, does not definitely believe in it until his son's death convinces him of its reality. But does it in fact exist?

An uncompromising follower of Verrall[1] would find little difficulty in showing that the Gift is illusion. The only proof of it offered is the death of Hippolytus, which the Messenger, Theseus, Hippolytus, and Artemis agree in attributing to it: Poseidon sent the miraculous wave whence the bull emerged that caused the prince's horses to destroy their master. But why not assume a natural submarine earthquake, one familiar result of which is an immense wave bursting upon the nearest shore? And yet, is it easier to credit the coincidence of a natural event with the prayer of Theseus than to credit a miraculous answer? Is not the coincidence itself miraculous? Not miraculous, but amazing. In the course of many generations such coincidences occur and give rise to the myths: the men who accept them are uncritical, but they are not lunatics and therefore must have had some excuse for their acceptance.[2] As for the monster, why should it not be an ordinary wild bull—they were frequent[3] enough in Greece—that has wandered down to the shore from the hills whither the Messenger saw it return (1248)? The myth-creating feat whereby it is said to emerge from the wave itself can be paralleled easily in folk-tales, such as that of the infant Merlin. The onlookers were predisposed by emotion and excitement[4] to find marvels everywhere: we hear, for instance, that this creature was "a sight that vanquished the gaze".[5]

[1] As was I when last writing on this topic a good many years ago (*Phil. Quart.*, vol. XV (Jan. 1936), pp. 46–52). It is much to be regretted that Verrall himself published nothing on our play.   [2] Cp. *ibid.*, pp. 50 f.
[3] And mentioned as familiar in, for example, Soph. *Ant.* 352.
[4] Vv. 1175–81.
[5] Vv. 1216 f.:
$$\epsilon i\sigma o\rho\hat{\omega}\sigma i\ \delta\grave{\epsilon}$$
$$\kappa\rho\epsilon\hat{\iota}\sigma\sigma o\nu\ \theta\acute{\epsilon}\alpha\mu\alpha\ \delta\epsilon\rho\gamma\mu\acute{\alpha}\tau\omega\nu\ \dot{\epsilon}\phi\alpha\acute{\iota}\nu\epsilon\tau o.$$

Or can these words mean rather: "When people looked at the bull he was too big to be seen": when the Messenger called his fellows' attention to the creature, their sight

All this seems reasonable enough, so far. But Euripides has used his utmost skill to invest the story with an uncanny atmosphere. The subterranean rumbling is like "God's thunder" (1201): the unearthly wave "presses against Heaven",[1] blotting out the farther shore, and "advances" towards Hippolytus' chariot;[2] the bull is a "savage portent",[3] whose bellowing filled all the land, whose look quelled the gaze.[4] Most unnerving touch of all, though it comes up to the car, there ensues no physical contact between it and any person or thing: like a spectre, it works through the self-destroying acts to which its victims are impelled; even its bellow has ceased; at last it vanishes "I know not whither in the rocky earth".[5] Are we not to conclude that Euripides offers us, as Virgil does at times,[6] the choice between a natural and a supernatural explanation of a strange experience? They are (as it were) intertwined, neither being unmistakably endorsed by him.

This equivocal impression is strengthened by the diction: Euripides gives us a series of pleasant hints that we can, if so minded, read this splendid narrative as an essay in a kind of poetry whose atmosphere is more congenial to marvels than his own.[7] On reading vv. 1223 ff.,

proved dimmer than his (*Phil. Quart., ut sup.*, p. 51)? Grube (p. 191) finds this "an ingenious but unconvincing 'Verrallism'". It is certainly odd enough, but not unique. Pindar (*Ol.* XIII. 113) sings that the victories won by the Oligaethidae are too numerous to be seen: μᾶσσον ἢ ὡς ἰδέμεν. (So Sandys.) Mrs. Thorne in *The Last Chronicle of Barset* (chap. XIV) says: "You must excuse me, Major Grantly, but Lady Hartletop is really too big for my powers of vision." Hippolytus, though he twice (1240 f., 1355 ff.) reproaches his horses, never mentions the far guiltier animal; nor does anyone else but the Messenger. Diodorus, who tells this story in some detail (IV. 62), omits the bull altogether and attributes Hippolytus' disaster to a contagion of distress: 'Ἱππόλυτος δὲ ἱππηλατῶν, ὡς ἤκουσε τὰ περὶ τῆς διαβολῆς, συνεχύθη τὴν ψυχήν, καὶ διὰ τοῦτο τῶν ἵππων ταραχθέντων καὶ ἐπισπασαμένων αὐτὸν κτέ.

[1] Vv. 1206 f. "Unearthly" is Murray's excellent word for ἱερόν, which has the Homeric meaning "huge"—ἀντὶ τοῦ μέγα (schol.).

[2] V. 1212. χωρεῖ suggests purpose.   [3] V. 1214: ἄγριον τέρας.

[4] Contrast the absurd particularity of Seneca (*Phaedra* 1036–48): its neck was blue, its forehead green, the horns parti-coloured, etc. So far from its being unseen or impossible to look at, the whole countryside is in panic, *nec suos pastor sequi meminit iuvencos*. Ovid (*Met.* XV. 509 ff.) sensibly keeps much closer to Euripides.

[5] It is not Verrall, but Weil, who remarks (on 1217): "Le taureau d'Euripide est-il un être réel ou un fantôme? On ne saurait le dire. Il ne touche ni le char, ni les chevaux, à plus fort raison n'est-il pas blessé par Hippolyte. Il ne fait que se montrer, il fascine, il agit par la terreur de sa présence, et il disparaît soudain, comme il était venu." It is exactly like the three *symbolical* wild beasts that terrify Dante (*Inferno*, Canto i).

[6] E.g., in *Aen.* VII. 341–91, the Fury's attack and Amata's natural emotion are each enough, without the other, to explain the queen's conduct.

[7] In Bradley's *Shakespearean Tragedy*, pp. 389 f., a parallel is drawn between the diction of *Macbeth* and the Player's speech in *Hamlet*. "He may have seen in the bloody story of Macbeth a subject suitable for treatment in a manner somewhat nearer to that

αἳ δ' ἐνδακοῦσαι στόμια πυριγενῆ γναθμοῖς
βίᾳ φέρουσιν, οὔτε ναυκλήρου χερὸς
οὔθ' ἱπποδέσμων οὔτε κολλητῶν ὄχων
μεταστρέφουσαι,

we feel at once that here is an unusual jewelling of the language: πυριγενῆ and κολλητῶν are notable instances of the *epitheton ornans*.[1] To these may be added ἀκτῆς κυμοδέγμονος in the very first line, ἁλιρρόθους ἀκτάς and τμητῶν ἱμάντων, together with others, such as ἵππους ζυγηφόρους and φόβος νεανικός, which are in this connexion of doubtful value. In v. 1247 the phrase δύστηνον τέρας has excited objection:[2] to call the fatal bull an "unhappy miracle" may be natural in a critic, as the preceding pages have hinted; but not in the speaker. δύστηνον should apparently mean "guilty", but seems to have that sense nowhere else in Euripides. Now, can we point to anyone who writes brilliantly elegant narrative, studded with ornamental epithets? Is there any dramatist in whom Euripides can be supposed to have taken keen interest, who combined poetic genius with a commonplace theology, who believed for example that human curses could enlist for their fulfilment the omnipotence of gods? The brilliance that irradiates this narrative is largely due to adroit imitation of Sophocles: such things as στόμια πυριγενῆ and κολλητοὶ ὄχοι cannot but recall ἐπισχὼν χρυσόνωτον ἡνίαν[3] and many other phrases. The evidence of δύστηνον τέρας is at least equally striking.[4] The whole narrative, though not at all points Sophoclean—to this we shall return shortly—has, then, a distinct flavour of that poet. We know that this version of *Hippolytus* is a rewriting of an earlier work, which was marred by certain "improprieties".[5] Perhaps critics had held up the example of Sophocles' *Phaedra* of Seneca, or of the English Senecan plays familiar to him in his youth, than was the manner of his own mature tragedies."

[1] Schmid (p. 427, n. 1) reports on the authority of K. H. Meyer (Diss. Münster, 1913, 69, 1) that of Euripidean plays *Hecuba* has the largest (*Heracleidae* the smallest) number of *epitheta ornantia*. My remarks here are inspired by nothing more scientific than an impression renewed each time I read this narrative: ἐκρύφθεν counts for much more than one ingredient in a percentage. Of course such things occur elsewhere in Euripides. The most striking (*Heracles* 65 f.) is Sophoclean not in its diction but in its imaginative quality:

ἔχων τυραννίδ', ἧς μακραὶ λόγχαι πέρι
πηδῶσ' ἔρωτι σώματ' εἰς εὐδαίμονα.

[2] Paley, followed by Hadley, calls it "very inappropriate".
[3] *Ajax* 847. For τμητῶν ἱμάντων (1245) cp. Soph. *El.* 747, τμητοῖς ἱμᾶσι—and (see below) *Il.* X. 567, εὐτμήτοισιν ἱμᾶσιν.
[4] Cp. Soph. *El.* 121: ὦ παῖ παῖ δυστηνοτάτας Ἠλέκτρα ματρός, and Jebb's note. *El.* 806, which he quotes, is a still clearer example.
[5] The shorter Hypothesis says: ἐμφαίνεται δὲ ὕστερος γεγραμμένος· τὸ γὰρ ἀπρεπὲς καὶ κακηγορίας ἄξιον ἐν τούτῳ διώρθωται τῷ δράματι. Unfortunately this seems to be all that

before the offender's eyes; perhaps he heard comments of Sophocles himself like that reported by Aristotle.[1] Euripides seems to have answered brightly: 'Very well: you shall have an edifying and beautiful play. I will even give you a Family Curse. The gods shall appear to rule the action, and though the Spirit of Olympian Religion may not wear continuously the facial expression that you have in mind, at any rate the language shall be of the finest quality.' This language is seen at its best in the narrative before us. There is just enough[2] of Sophocles to convey a demure little acknowledgement of the Laureate's pre-eminence. But Euripides goes farther. The style is Sophoclean with a delightful admixture of more distinct archaism than Sophocles, so far as we know, saw fit to employ.

Near the beginning occur the lines (1196 f.):

εἰπόμεσθα δεσπότῃ
τὴν εὐθὺς Ἄργους κἀπιδαυρίας ὁδόν,

"we followed our master along the road leading directly to Argos and Epidauria". The use of εὐθύς startles one, since εὐθύ is the only form known in Attic for this prepositional meaning. It has defied emendation.[3] Has Euripides, then, written bad Greek? No: this is bad Attic; but Homer can say ἰθὺς Διομήδεος, ἰθὺς κίεν οἴκου, and so forth freely. The Athenian is simply marking the obsolete opinions of the speaker by a touch of obsolete idiom.[4] In a moment we find this:

ἔνθεν τις ἠχὼ χθόνιος ὡς βροντὴ Διὸς
βαρὺν βρόμον μεθῆκε....

we can affirm with confidence. Scholars disagree as to which came first, *Phaedra* or the second *Hippolytus*. In any case "we know little or nothing of the *Phaedra* of Sophocles which helps us to discover its character" (Pearson, *The Fragments of Sophocles*, ad loc.).

[1] See p. 14 above.

[2] Pohlenz (p. 279) would make an important addition, of a completely different type. "Der äussere Aufbau des Stückes erinnert an sophokleische Kunst": despite Hippolytus' continued presence and importance, Phaedra dominates the interest throughout, introducing by her letter an entirely new action. But may we confidently describe this method as Sophoclean? Alcestis was probably created before Deianira, whom Pohlenz names as an example.

[3] Photius objected to it as a solecism. Hartung and Blaydes wished to read τὴν εὐθύ τ' Ἄργους, but the misplacement of τε is objectionable. Dindorf would write τὴν εὐθὺ Ἄργους, with an incredible hiatus. If ugliness is to be allowed, why not εὐθὺ κἄργους? In *I.A.* 1356 the manuscripts give κἀργόθεν.

[4] A charming instance of this method is provided by *Heracleidae* 539 ff., where Iolaus, who believes Heracles a son of Zeus, uses antique language to Heracles' daughter:

ὦ τέκνον, οὐκ ἔστ' ἄλλοθεν τὸ σὸν κάρα,
ἀλλ' ἐξ ἐκείνου σπέρμα τῆς θείας φρενὸς
πέφυκας Ἡρακλῆος.

The Homeric form Ἡρακλῆος was "emended" by Elmsley to Ἡράκλειος.

The strong alliteration strikes our ear as an archaic device, recalling such things (far better than this, no doubt) as χύντο χαμαὶ χολάδες[1] and τριχθά τε καὶ τετραχθὰ διέσχισεν ἶς ἀνέμοιο.[2] Later we find the Homeric ἱερός.[3] This antique patina is preserved by similar devices, slight but definite, throughout the story. In v. 1218, εὐθὺς δὲ πώλοις δεινὸς ἐμπίπτει φόβος, the last word has not only its Attic meaning of "fear", but also the Homeric, "stampede". The horses are not merely terrified: they begin to bolt.[4] Later appears the most surprisingly archaic word, ἔκρυφθεν.[5] And all this, we should remember, in a passage copied and recopied by scribes who regarded it as meant for good poetical Attic. We may well surmise that many other antique features have been obliterated by "obvious corrections".[6]

Nothing more need be said of the Messenger's speech in general or of Poseidon in particular, whose Gift of Prayers and its outcome we may view with as much awe as our temperament and taste in drama may suggest.[7] It has no clear bearing upon the theology of our play.

So far, then, we have studied a drama purely human, however solemn and affecting, an example upon a conspicuous stage to remind us that sorrow falls upon man not only through transgressions that he could avoid, but also through good-nature, as in the pleadings of the Nurse, and actually through his virtues, like the insistent chastity of Hippolytus and the self-respect that brought Phaedra to destroy the man who might injure her good name. Such is the first impression made by these events. Well may the women of Trozen exclaim[8] that the bread of Man is

---

[1] *Il.* IV. 526.   [2] *Od.* IX. 71.   [3] See above, p. 92.

[4] This is plain from the way in which the experienced (1219 f.) driver behind them deals with the φόβος. Instead of soothing them with his voice "he snatched the reins and pulled like a sailor on the oar, fastening the thongs round his waist". That the team has already broken from a walk into a gallop is proved moreover by the non-interference of the grooms, who have hitherto been walking at the horses' heads (see vv. 1196, 1243 f.).

[5] V. 1247. Nauck's suggestion, ἵπποι δὲ φροῦδοι, and Weil's ὄχος δ' ἐκρύφθη do little more (so poor are they) than emphasize the correctness of the received text.

[6] See Murray's *apparatus* for σίδαρος and σίδηρος in v. 76. Some manuscripts give ἀρβύλῃσιν (accepted by Valckenaer) in v. 1189. Perhaps in v. 1197 ἰθύς (cp. p. 94 above) should be read in place of εὐθύς. Modern editors admit only when compelled even the one epic licence regularly allowed in such ῥήσεις. All read χωρεῖ in v. 1212, where χώρει (= ἐχώρει) might well stand. See further Verrall's note on *Agamemnon* 582, where he reads Τροίην after the Laurentian MS.

[7] "Poseidon does not appear in this story as a god of any special significance. His 'gift of prayers' ... is a mere piece of mythological mechanism used to enhance the dramatic effectiveness of Theseus cursing his son." Grube, p. 178, n. 2.

[8] V. 367: ὦ πόνοι τρέφοντες βροτούς. So Spenser writes (*Daphnaida*, 375): "My bread shall be the anguish of my soul."

sorrow! Entangling his feet in his righteousness no less than in his sin, he stumbles unceasingly: διέφθαρται βίος. All seems chaos; and, if ever he fancies that it has begun to grow coherent and intelligible, the Universe appears organized for the defeat, not the encouragement, of human effort towards good. Does solace lurk anywhere in Euripides' presentation? At once we turn our eyes to the theological background. Does he set the story in a new perspective?

Artemis baffles us at first and perhaps to the close, inspiring us with a strange blend of annoyance, amusement, and admiration. Instead of contenting herself with the speech of solace and prophecy which, though marvellously beautiful, can be matched technically elsewhere, or with conversation of a frigid explanatory tenor, which also is familiar, she joins with Hippolytus in what one is tempted to call a quite human talk. By her greeting to the wounded prince,

> Unhappy man, disaster's yoke-fellow,
> Slain by thine own nobility of soul!

and by her other words of sympathy does she not become a regular "character of the play"? What are we to think of her?

Again and again she speaks words unsurpassed in loveliness by any that our poet has left us. "Excessive beauty of speech", however, as we are warned by this very drama,[1] "is the ruin of society and the family." It is just as often a menace to clear thought. If we are to appraise the dramatic and personal value of the goddess, we shall be well advised to look into the substance as well as the manner of her speeches. Artemis is the spirit presiding over wild free animal life, over the solitudes untouched by scythe or grazing sheep, and over human hearts as virginal.[2] She is no mighty exponent of divine dispensation like the Delphian Apollo; she cannot claim Athena's sovereign intellect. It is with misgiving, then, that we find her lightly assuming the right to speak with authority like theirs. On so simple a topic as classical mythology—simple at any rate for gods—Artemis proves sadly uninstructed. She names Theseus the son of Aegeus (1282 f.), whereas the king himself calls Poseidon his father. Though the goddess should be better informed than the mortal, who has indeed known moments of doubt concerning his divine parentage,[3] yet

---

[1] Vv. 486 f.:

> τοῦτ' ἔσθ' ὃ θνητῶν εὖ πόλεις οἰκουμένας
> δόμους τ' ἀπόλλυσ', οἱ καλοὶ λίαν λόγοι.

[2] Otto (*ut sup.*, pp. 102–15) deals fully and most attractively with this.

[3] Vv. 1169 f. See above, pp. 88 f., and cp. Isocrates, *Helen* 211c: Θησεύς, ὁ λεγόμενος μὲν Αἰγέως, γενόμενος δ' ἐκ Ποσειδῶνος.

the prompt fulfilment wrought by the sea-god, when invoked as Theseus' father, ought (one would suppose) to convince Artemis that she is mistaken, although her address is no casual periphrasis, but marked as a compliment by the word εὐπατρίδαν: "upon thee do I call, son of a noble sire, even Aegeus". A blunder it certainly is, for to our amazement Artemis herself, when discussing the Gift of Prayers, changes her mind (1315): "Art aware that thou hast three certain gifts *from thy father*?" This emendation might be satisfactory, were it not that she changes her mind again[1] when she has forgotten the point. Her self-contradictions are intelligible enough, however stupid. Stories of men to whom tradition gave two fathers, a god and a mortal, were familiar; and *Heracles* in particular gains overpowering effect from the ambiguity. Artemis belongs to an age, to a state of mind, which felt no need to solve the puzzle: indeed saw no puzzle.[2] For critical minds in a later age she is a crude anachronism.

The same nullity clings to her moral judgements. As soon as she appears, her mouth is filled with grim taunts concerning the ruin that Theseus' folly has caused, and with suggestions as to suicide or transformation into a bird, since he is not fit to live among righteous men. On this easy theme she waxes copious, calling her wretched auditor a villain and laying upon him complete responsibility for his son's fate. She even brings in Poseidon, who (if we are to believe her) agrees in condemning the use to which the Gift of Prayers has been put. In a moment, however, we learn that the extraordinary openness of mind wherewith she examines Theseus' parentage extends to his conduct. No sooner has he uttered his second desperate groan than Artemis makes a complete *volte-face*:[3] Cypris alone is responsible; Theseus' ignorance exonerates him; it

---

[1] V. 1431: ὦ γεραιοῦ τέκνον Αἰγέως.

[2] In the Homeric *Hymn to the Dioscuri*, they are called Διὸς κοῦροι in the first line and Τυνδαρίδαι in the second. On Ibycus fr. 3, 20 ff. (Diehl) see Sir Maurice Bowra (*Greek Lyric Poetry* (1936), p. 267): "Here mythology is confounded. Agamemnon is made both the son of Pleisthenes and of Atreus. The two versions were current in the sixth century. . . . Ibycus gaily combines the two competing fathers in the same sentence, and it is hard to resist the feeling that this happy disregard of accuracy is deliberate. By it Ibycus indicates that he is no longer concerned with mythology. For all he cares, Agamemnon may be the son of both." Bacchylides (XVI. 15 f.) calls Theseus Πανδίονος ἔκγονος (Pandion being Aegeus' father), though the whole point of the dithyramb is that Theseus is Poseidon's son and proves it by his diving adventure. (Jebb on v. 36 writes: "The key to the confused legend is that Aegeus and Poseidon were originally identical.")

[3] Vv. 1325–37. This ineptitude can, it is true, be matched. In *Rhesus* the Muse first (893 f., 906 ff.) blames Odysseus and Diomedes for her son's death, then (938 ff.) lays the guilt on Athena and acquits the two Greeks. But in the last passage her language shows that she is half-hysterical.

is natural to err when the gods send error. The aged Huntsman of Hippolytus opines that the gods ought to be wiser than men; his hinted doubt must have been strengthened by Artemis' essays in ethical philosophy.

When, therefore, she proceeds to say "for gods there stands a law as follows", announcing a statement (*ex cathedra*, of course) on theology, we feel that we should prefer not to listen. The "law" proves to be this: "None seeks to thwart the eagerness of another's will: we ever stand aside. For, be sure, had I not feared Zeus, never would I have incurred the shame of permitting a man to die who of all mortals is dearest to me."[1] Aphrodite, we gather, by conceiving murderous wrath against Hippolytus, secures what can only be called an option on his life, and therefore Artemis can do nothing to save him. All might have been well if she had "got in first", warning her sister betimes that the prince was dearest to her of all mankind, and that she desired his continued society with "eagerness of will". The truth is that Artemis has heard something of what philosophers say about *moira* and the allotted spheres of individual deities,[2] but her studies have been hurried and defective. *Moira* is a system of government, not the establishment of anarchy; but in her ardour to explain she does not hesitate to saddle Zeus himself with this curious doctrine.[3] However that may be, granted anarchy, she intends to enjoy it: though she may not save Hippolytus, she can and will destroy Adonis, the favourite of Aphrodite. Let heart-broken father and dying son console themselves with that!

If her hearers do accept this revelation, they find on second thoughts that they have its proclaimer herself against them; for whatever mortals may think about the Gift of Prayers, Artemis a moment ago has clearly taken it for genuine. But what would Poseidon have done had Theseus used it to impose on him some act which interfered with the "enthusiastic wish" of another deity? Indeed, according to one account[4] he availed himself of the Gift to win his own return from Hades. If that is not trespass upon another god's prerogative and sphere, where shall such

---

[1] Vv. 1328 ff. The awkward phrase προθυμίᾳ τῇ τοῦ θέλοντος is oddly like the contorted language of an examinee struggling to recall his lecture-notes: "the keenness of one who has got a wish". Artemis is completely out of her depth.

[2] See F. M. Cornford, *From Religion to Philosophy* (1912), pp. 15 ff., etc.

[3] V. 1331, Ζῆνα μὴ φοβουμένη. Grube (192 f.) emphasizes this brief phrase, expanding it thus: "We must suppose that Zeus had granted Aphrodite's demand for vengeance on Hippolytus, and that therefore Artemis was afraid of his displeasure if she should venture to interfere." Why, then, does not Aphrodite in the prologue quote this vital permission instead of using the accents of unchallenged sovereignty?

It is scarcely worth while to add that this "law" is flouted in *Helen* 27-36—and indeed by Ovid (*Trist.* V. iii. 45 f.).   [4] So the scholiasts; see above, p. 88, n. 1.

trespass be found? But no misgiving disturbs Artemis: the celestial Monroe Doctrine and the unconditioned grant of Poseidon do not clash in her thought. Why? Because her being, power, and importance, her very meaning, belong to the world of instinct and emotion: she has naught to do with any system, or even idea, of rational congruity.

For, if she believes in the Gift wherewith she upbraids Theseus, why does she not call on him to follow that belief, which he now shares with her? Why should he not, having learned his son's innocence, instantly offer another prayer that shall reverse the doom? Has Theseus another chance? Has he in the past used his two other prayers, or has he not?[1] Before Artemis appears the point troubles no one; and if by any chance it had been thrust upon our attention, we should have replied: "It matters nothing with which prayer Theseus has doomed his son: he intends his death and has so secured it." In the epilogue all is changed. Theseus has vindicated righteousness and the ways of Heaven, so he thinks. But Artemis' first speech reveals his error. He is overwhelmed beyond speech: only a single groan escapes him. We are numb with grief for him . . . but—is there not some way . . . ? Then Artemis plunges forward (1313 ff.): "Knowest thou of three certain prayers given by thy father?" The callous jauntiness of her tone would enrage auditors less preoccupied; but she brings hope. The *three* Prayers! Is there another chance? First, by the emphasis of position and assonance she throws two words to the front:

ἆρ' οἶσθα πατρὸς τρεῖς
ἀρὰς ἔχων σαφεῖς;

"Three Prayers, Theseus, not one only! And all certain of fulfilment!" Of course; but has he any part of the Gift still unused? She continues: "One of those prayers hast thou—oh, base!—taken out for thine own son's ruin." Her language makes it certain that Theseus has today for the first time made use of the Gift. Our agonized suspense, then, is over: let him restore Hippolytus,[2] and on the instant! Nothing has been heard

[1] He has, in fact, two prayers still available; see above, p. 88, n. 1.

[2] We need not trouble ourselves with the fact that, if the Prayers are certain, Hippolytus *must* die: the second Prayer could bring him back to life.

If one suggested further that the third Prayer should restore Phaedra also, the reader would be disgusted with a notion so painful and absurd. (That is in fact true of the proposal about Hippolytus also.) This shows what is wrong with the Gift altogether. The fundamental triviality of such a conception means death to sound dramatic art, and indeed to any good art. One need scarcely add that Euripides disregards the story (Virgil, *Aen*. VII. 765 ff.) in which Hippolytus was restored as Virbius by Artemis.

See further A. Lesky (*Deutsche Literaturzeitung*, 1930, 1169) and H. Herter, "Theseus

of any law against redressing the effect of one Prayer by a second.¹ But not a word about this obvious remedy falls from the lips that have just revealed its possibility. Artemis is content to ramble on, forgetting her own fierce condemnation of Theseus, with welcome but unexpected friendliness discussing his innocence as a victim of Aphrodite and of Phaedra, expounding the "option" system aforesaid, the sympathy of Heaven with righteous men, and the destruction meted out to wrong-doers. Whatever be the truth concerning the Gift, she who here describes it cannot see the plain meaning of her own description.

Such, so far as we have read, is Euripides' account of "the goddess Artemis". She has not defended her favourite, nor can she save him now, her sole attempt at energy being a promise to destroy another innocent person later. We may believe if we can that the promise will be fulfilled, supposing she remembers it in an hour's time. She can discuss nothing intelligently, knowing and understanding just enough to expose her own futility. Any woman in Athens would have cried: "Raise thy voice again, Theseus, in a second and better prayer."² So far, Artemis shows herself not a goddess or a fiend, not even an imbecile: she is a nullity, a radiant emptiness.

But radiant she is. When we pass from her scene with Theseus to her conversation with his dying son we breathe an air in which our fault-finding expires. Think again of Hippolytus' greeting:

> ἔα·
> ὦ θεῖον ὀδμῆς πνεῦμα· καὶ γὰρ ἐν κακοῖς
> ὢν ᾐσθόμην σοῦ κἀνεκουφίσθην δέμας·
> ἔστ' ἐν τόποισι τοισίδ' Ἄρτεμις θεά.

> Ah!...
> Celestial fragrance! In the depth of woe
> I feel thy presence and forget my pain.
> Upon this ground stands heavenly Artemis.

der Athener" (*Rhein. Mus.*, N.F., vol. LXXXVIII (1939), pp. 314 ff.): the criticism that neither the reader nor Artemis can think of such reversal by a second prayer is surely to be answered by asking why, then, does the poet put such suggestive words into Artemis' mouth? Cp. n. 2, below.

¹ This use of the Gift appears to be frequent. A coarse but neat poem of Prior illustrates the idea excellently. Mr. Charles Morgan quotes a more decorous version. *Reflections in a Mirror*, Second Series (1946), p. 79.

Schlegel writes *à propos* of Racine's play: "Il pouvait révoquer ses vœux addressés à Neptune." *Comparaison entre la Phèdre de Racine et celle d'Euripide, Œuvres*, etc. (Leipzig, 1846), vol. II, p. 404.

² The Chorus-Leader exclaims (891): "O king, in Heaven's name revoke this prayer!"

Or listen to his wistful adieu, where heartbreak quivers into music: χαίρουσα καὶ σὺ στεῖχε, and the rest. Hardly less magical are those lines[1] in which Artemis herself, that Artemis whom we have mocked, promises to her dying acolyte an immortality of sad yet beautiful remembrance.

> But, hapless youth, on thee will I bestow
> Majestic honours paid by Trozen town
> In recompense of these calamities.
> Damsels unwedded shall their tresses shear
> For thee on marriage-eves through endless time,
> Rich harvest offering of tears and woe.
> Virgins shall tune their solemn minstrelsy
> For ever, nor shall Phaedra's love of thee
> Fall into silence and be named no more.

In face of this, must we not struggle to forget our earlier rebukes?

No: the absurdity and the loveliness are equally undeniable. Such contrasts are an essential of Euripides' mind and art.[2] They distress many of us so gravely that we strive to ignore one of the clashing elements: the absurdity, as a rule. But that will not serve: what he has written he has written. All the great Attic writers, who have never been surpassed as artists no less conscious than successful, understood clearly how much virtue lay in fine language. They did not believe that splendid phrasing compensated for badness of heart or weakness of head. Euripides seems to enjoy bestowing literary excellence, as a kind of sardonic apology, upon characters who despite their language, sometimes indeed by means of it, are unconsciously but fatally condemning themselves. How eloquent is Jason's reproof of Medea's ingratitude, how moving Admetus' language to his wife about bringing her back from Hades, how trenchant Menelaus' attack upon Agamemnon's mean ambition in the Aulid *Iphigenia*! The irony that Euripides traced in the Universe thus left strange marks upon his style. Hardly any other writer has combined such mastery of eloquence with such implacable distrust of it; but a parallel can be found in a playwright who not seldom reminds us of Euripides: Bernard Shaw, whose most notable exploit[3] of this kind occurs early in *Caesar and Cleopatra*, where the noble address beginning "Hail, Sphinx!

---

[1] Vv. 1423–30. Their charm is increased for readers who compare them with other passages (e.g., *Androm.* 1243 ff., *Ion* 1575 ff.) which technically serve the same aetiological purpose.

[2] See the first essay above, especially pp. 21–23, 45–47.

[3] Other good examples are found in the first act of *John Bull's Other Island*—and often elsewhere, for pricking bubbles is one of Shaw's chief amusements and chief services.

Salutation from Julius Caesar!" is followed by a charmingly absurd anticlimax.

What, then, becomes of the epilogue to which Artemis so strangely but so powerfully contributes? Condemn as we will her intellectual feebleness, we think quite otherwise of her emotional quality and meaning: on that side she is entirely credible as a goddess and (apart altogether from the beauty of her speech) by no means devoid[1] of both dignity and charm. Moreover, the structural function of this scene should be noted. Consider the epilogue of *Orestes*. Not only is Apollo incredible in himself: the reconciliation that he produces is incredible too, and would remain incredible if produced by some agency both intelligible and intelligent. Expunge Apollo with all his spuriousness and replace him by Solon or Pericles uttering the soundest argumentative eloquence: you are no nearer to procuring Orestes and Electra pardon from Argos for the murder of Clytaemnestra or to persuading Menelaus that a marriage between Hermione and Orestes is desirable or even tolerable. So in *Ion*: what plain and believable piece of information (whether conveyed by Athena or by a human friend) can be imagined that is capable of inducing a man, with Ion's character and in Ion's situation, to renounce his purpose, turn away from the temple-door and leave unprobed the divine statements he suspects to be lies? *Orestes* and *Ion* are melodramas: that is all.[2] In *Hippolytus*, a genuine tragedy, Theseus and his son are as natural, as vivid and convincing, at the close as throughout. Theseus' opinions and language, of course, have changed completely; but to cause this nothing was needed save a simple and credible piece of information: that Phaedra's dying message is a falsehood. And it is the *dea ex machina* who brings about this perfect close.

Artemis, then, must be accepted as a genuine *dramatis persona*, no less authentic than Hippolytus himself: so much, and no more. It does not follow that Euripides himself believed in her personal existence: while

---

[1] Her admirable qualities have, however, been somewhat exaggerated by sensitive scholars. P. Decharme (*Euripide et l'esprit de son théâtre* (1893), p. 388) writes of "Artémis qui voudrait pleurer, qui regrette que sa divinité l'en empêche". This points to v. 1396, less outspoken than the French. Certainly she holds Hippolytus dear (1333, 1398); but we must not drift into thinking her a victim of the calamity, as Hippolytus tries to believe her (see above, pp. 90 f.). Professor S. M. Adams (*Class. Rev.*, vol. XLIX (1935), pp. 118 f.) seeks to excuse her roughness to Theseus, and asserts that she "alters the attitude of Hippolytus" (yes: but only his attitude to his father). He sums up thus: "What Artemis does for Hippolytus she does also for the play. Pain and resentment fade, leaving behind them pity." Much of the agony vanishes, but both sorrow and indignation remain (1459–66); and the assuagement is due not to Artemis' qualities but to her revelation of the truth about Phaedra, a revelation dictated by the poet who would reconcile the two men. [2] See above, pp. 23–30.

writing this particular play he "puts her in", and thereby no more commits himself to belief in her divinity than Dickens commits himself to belief in a person called Christmas Past, or than Shakespeare (or whoever wrote that portion of *Cymbeline*) commits himself to belief in Jupiter. Indeed, we here light upon the reason for the absurdities in Artemis' remarks on theology, on Theseus' parentage and criminal folly. Speaking *ex cathedra*, she reveals herself as utterly spurious, a survival from days of uncontrolled superstition. But as Hippolytus' beloved companion she is authentic and divine. Euripides makes her thus real simply because she has complete reality for his hero: that reality is a basic fact of his play.

But why does he allow this disconcerting clash in his presentation of her? Having chosen to use artistically a person in whom he does not believe, why does he not treat her with more discretion? He would have found no difficulty, and we should have taken far more pleasure, in an Artemis who did not make us uneasy, who remained quietly emotional throughout, never allowing the question of brains to arise. The answer is simple but unusual. It may be worded in several ways. "Take what genius gives you and be thankful." "Euripides is a notoriously uneven playwright." "He never read Aristotle: if in the course of composition a quaint fancy struck him, down it went into the play, and a fig for consistency!" Anyone who considers the prim expostulations uttered by the Spirit of Frenzy against Hera's injustice,[1] or the ode in *Electra* that so gracefully tells the legend of the Golden Lamb only to brand it in the final stanza as a lie,[2] and other such gambols, will agree that Euripides, in the deepest sense of the words, wrote his dramas to suit himself. Such discord in the presentation of Artemis (like many other discords in his work) is, then, best explained by recognizing that Euripides was a philosopher as well as a poet, and that the two sides of his nature often show themselves in frank opposition. Even when he presents a goddess as a needed and impressive participant in the dramatic action, he allows his irrelevant rationalism to hang upon her a label saying: "This is merely a puppet at which you need look only for a moment: it will soon be tossed back into the box and forgotten."

If we turn now at length to Aphrodite, the contrast between her and Artemis is clear and impressive, perhaps shocking, in character, emotions, aims, and significance for mankind. Nevertheless, they are alike in this, that Euripides has used the same strange method of portraying them.

Aphrodite, who speaks to none of her victims, is at first displayed by her soliloquy as a tremendous figure: making no claim upon our love or

[1] *Heracles* 843 ff.   [2] *El.* 698 ff.

admiration, she is yet a goddess in her power, her will, her import for us and our world. In her might and relentless cruelty there dwells "something of the sea" that gave her birth and across which Phaedra, dogged by her unseen curse,[1] voyaged from Crete. There seems nothing irrational in such a Being, so imagined, and we are to believe (are we not?) that she and her like do rule the Universe. But as we hear her speech to the end doubt steadily grows. Why should this eternal omnipresent Power concern herself with times and places, opportunity and machination? Why this profusion of detail about the petty human creatures whose strength means to her no more than their happiness? Instead of this artful precise arrangement of the snare, surely the mere emanation[2] of her will should suffice to humble Hippolytus, to shrivel him on the instant. But the world-goddess who awed us in the opening sinks before the end to language that, except for its neat style, might have been uttered by some malicious abigail of the Athenian court.[3] Euripides, we

---

[1] Vv. 756–62. It can hardly be doubted that Murray has rightly understood this weird passage: otherwise the second sentence is condemned to flatness surely impossible in so wonderful an ode. He translates:

> And there, where Munychus fronts the brine,
> Crept by the shore-flung cables' line,
> The curse from the Cretan water!

His note runs: "A curse or spell must have come with her from Crete. It was difficult for a curse to come from one country to another. Exactly like infection, it had to be somehow carried. The women suggest that it came with Phaedra in the ship, and then, when the ship was moored in Munychia, the old harbour of Athens, it crawled up the cables to the shore."

On the whole ode see H. F. Graham's attractive paper (*Class. Jour.*, vol. XLII (1947), pp. 275 f.).

[2] It was pleasant to find my thought anticipated by D'Annunzio. In *Fedra* I. 799 ff. Phaedra hurls passionate defiance at the silent goddess, but suddenly collapses:

> No. Ti cedo. Invitta,
> invitta sei. Mi snodi le ginocchia,
> mi dirompi la spina
> sol con lo sguardo.

Cp. *Tro.* 985 f. (of Aphrodite):

> οὐκ ἂν μένουσ' ἂν ἥσυχός σ' ἐν οὐρανῷ
> αὐταῖς Ἀμύκλαις ἤγαγεν πρὸς Ἴλιον; . . . .

[3] So in Apuleius (*Met.* IV. 84) this same goddess (as it happens), while describing herself as *elementorum origo initialis*, grumbles venomously against the mortal girl Psyche.

Grube, however, writes (p. 197): "The reality of her existence is so clear that the details of the presentation are relatively unimportant, nor are these so inconsistent with the Greek idea of godhead as to require us to look for satirical intent." But there was more than one Greek idea of godhead. Euripides begins with the Aeschylean: his goddess shows at first no less majesty than Athena in the *Eumenides*. Can we imagine Athena proceeding to describe a programme like Aphrodite's? The presentation here contradicts not only other ideas, but itself also.

see, presents Aphrodite, as he presents Artemis, by a method reminding us of Theseus' odd wish[1] that every man had two voices, one to contradict the other. Like her sister, Aphrodite is used by the playwright as a genuine character of his tragedy, but at the same moment labelled by the philosopher as a spurious deity.

Here is no confusion of thought or aim. He did not believe that the traditional gods existed: for him they merely symbolized the permanent facts of the Universe and of human life.[2] No doubt drama, by its very nature, is compelled to use persons whom the spectator can accept as in some degree resembling himself. Nevertheless 'Artemis' meant for Euripides not a wondrous female figure, but the unfettered energy of non-human existence, and "the splendour of the God-haunted countryside". She is the life, withdrawn and rapturous, followed by dedicated human beings who are embarrassed among men and women but find their true selves by consorting with what others feebly and briefly call 'Nature', rendering their human hearts fit for this companionship by a chastened life, an *ascesis* that seems to others stupidity or pride. Such a man, thus ill at ease in the market-place, thus serenely blissful in woodland or secluded meadow, thus proud under the world's eyes, was the son of Theseus and the tameless Amazon.

'Aphrodite', far better understood by Theseus and by most others, stands for the quenchless instinct that heaves itself ceaselessly outward, the creative stress that urges all animal life and must be served with gladness by Man, its highest offspring. It speaks to him with the most intimate and urgent voice of all, summing in one appeal the vitality, the colour, the charm and significance of all that surrounds his way. But soon a change passes over his spirit, a change unavoidable because he is a creature swayed not only by instinct but also by imagination, conscience, and intellect. He begins to imagine this dominant stress as a Person whose will lies irresistibly upon him: Aphrodite the Sea-Queen, wonderful and ruthless like the ocean, bringing joy or pain with indifferent hands. On other forces, too, thus moulding his life he confers personality. But when

---

[1] Vv. 925-31.
[2] So much, of course, has often been said. Euripides' own contemporary Prodicus voiced it plainly (Sext. Emp. IX. 18). For our own day it suffices to quote Pohlenz (p. 283): "Euripides glaubt nicht an die Aphrodite der Volksreligion, die zur Befriedigung eigener Rachsucht Unschuldige schuldig macht, glaubt schwerlich an ein persönliches Wesen, das solche Leidenschaft im Menschen hervorrief. Aber die Macht, mit der diese den Menschen zwingt, kennt der Herzenskünder wie kein anderer, und für den Gestalter war es ein einzigartiger Vorteil, wenn er die Göttin des Volksglaubens einführen konnte, die sofort in jedem Zuschauer bestimmte plastische Vorstellungen erzeugte."

poetical imagination has done its work, what then? As man grows mature, his moral sense intervenes and applies to these Beings the standards of conduct that he has evolved, often condemning them, on their record, as unworthy of respect. Such is the price paid for indulging the poetical imagination before it begins to be curbed by the moral imagination. That sexual passion often causes anguish and sin, though a terrible fact, need not endanger religion; that personal gods, possessing knowledge, power, emotion, and will, should work such evil makes the Universe a nightmare.

But now Euripides enters, wielding yet another instrument that his fellows have here forgotten to use: the intellect. 'What these gods (according to legend and other fancies) say, do, and command others to do proves them not evil gods or idiot gods, but simply no gods at all.[1] Let us put them back into their rightful place. They are forces, blind forces; to worship them is to embrace ruin. What, then, are we to do in face of them? Some we must endure as best we may: who can bridle the hurricane or defy the earthquake? But others there are that we cannot indeed annul, yet may learn to bridle and turn into the means of good: man's own passions, the instincts of his heart, the energies of his own body.' Independent entirely of man's control, Aphrodite is a figure to darken the sun and make life a torture-chamber. Entirely subdued to his will, such instincts or powers become nerveless slaves, leaving his life a mechanical round of easeful accomplishment. But neither of these propositions is the fact, and herein lies, not only the tragedy of Euripides, but the tragedy of all dramatists, indeed the very marrow of life as a high enterprise worthy of human acceptance. That our fates are in our hands but ever and anon leap from the careless fingers, that our instincts may be harnessed but must never be chained however frightful the consequences of their complete enfranchisement—this it is that makes life an art, not a science on the one hand or a chaos on the other.

If these ideas concerning Artemis and Aphrodite are sound, we should not find it difficult to answer the query, Where lies the source of this play's action: in the deities or in the mortals? Scholars have offered very different replies. At one extreme stands Méridier, who writes: "It would be a complete misunderstanding of the spirit of the drama to see in it a human action flanked at each end by two artificial apparitions. *Hippolytus is a religious tragedy* . . . that is a vital point and cannot be too strongly emphasized."[2] Schmid adds that the mortal characters are mere "supers"

---

[1] Cp. frr. 286 and 292, especially the famous last line: εἰ θεοί τι δρῶσιν αἰσχρόν, οὐκ εἰσὶν θεοί.

[2] *L'Hippolyte d'Euripide* (1931), p. 206 (his italics). Kitto says: ". . . the real unity

without knowing it, and "are therefore freed from all personal guilt".[1] At the other extreme Wilamowitz writes that Aphrodite is unnecessary to our understanding of the action; to suppose that the human deeds and suffering are due to God or fate or accident is a blunder unworthy of refutation: the mortal characters are fully responsible for their own conduct.[2] Two views may be added that lie between these extremes. Lesky[3] is rather closer to the second: there are two planes of action—gods working above, events happening in human lives below. Grube's view is nearer to the first: "... the main conflict is not the struggle in Phaedra's heart, it is not even that between her and Hippolytus; rather it is between Aphrodite, with her representatives, the nurse, Phaedra, later Theseus, on the one hand, and Artemis-Hippolytus on the other."[4]

Our present study suggests yet another view. On the face of it, there are two sequences of action: the divine and the human. These are in cold theory separable, and they cannot both be completely true. If the first is authentic, Phaedra and the others must join the "puppets of fate",[5] those

lies not in [Phaedra's] fate but in what Aphrodite is doing. ... The logic of the plot and the unity of the action obviously reside in the underlying conception and not in the tragic mind of either Phaedra or Hippolytus." *Greek Tragedy* (1939), p. 204.

[1] P. 384.
[2] *Griechische Tragoedien übersetzt*, vol. I, pp. 109 f., e.g.: "Diese Menschen haben ihre Handlungen selbst zu verantworten, sind ihrer Geschicke Urheber selbst, genau so weit wie wir Menschen es überhaupt sind."
[3] *Die griechische Tragödie* (1938), p. 158. (He points to a parallel in Apollonius' description of Medea's love-story.) His theory attributes to the whole complex work the Virgilian treatment of details mentioned above (p. 92).
[4] P. 19. He makes it plain that he thinks Aphrodite and Artemis altogether predominant. The passage quoted above proceeds: "Aphrodite's attack is in two distinct waves, of which the first culminates in Hippolytus' interview with the nurse, the second in his first scene with Theseus...." And in pp. 182 f., he ably exhibits the manner in which the goddesses are kept in our minds throughout: that is remarkable, true; but the human actors are vastly more prominent.
[5] This topic is best studied in Sophocles. Oedipus commits two frightful acts. Why? He does not intend them. Nevertheless (so we often say) he is condemned by Heaven to commit them: if that is true, he is "a puppet of fate". But it is not true. Sophocles shows clearly that Oedipus' acts arise from his character, from the deeds of other human beings, and from accident. In their origin they are precisely like the acts of everyone else. What, then, of Heaven's alleged *fiat*? The idea that the gods force such conduct upon him is plainly false. When their oracle speaks, he is not only unborn: he is not even conceived (cp. *Oed. Col.* 964–73, and Jebb's note on 972). Therefore the gods are not commanding him, in the genuine sense of the word "command"; for he can neither obey nor disobey, since he does not exist. They are only prophesying: the oracle is not a *fiat*, but a *fiet*. (In *O.T.* 788–93, χρείη is shown by the following future optatives to mean "I was to", in the sense of mere statement, as in 1110 f. and often. To that passage *O.T.* 1329 f.: Ἀπόλλων ... ὁ κακὰ κακὰ τελῶν ἐμά, refers in language distorted by the speaker's agony.) Thus we find ourselves outside the problem of fate and free will, envisaging a different matter: divine foreknowledge, not divine

notorious phantoms that would make tragic art impossible, and owe whatever English[1] vogue they have mostly to the aberration of our greatest novelist.[2] The "divine sequence" must therefore be rejected: even if we were to grant that Euripides anywhere accepts the "puppet" theory, we could not believe it here. Would he have lavished all his powers on the greatest feats of characterization that he ever achieved, only to imply in the end that character counts for nothing in human fortunes? Therefore the second "sequence" only is authentic, forming of itself the body of the play. The "divine sequence", then, must be one of three things. Is it a mere irresponsible flourish like the Fairy Queen in the old Christmas pantomimes? That description may suit some of Euripides' work, like Thetis in *Andromache* and the Twin Brethren in *Helen*; it is utterly unsuitable to this tragedy. Is it a transparent imposture, such as Verrall believed Euripides to have written for sundry other plays, whether to make them fit for the religious festival or to avoid accusations of impiety? That is less absurd, but cannot be seriously alleged, if only because Artemis, during part of her appearance, acts as a technically normal *dramatis persona*. We must accept the third possibility, that it is a comment on the "human sequence".

But that human story has been told in human language of a precision, a clearness and beauty rarely equalled. What comment or development can it need? For us, perhaps, none. For the poet's own place and time surely some addition, or he would not have given it. Let us note that whereas this tragedy gained the first prize, *Medea*,[3] produced only three years before, was placed third. Both plays are immensely effective: what can have caused such a difference in the awards? Had it been some striking event or action or experience of the poet's own, irrelevant to dramatic art but providing a curious anecdote, we should find it somewhere in the subsequent literature. Since that is lacking, we are justified in assuming that Athens esteemed *Hippolytus* far more than *Medea*.[4] Why?

ordinance. At that point we may reasonably imitate Sophocles and probe no farther: his play is based on a mystery that must be left a mystery; its action is human.

[1] Upon other students and writers the paramount influence has no doubt been that of Schlegel, who in his *Comparaison* (p. 387) calls fatality the "pensée fondamentale et motrice dans la tragédie grecque".

[2] It is plain from, for example, the famous ending of *Tess* and his own entry, in *Who's Who*, of the year in which he began to study Aeschylus, that Thomas Hardy thought he derived his notion of the divine government from Greek tragedy.

[3] One would be glad to draw in here the earlier *Hippolytus* (Καλυπτόμενος) and Sophocles' *Phaedra* (see above, pp. 93 f.); but it is better to resist the temptation, as we know too little of them.

[4] Schmid (p. 389) will have it that we cannot tell what the public thought of our tragedy in 428 B.C., because two plays of the victorious trilogy are lost. Why did they

In both we find masterly characterization, superb tragic power, terrible crime springing from a woman's agonized resentment of masculine callousness and complacency. But *Medea* contains no god[1] or goddess: we must understand Medea and Jason purely by means of their own (and our own) experience and characters. For fifth-century spectators the task, it seems, was at that moment too great, being (as regards Medea) too novel. Three years later, Euripides demanded less of an audience mostly not at ease with general ideas, not alert to realize passions in the abstract as forces no less powerful in Athens than in Corinth and the East. That is a constant weakness of popular imagination, which must set ideas upon two legs if it is to make anything of them: hence the mythology of Uncle Sam, John Bull, and Santa Claus. In *Hippolytus* Euripides supplied what the earlier play lacked. By introducing the persons Aphrodite and Artemis he irresistibly led his hearers to view Phaedra, Hippolytus, and Theseus as not only vivid and exciting people but also as types of humanity and therefore capable of a more intimate, more permanent, appeal to each man and woman on the benches.

He thus performed in a manner peculiar to himself the miracle that all great dramatists perform, who by universalizing their characters make them more intelligible and more real than one's next-door neighbour. For him the process meant using mythological figures that were ready to his hand because familiar to Athenians as objects of awe and worship. That he himself did not believe in those deities mattered nothing: they were only instruments employed in a complex artistic work that was not theological but human from top to bottom. The method proved successful. By awarding him the first prize his countrymen showed that they understood his new method in dramatic art. Thereafter he felt able to address them as adepts who would instantly take his meaning. Later works make this plain. Contrast the elaborate presentation of Aphrodite and her meaning here with Hecuba's curt and merciless rationalism in the *Troades*. When Helen excuses her elopement with Paris by alleging the compulsion of Aphrodite, Hecuba answers: "My son was most glorious in beauty, and your mind at the sight of him became the love-goddess."[2]

disappear, if they were in the public view as good as or better than *Hippolytus*? Moreover, as he himself remarks, Aristophanes echoes *Hippolytus* in the *Knights*, *Wasps* and *Frogs*; the second Argument, too, says τὸ δρᾶμα τῶν πρώτων.

[1] In vv. 1321 f. she tells Jason that her grandfather the Sun-God has given her a chariot; but (like Poseidon) he does not appear, and does not help to explain any aspect of the tragedy.

[2] Vv. 987 f.:

ἦν οὑμὸς υἱὸς κάλλος ἐκπρεπέστατος,
ὁ σὸς δ' ἰδών νιν νοῦς ἐποιήθη Κύπρις.

Few would have understood such a quick slashing-away of pretentious verbiage[1] had not our play already been heard, pondered, and discussed.[2]

This tragedy, then, is entirely human. Very well: why did Euripides write it? He was urged by two thoughts, from which as he worked one magnificent conception emerged.

The first is the grim muddle that we make of life, no less by our virtues than by our faults. At times, indeed, one may wonder which are the faults and which the virtues. Hippolytus' holiness becomes one source of Phaedra's despair and so of her dreadful letter, another being her own valiant self-respect, and her love for her children yet another. We have no need of supernatural interference! But over this hope-abandoned landscape the poet's other thought sheds a transforming light. True it may be that if we look only at morality, at ignorance and folly, ponder nothing but the outcome of conscious effort, we shall condemn life as a woeful labyrinth into which we have been hustled at birth. But, in spite of all, men cling to life by an instinct that outfaces reason and finds joy in survival. This instinct means that mere existence is good, not evil: beneath all defeat, more ultimate even than right and wrong, endures the simplest and greatest of all victories, that we *are*. It is the very heart of poetry: all poetry that transcends mere verse, whatever else it may neglect or fail to achieve, declares for us and strengthens in us the zest of being alive.

This at once explains the paradox that we enjoy tragedy. Often we cannot easily tell how the pleasure is created: but in *Hippolytus* we can see the method plainly enough. Euripides has used language that makes the whole story extremely *interesting*, indeed (to use a word still more hackneyed) thrilling: we follow the play with an eagerness that the events, if otherwise portrayed, might well have failed to arouse. He has made it beautiful also, beyond any other of his extant works, despite the evil wherewith it is loaded. His mighty hand keeps the balance even. Aphrodite's hideous speech is at once followed by Hippolytus' prayer to his own goddess, radiant at once with poetic loveliness and that fusion of emotion with intellect whence springs the true religious mood. Artemis

---

[1] The same *ad hoc* theology is aired by Jason (*Med.* 527 ff.) but ignored by Medea, unlike Hecuba.

[2] Aristophanes would of himself be a sufficient witness that Euripides was thought to have trained his audience in sound appreciation of tragedy; see especially *Frogs* 957, 971–9. A distorted echo of these discussions is uttered by the widow who complains that her business as a florist has gone down more than 50 per cent since Euripides persuaded "the gentlemen" (τοὺς ἄνδρας) that the gods do not exist (*Thesm.* 445 ff.).

herself utters over him whatever consolations she can give in words so entrancing as to seem well purchased by the death of the body. Even Theseus at his darkest moment can magically transmute anguish into poetry. No less constantly do the lyrics quiver with this sense that life's beauty glows everywhere about us. News of Phaedra's illness has reached the Trozenian women not, as in *Medea*, from the spring whereby old men sit at chess, but from a pool below the cliff-face down which gushes water of the remote ocean. Here at once is heard the insistence on romantic beauty and the hint of far peaceful regions so exquisitely sung in the ode that dreams of Adriatic waters and the apple-boughs of fairyland. But this beauty is fragile, the glow is fringed with darkness. The song just mentioned passes back from the Hesperides to dreadful bodings of Phaedra's self-inflicted death. So the Nurse too utters a weird trance-like expression of life's mingled sweetness, yearning, and pain. Euripides shirks nothing.

IV

THE *SUPPLICES*

IF we are to make anything of this bewildering play,[1] we must resort to a humdrum catalogue and explore its oddities one by one.

A. THE CHORUS

Who are these Suppliant Women? That is the question King Theseus asks of his mother when he first enters and sees them grouped round her in tears, with shorn heads and dressed as mourners. She replies (100 ff.): "My son, these women are the mothers of the seven chieftains who were slain at the gates of Thebes." She has said as much in the prologue (11 ff.) and the Chorus sings (963 ff.): "Seven mothers, seven sons we bore to our sorrow, men high-famed among the Argives." That seems a most simple, natural, and effective idea: the poet has made the sorrowing mothers into a chorus begging the aid of Athens, just as Aeschylus formed the chorus of his own *Supplices* from the Danaids who seek the protection of Argos.

But a difficulty at once appears.[2] Aeschylus' chorus numbered fifty, exactly the number of the Danaids; in Euripides' day the tragic chorus had only fifteen members: how can that number represent a group formed of seven persons only? If there was any numerical datum familiar to everyone in the theatre it was this, that the chieftains who led the assault on Thebes numbered seven. It is unnecessary to adduce other passages from Greek literature, such as the *parodos* of *Antigone* and the very title of Aeschylus' play: the drama before us mentions that number repeatedly. Modern popular knowledge contains perhaps only one analogous and equally familiar number—that of the Disciples. Conceive a dramatist of today who should stage a tragedy based upon the Gospels

---

[1] We must regret that Verrall published no essay on it. In *The Bacchants of Euripides* (1910), he writes (p. 272): "The *Suppliants* of Euripides will be found, in almost any investigation of tragic or Euripidean practice, to provide a surprise."

[2] Lesky, at least, faces it (*Die griechische Tragödie* (1938), pp. 170 f.): "Den Chor bilden die Mütter der Gefallenen mit ihren Mägden, und wir müssen es hinnehmen, daß diese Scheidung in dem üblichen Chore der 15 Sänger mehrfach verschwimmt und auch die Siebenzahl der Mütter und der Leichname rational aus dem Mythos nicht zu belegen ist, da beispielsweise Polyneikes nicht unter diesen, Iokaste nicht unter jenen sein kann. Wir haben es zu verstehen, daß der Dichter die Mütter der Sieben förmlich als kollektiven Begriff in das Spiel einführt." See p. 162, n. 5, below.

and introducing that well-known company. Every eye in the audience would instinctively count them as they filed in. Imagine the universal stupefaction when Iscariot with his red hair and money-bag was followed by a thirteenth man, by a fourteenth, and so on, up to (let us say) a twenty-fifth![1]

Of this folly, however, the author himself was, it seems, not unaware. He has made an attempt to reinforce the seven mothers by a bevy of attendants. They are called upon once (1115 ff.) by the mothers to assist their aged steps, but are otherwise not heard of,[2] save that they add two stanzas to the first song (71–87). It is an astonishingly crude attempt to "have it both ways"—to secure a natural chorus appropriate to the most familiar fact in the story, and also to employ the official number of performers—resulting in an absurd lopsidedness[3] since the attendants must be hopelessly eclipsed by the mothers.[4] But, after all, the attempt fails. Seven mothers and seven attendants leave us with one chorister unallotted;[5] he cannot unearth an eighth mother, and it is against common sense and symmetry to believe that one mother has two followers while the other six have but one each.

Even this is not all. Since these mourners are to receive the ashes of

[1] Eugen Petersen (*Die attische Tragödie als Bild- und Bühnenkunst* (1915), p. 503) is content to write: "die flehenden Mütter, die, in der mehr im Namen als in der Sache gegebenen Siebenzahl mit ebensoviel Dienerinnen...." Wilamowitz (*Der Mütter Bittgang*, p. 30, in *Griechische Tragödien übersetzt*, 2nd ed., Vol. II) is obscure and confused about the handmaidens.

[2] Vv. 275 f. are spurious on any view. See p. 155 below.

[3] The lyric is itself open to the same censure: the mothers sing four stanzas in the majestic ionic metre; then the more numerous handmaids sing but two, in the simpler trochaic. Note also 86 f., "may death bring me oblivion of these woes", which is foolish exaggeration in the mouths of mere sympathizers. Who would not gladly see these two stanzas expunged? But why, then, were they inserted?

Concerning the handmaids in Aeschylus' *Supplices* we learn only that there is one for each Danaid (977–9).

[4] There is no question here of a subsidiary chorus as in *Hipp.* 61 ff., 1104–10, 1120–30: we must make up a normal chorus of fifteen. (The boys, of course, do act as a subsidiary chorus.)

[5] Boeckh indeed (*Graecae Tragoediae Principum*, pp. 75 ff.) was content with fourteen. Hermann (preface to his edition, pp. xvi f.), but no one else, followed him: proposing, in order to conceal the fifteenth chorister's absence, that the chorus were arranged thus, with a gap in their midst which the audience would hardly notice:

```
•   •   •
•   •   •
•       •
•   •   •
```

Elmsley (reviewing Hermann in *Class. Jour.*, vols. XVI, XVII, on vv. 88 and 71) held that the chorus consisted of seven mothers, seven attendants and a chorus-leader.

their sons, and since two corpses—those of Amphiaraus and Polynices—were, according to tradition and this very play,[1] not recoverable with the rest, we cannot believe in the presence of seven mothers. Clearly, that scene near the close, where the lads[2] bring in the urns containing the bones of the chieftains and present them to the aged women should, and quite easily could, make a simple, beautiful, and touching spectacle. What, then, becomes of this tableau if five sons with five urns confront seven grandmothers? Some avoid this foolish situation by accepting the facts as to Amphiaraus and Polynices and by therefore postulating only five mothers, each with two attendants.[3] Though by this *tour de force* we are somewhat overloaded with attendants, we do obtain symmetry in numbers; but we thereby turn our backs upon the author,[4] who never

---

[1] Adrastus delivers brief funeral speeches on the other five only (860–908); then Theseus says (925–7) that Amphiaraus' body is not available, and clearly implies (928–31) the same of Polynices. Paley on *Helen* 1261 (στρωτὰ λέκτρα) writes: "An empty bier represented the bodies of those who were absent. And hence perhaps it is, that in the Supplices, v. 1207, mention is made of *seven* pyres of the Argive chiefs, though Amphiaraus and Polynices were not included among the bodies brought on the stage. Their places may have been taken by similar empty litters. Pflugk well compares Thucyd. ii. 34." This is ingenious but very doubtful; in any case it does not help the urn-presentation.

D'Annunzio (*Fedra* I. 602) coolly writes of "le *sette* urne di bronzo".

[2] Grégoire in his edition of the play writes (p. 101): "Le groupe des Épigones pourrait donner lieu à des observations encore plus embarrassantes [*sc.* than those concerning the number of mothers]. Diomède, fils de Tydée est absent (v. 1217), et les os de Capanée, de Polynice et d'Amphiaraos n'avaient pû etre recueillis. D'autre part, Aigialeus, fils d'Adraste, est présent, et s'il porte une urne, ce n'est certainement pas celle de son père. Mais le nombre de *sept* n'est jamais mentionné à propos des enfants. Ils n'étaient, en scène, que trois ou quatre."

[3] This view was first put forward by C. A. M. Axt (*Quindecim in Euripidis Supplicibus esse chori personas*, 1826). Its elaboration by R. Arnoldt (*Die chorische Technik des Euripides* (1878), pp. 72–76), who seems not to have read Axt, has met with much acceptance. He sees the mothers as one rank of the chorus, the attendants as two.

[4] Arnoldt of course does his best (pp. 75 f.) to dissolve this mountainous obstacle. (i) vv. 963 ff.: ἑπτὰ ... ἐν Ἀργείοις (see above) are the chief argument of Boeckh and Hermann. But they *must* be taken loosely, for not all the Seven were born in Argos. (ii) Athena's remark (see below) shows, since there were in fact only five corpses, that we cannot press ἑπτά: that number was a datum of the legend. In the same way *I.A.* 1054 f. mentions fifty Nereids, but Thetis ("first of Nereus' daughters", *ibid.* 1078) is at the moment not among them, for they are dancing in celebration of her wedding. So in *Androm.* 1266 ff. she intends to fetch the fifty Nereids. (iii) Hermann (*Aeschyli Tragoediae*, vol. II, p. 649) rightly says that Aeschylus' chorus of 12–15 could not correspond numerically to the Furies or to the fifty women in his *Supplices* and *Danaides*.

Much that seems obvious could be said in reply to all this; but it is surely enough to remark that, even if Arnoldt's arguments are sound, we are left with the stubborn fact that our poet goes out of his way to emphasize his impossible seven. Why, for instance, does the Messenger (755) drag in the unneeded numeral? Why does Athena (1207) not say τῶνδε instead of ἑπτά?

mentions the number five, preferring his own incredible arithmetic from beginning to end of the affair. So obstinate, indeed, does he prove, that he causes Athena at the close to support it. In her directions to Theseus (1207) she mentions "seven"; but, alas, makes a sad muddle: her phrase "seven pyres of the dead"[1] shows that she has forgotten the king's instruction to Adrastus (934–6) that Capaneus is to have a separate pyre, the others but one in common, which gives in the end a meagre total of two pyres.

So much for the number of the Chorus: seven are not enough; seven *plus* eight are absurd; five *plus* ten contradict the poet's own statements. If now we ask "Who are they?" in the personal sense, we meet another surprise. Of all extant Greek tragedies this alone contains a chorus that is not homogeneous. Elsewhere they are all Ocean-nymphs, all Salaminian sailors, all Trojan women, and so forth. Here they are individuals. An attempt is, indeed, made to confer on them the normal homogeneity: none of them speaks as a separate authentic person.[2] They are again and again described simply as Argive women[3]—once indeed, madly enough, as "Argive girls".[4] This is untrue; several of them belonged to other States: we are practically told (888 ff.) by our erratic dramatist that Atalanta was an Arcadian; Iocasta belonged to Thebes, Periboea (Tydeus' mother) to Calydon.

Despite this attempt at anonymity, we cannot forget, and surely few in the audience could forget, that some of the Seven Mothers are famous. We are to understand that Iocasta is present as a chorister, singing away with the rest about wounds and grief, with no allusion by herself or any other to her unmatched sorrow, and even joining in the normal lamentations over ill-starred marriage and motherhood.[5] If this jars us

---

[1] Petersen (*ut. sup.*, p. 507) quotes Athena with impolite inverted commas: "bei den 'sieben' Leichenbrandstätten". Welcker (*Die griechischen Tragödien*, p. 575, n. 5) makes a desperate and absurd attempt to set things right: "Euripides ... hat einen andern siebenten Anführer an die Stelle des Polynikes gesetzt, so wie einen auch für den Amphiaraos."

[2] That the lyrics are sometimes divided between individual singers (see Murray's text) is of course no bar to this statement. That happens in other plays also. The performer sings his tiny solo merely as a chorister.

[3] Vv. 9, 365, 957, 965, 1165.

[4] V. 1073, Ἀργείων κόραι.

[5] Vv. 786 ff. Axt (*ut. sup.*, p. 3) has certain ghastly remarks on Iocasta's return from the dead, e.g.: "Profecto, si septem mulieres in scenam prodiissent, nescio, an non spectatorum oculi, cuinam earum collum laqueo detritum esset, curiose quaesisset." Hermann (on 912) writes: "Nescio, an haud satis apte hic Atalantae mentionem fecerit, cuius quum nomen audirent, spectatores non poterant non oculos in chorum convertere, ut nobilem quondam venatricem, arcu sagittisque spoliatam, inter grandaevas ducum matres agnoscerent."

unpleasantly, what shall we say of Euadne's scene? Her father Iphis witnesses her suicide with anguish, then utters a long adieu to happiness. Meanwhile his wife,[1] who watches it also, stands by as a member of the Chorus. Neither her husband nor her daughter throws her a word of love, pity, or farewell. She herself shows no interest whatever in this agonizing scene, except that, apparently, she joins her colleagues in the brief lyric condolence (1077 ff.): "Alas, unhappy! Thou hast a share of Oedipus' fate, aged man, both thou and my wretched city." "My city"—and not a word about herself! In our amazement we can hardly spare a thought for the fact that another woman, the mother of Capaneus, upon whose pyre Euadne has thrown herself, shares this revolting stoicism.[2]

Two more facts about the Chorus await notice: strange, though less disconcerting than those already examined.

Before the first line is uttered, a tableau has been already set: Aethra seated in the background, with the Chorus grouped before her; further away, the muffled figure of Adrastus stretched upon the earth, surrounded by the sons of the slain chieftains. So far, this opening has a few parallels[3] in extant Greek tragedy. But we soon learn that important action—and (as it were) a part of the play—has already occurred: the Mothers have not only uttered their appeal to Aethra but have also made her "prisoner" by ritual bonds of their suppliant boughs. Such presentation is unique,[4] because highly confusing. If, as in a modern play, "the curtain rose" just before the first line of our text, all would be well; but no curtain was used in Greek theatres of the classical period.

They utter the final anapaests (1232 ff.): "Adrastus, let us go, and give our oaths to this man and to his city: the toils which they have already endured for us are worthy of our reverence." This refers to the covenant of alliance between Argos and Athens. Some of these women do not even belong to Argos. In any case what have women to do with this transaction? Such affairs concern men alone. They have forgotten

[1] The mother of Eteoclus, who was Iphis' son and Euadne's brother.

[2] Wilamowitz (*Der Mütter Bittgang*, pp. 30 ff.) mentions all the difficulties so far noted, but brushes them airily aside: for example, "Die Siebenzahl hat nur die Bedeutung der konventionellen Zahl, die fast gleich einem Namen ist: es waren eben die Sieben gegen Theben". Why then does the poet continually mention it instead of giving it once only (if that)? See p. 162 below.

[3] In *P.V.*, *Heracleidae*, *Hecuba*, *Heracles*, and *Orestes* physical action occurs before dramatic action begins and is ignored by the audience, precisely as we ignore the noise of scene-schifters. But here the tragedy itself begins (so to speak) before it has started: the "imprisonment" of Aethra is part of the action and the audience are welcome to watch it, though the appeal of the Mothers is unuttered.

[4] Cp. Grube: "The peculiar difficulty here is that previous conversation has just occurred." *The Drama of Euripides* (1941), p. 229.

Aethra's words at the opening (40 f.): "It is proper that women who are wise should do all business through men." Still more notable, they ignore what Athena herself said two or three minutes ago (1188 ff.): "First exact an oath. It must be sworn by Adrastus yonder: he, being king, has full authority to take the oath on behalf of the whole Argive land."

Contemplating this medley of puzzles, some only mysterious, others apparently as deliberate as fantastic, can we bring up any fact or theory to save us from the conviction that the *Supplices* has nonsense at its very root? At present, no; and it may well be that here is the reason why scholars have usually[1] said so little that is valuable about this play: half-consciously (we may surmise) they feel that, did they scrutinize it as thoroughly as *Medea* or *Hippolytus*, they would be forced to condemn Euripides not merely as the botcher that Swinburne called him,[2] not even as the charlatan pilloried in the *Frogs*, but as one who, fine poet though he was, here tottered upon the border of insanity. Still, we must not lose heart, however puzzled. Elsewhere Euripides shows himself anything but an imbecile; and the monsters now wallowing in our net will—especially when joined by others yet at large—suggest a view of the *Supplices* that triumphantly saves his reputation.

We may already draw some encouraging conclusions. Whoever insisted that his chorus contained but seven persons,[3] whoever used a scene

[1] Grube's treatment (pp. 229–43) is one of the few exceptions. He frankly states many of the difficulties noted above or to be mentioned later. But even he draws no conclusions from them. Kitto (*Greek Tragedy* (1939), pp. 221–9) brings out most of the play's merits, and is especially good on "the central tragedy of man, his capacity for intelligence and self-control, his domination by unreason and folly" (p. 228). But, save for remarking (p. 222) that "we could willingly spare the Funeral Speech of Adrastus" and noting (pp. 227 f.) the inferiority of Athena to Theseus, he mentions none of our problems. Grégoire's edition, admirable for its precision and vivacity, notes few of them.   [2] See p. 1 above.

[3] There is some evidence for a much later use of that number: a comic chorus of seven at the Delphic Soteria and a tragic chorus of seven at Cyrene. See Wieseler, *Theatergebäude*, pp. 99–102; Lüders, *Die dionysischen Künstler*, pp. 118, 189–97; Haigh and Pickard-Cambridge, *The Attic Theatre* (3rd ed.), p. 290; Haigh, *Tragic Drama of the Greeks*, pp. 451–3.

A passage in Diodorus (XIII. 97) seems to have been neglected in this connexion. Concerning the battle of Arginusae he writes: τῶν δ' Ἀθηναίων ὁ στρατηγὸς Θράσυλλος, ὃς ἦν ἐπὶ τῆς ἡγεμονίας ἐκείνην τὴν ἡμέραν, εἶδε κατὰ τὴν νύκτα τοιαύτην ὄψιν· ἔδοξεν Ἀθήνῃσι τοῦ θεάτρου πλήθοντος αὐτός τε καὶ τῶν ἄλλων στρατηγῶν ἓξ ὑποκρίνεσθαι τραγῳδίαν Εὐριπίδου Φοινίσσας· τῶν δ' ἀντιπάλων ὑποκρινομένων τὰς Ἱκετίδας δόξαι τὴν Καδμείαν νίκην αὐτοῖς περιγενέσθαι, καὶ πάντας ἀποθανεῖν μιμουμένους τὰ πράγματα τῶν ἐπὶ τὰς Θήβας στρατευσάντων. Seven men to act the *Phoenissae* and seven the *Supplices* unmistakably mean choruses: in both plays there are more than seven *characters*, and in both three *actors* would as usual suffice. Note also καὶ τῶν ἄλλων στρατηγῶν ἕξ:

whose opening was absurd without a curtain, did not write for the fifth-century Athenian theatre. The man responsible for these two features had in view a private audience,[1] or he was one of those ἀναγνωστικοί[2] who wrote for the study, not the stage, and therefore were at liberty to indite attractive drama that would never have been accepted by the archon for performance had they been so misguided as to offer it.

B. FOURTH-CENTURY FEATURES

(a) War and Society

The political statements in the *Supplices* shall be divided into two groups: the passages (next to be considered) that prove no more than that Euripides, merely because he died in the fifth century, cannot have written them; and those (to be postponed) so foolish that, whatever their date, we cannot make him responsible for them without contradiction of everything else that we know about him.

The passages now to be studied are these:

(i) vv. 267–70 (the Coryphaeus): "Nay, do not so! A wild beast finds refuge in the rock, a slave at altars of the gods, and city cowers up to city, tempest-driven: for in human life nothing has enduring happiness."

(ii) vv. 481–93 (the Theban Herald): "When the people vote about war, each man forgets the prospect of his own death, but imagines this calamity as lighting on some other. If death stared each in the face at the moment of voting, Hellas would not be perishing of war-madness. And yet every man of us knows the better of two considerations, and how much better for mankind is peace than war. . . . These thoughts—oh, base!—we fling away to take up wars: a man enslaves a weaker man, a city a weaker city."

(iii) vv. 745–9 (Adrastus): "Ah, ye who overstrain the bow! Ah, vain mortals, who suffer many ills—aye, and justly—events, not your friends,

---

seven are taken from a larger group, which implies that seven is the correct number. (These groups of seven are said to act the plays because officially the chorus was the play.) This story does not however necessarily contradict the otherwise complete *argumentum ex silentio* about fifth-century choruses of seven: it may be far later than the battle.

[1] See above, pp. 33–36.
[2] Ar. *Rhet.* III. xii. 2 (413b). Cope (*ad loc.*) takes ἀναγνωστικοί to mean "that write to be read as well as acted or rhapsodized". (Similarly M. Croiset, *Histoire de la littérature grecque*, vol. III, pp. 384 f.) But that would be hardly worth reporting; they must have been genuine "closet-dramatists": cp., e.g., J. P. Mahaffy (*History of Classical Greek Literature*, vol. I, p. 396) and W. von Christ (*Geschichte der griechischen Litteratur*, p. 238).

control you. And ye city-states, when reason might bring you clear of sorrow, decide affairs not by reason but by slaughter."

(iv) vv. 949–52 (Adrastus): "Ah, unhappy mortals, why get you lances and go about to slaughter one another? Nay, stop your miseries and keep your towns, living quietly with your neighbours."[1]

That these outcries are alien to the spirit of fifth-century Athens as elsewhere revealed in her history and literature, but in full accord with fourth-century temper as so revealed, cannot be questioned. In the latter period mankind met one of those disasters that prove permanently irretrievable. At Aegospotami Athens had lost her nerve; at Chaeronea she lost her soul. An era of collapse destroyed the practice and the possibility of the civilization voiced in Pericles' Funeral Speech and so gloriously lived by Athens in her prime; it killed the spiritual valour, the buoyant self-confidence, the gusto for life as both an art and an adventure that, despite all crimes and follies, had made Athens great. This change found its earliest and (because unconscious) most startling expression in Aristophanes: whoever reads *Plutus* immediately after the *Frogs* is horrified by the loss consummated during those seventeen years. The fourth century rumbles hollowly under the efforts of men superbly astute, but disillusioned if not desperate, to rebuild something of a greatness that is for ever lost. Set the *Eumenides* beside the *Republic*, Pericles beside Demosthenes, compare the speeches in Thucydides with Isocrates' manifestoes, the Egyptian and Sicilian expeditions with the resistance against Macedonia, and you perceive that politics are no longer a passionately felt and gallantly performed function of Athenian life, but a new science, studied and promulgated by a few experts, some aloof and therefore frigid, others concerned and therefore worried and shrill. The statesman's first duty is no longer to guide enthusiasm but to create it, his aim no longer to aggrandize Athens at the expense of Argos or Thebes, but to save and protect Greek civilization. The central thought of the ablest and most original minds is now not rivalry, but mutual help. Pericles rose to power by combating the philo-Laconian policy of Cimon. Demosthenes' ceaseless cry is: 'Forget the injuries that Sparta, Thebes, and other Greek states have inflicted upon you: alliance with them against the non-Hellenic Macedonian offers the sole hope not only for Athens but also for the Greek world, on the safety of which her own safety depends.' He was ultimately at one with Isocrates, though the latter's philosophic poise allowed him to include Philip and Alexander in his pan-Hellenic

[1] In v. 951 Wecklein's μὴ δῆτ' is immensely preferable to the MS. παύσασθ', which is bad idiom before ἀλλά.

scheme, and to express completely and clearly the idea of "a Greek nation"; ἅπασαν τὴν Ἑλλάδα πατρίδα νομίζειν, "to think all Greece your fatherland".[1]

The four passages quoted above from our play are clearly alien to the fifth century and as clearly appropriate to the fourth: not to whatever elements therein were constructive, but to the sense of defeat and decadence.[2] All is true, all terribly moving and urgent; but compare it even with those sinister chapters where Thucydides[3] depicts the infamies engendered by war, and you feel as if you had stepped from the council-chamber of statesmen into a hospital for consumptives. Still more to our purpose, when Euripides himself pauses elsewhere for a diatribe upon the folly or wickedness of mankind,[4] he does not use this shrill plaintive tone. If our author is Euripides, then Euripides has changed very oddly—but only for a moment: at the close we find these appeals contradicted by a goddess, the patroness of Athens and deity of wisdom itself, who urges

[1] *Phil.* 108a. He is urging Philip to imitate his ancestor Heracles, the defender of all Greeks. That this idea is new the rest of the paragraph shows; moreover, a few lines later Isocrates, speaking of his own position, uses τὴν πατρίδα in the normal sense of "my country, Athens". The assertion that all Greeks have common interests is of course frequent. Cp. for example Dem. *De Corona* 263. 6 ff.: οὔτ' ἐν τοῖς Ἑλληνικοῖς ... κοινῇ πᾶσι τοῖς Ἕλλησι συμφερόντων, and see A. W. Gomme, *Essays in Greek History and Literature* (1937), p. 14: he quotes Poseidippus (third century B.C.), Ἑλλὰς μέν ἐστι μιά, πόλεις δὲ πλείονες—"it was a commonplace". (Polybius, IV. 79. 1, testifies to a strong instance of the opposite feeling: the people of Triphylia, when it was invaded, began to fear περὶ τῶν ἰδίων πατρίδων—not even Triphylia, but each his own village.)

[2] The asylum idea is worded by Isocrates, *Phil.* 88c, *De Pace* 186d; Aeschines, *In Ctes.* 72. 39; Demosthenes, especially *Phil.* I. 42. 21 ff.: κατέπτηχε μέντοι πάντα ταῦτα νῦν, οὐκ ἔχοντ' ἀποστροφὴν διὰ τὴν ὑμετέραν βραδυτῆτα καὶ ῥᾳθυμίαν, ἣν ἀποθέσθαι φημὶ δεῖν ἤδη; with κατέπτηχε cp. *Supp.* 268 f.:

πόλις τε πρὸς πόλιν
ἔπτηξε χειμασθεῖσα.

The other topics—the miseries and the degradation of Greece—are of course often mentioned, for example in Isocrates' vivid Ninth Letter and the great passage of Aeschines, *In Ctes.* 72. 23, beginning τοιγάρτοι τί τῶν ἀνελπίστων καὶ ἀπροσδοκήτων ἐφ' ἡμῶν οὐ γέγονεν; See also Isocrates *De Pace* 167d for the stupefaction wherewith "some observer from afar, not yet infected by our corruption" will gaze upon the mad degeneracy of Athens.

[3] III. 82–84.

[4] It is strange that this "philosopher on the stage", often as he deals with war, scarcely ever passes beyond pictures of death and captivity to condemn war as a crime committed by humanity upon itself and as a denial of civilization. Indeed, there is but one such utterance: *Helen* 1151–7. It reminds us of our four passages; but note the differences: its tone is scornful (ἄφρονες, ἀμαθῶς), not pathetic; the demand for universal humaneness is barely audible; the metre is lyric. Also, in *Phoen.* 515–17 discussion is briefly recommended instead of the sword. This is all that we glean from the humane genius who wrote the *Heracleidae*, *Hecuba*, *Troades*, *Phoenissae*, and the Aulid *Iphigenia*, to set beside no less than four passages in the *Supplices*.

the young sons of the slain chieftains to carry the murderous quarrel into yet another generation.

(b) Fortune

Much has been written about tyché (τύχη, "chance", "fortune") and fortuna (with or without capital letters) in Greek and Roman thought and superstition, literature and art; but we need concern ourselves here with only one phase of this long and curious history.

Greek literature earlier than the fourth century of course remarks times without number (often with a quaint implication of momentous discovery) that tyché is unstable. But scarcely ever do we find anything more subtle. Pindar, to be sure, apparently deifies it, but his rich phrases mean nothing more than yet another proclamation that we do not know the future. Sophocles, in a far more imaginative passage,[1] makes Oedipus say: "But I, holding myself the child of Fortune the bountiful, shall never come to dishonour. She, she is the mother that bore me; and the months that share my birth have set my feet now in lowly, now in exalted place." Even these superb lines present no doctrine about tyché, only the defiant mood voiced in Tennyson's simpler words: "Too proud to care from whence I came".

But in the fourth century there appears for the first time a new and far less nebulous conception: not that Fortune is a goddess (this was to come later) or merely a vague external power, but a positive, not negative, factor that is as truly part of a man's life as his vices and virtues, as truly part of a nation's life as its institutions and laws.[2] Earlier belief had made it an external whimsy that fulfils or thwarts desire or purpose: the new age saw in it a definite asset in one man's career, a definite liability in another's, that can be detected and then counted upon as having a known quality and effect. The fullest expression of this idea is uttered by Demosthenes in a passage[3] that shows it in the act of developing from a crude popular notion into a complex doctrine.

Conspicuous among the varied proofs of my opponent's brutal malignity stand his remarks about fortune. I think it a general rule that anyone who twits another therewith, forgetting that both of them are human, is a fool. Even

---

[1] O.T. 1080–3.
[2] Cp. Dem. De Corona 316. 24 ff.: πόσῳ δικαιότερον καὶ ἀληθέστερον τὴν ἁπάντων, ὡς ἔοικεν, ἀνθρώπων τύχην κοινὴν καὶ φοράν τινα πραγμάτων χαλεπὴν καὶ οὐχ οἵαν ἔδει τούτων αἰτίαν ἡγεῖσθαι; Here τύχη is plainly differentiated from the actual events, and φορά makes that distinction between "tendencies", "trends", etc. and the actual characters and conduct of real individuals which is so disastrously frequent in our own day. [3] De Corona 311. 7–312. 10.

those who believe themselves most prosperous and endowed with the best fortune do not know whether it will endure unchanged till nightfall: with what face, then, can they discuss it or insult others on that ground? . . . To me the fortune of our country appears good, and I see that the oracle given to you by Dodonaean Zeus supports me; but that of mankind in general, now dominant, is harsh and terrible: for who in the Greek world or outside of it has not suffered many sorrows in our time? That we chose the noblest aims and prospered better than those very Greeks who imagined that by deserting us they would live happy ever after, I attribute to the good fortune of my country; our mishaps and occasional disappointments I interpret as her inevitable share in mankind's universal fortune; but the particular fortune of each individual among us, including myself, I think no part of the national assessment. Such is my claim herein, which seems to me, and (I believe) to you, both realistic and righteous; but my opponent asserts[1] the fantastic doctrine that my trivial and sorry personal fortune overrides the good and mighty fortune of our country.

In the *Supplices*, but nowhere else in the Euripidean *corpus*, we find, not indeed as full a statement as that set forth by Demosthenes—whose rather wordy exposition suggests that he propounds a more elaborate idea than was then familiar—but the same conception of Fortune's quality and (one might almost say) her system[2] of dealing with mankind. "But thee, Adrastus, I bid stay here and not mingle thy fortunes with mine. For I, with my own guardian spirit, shall take the field as a fresh commander with a fresh sword."[3] He is to avoid the interference of another's *tyché* and deal with Thebes entirely *de novo*.

Observe, moreover, that even through the masterful and defiant sentences of Demosthenes an undertone is heard, rising from that *malaise* described above: this is a cowed and feverish generation.

(c) *Literature*

There is, of course, no point in assembling mere parallels. If we are to prove that some portions at least of the *Supplices* belong to the fourth or a later century, what we need is passages that are, not parallels of, but undeniable quotations from, work known to have been written later than the fifth century.

Theseus near the close of his long preachment to Adrastus briefly dis-

---

[1] Aeschines *In Ctes.* 73. 9 ff.

[2] Not that the "system" need be endorsed or admired. The Middle Comedy writer Apollodorus of Carystus (fr. 5) attributes to Chance not only stupidity but also "a complete lack of education" (οὐδὲ παιδείαν ὅλως εἰδυῖα)!

[3] Vv. 589 ff. Vv. 226 ff. are very similar. V. 249, αὐτὸς πιέζειν τὴν τύχην, ἡμᾶς δ' ἐᾶν, perhaps points in the same direction.

tinguishes three sections of the people;[1] one of them is thus described (240 ff.):

οἱ δ' οὐκ ἔχοντες καὶ σπανίζοντες βίου
δεινοί, νέμοντες τῷ φθόνῳ πλέον μέρος,
ἐς τοὺς ἔχοντας κέντρ' ἀφιᾶσιν κακά,
γλώσσαις πονηρῶν προστατῶν φηλούμενοι.

"And those who are made dangerous by their poverty and lack of livelihood, and whose ruling passion is envy, plunge evil goads into the rich, being misled by the tongues of wicked champions." The third line would normally mean "they wickedly goad the rich": that is, urge them on to some foolish or disastrous action. But that is certainly not the author's intention, nor has any reader (surely) ever supposed that it was. He plainly has in mind drones killing bees and stealing their honey. For this κέντρ' ἀφιᾶσιν is quite insufficient: even if κέντρα always meant "stings", we should expect more explicit language. Why then has he written thus, and why do we at once understand him aright? Because both he and we[2] have in mind the most brilliant and celebrated description of the types into which a mass of citizens may be divided, a description wherein this same metaphor appears without ambiguity. In the Eighth Book of his *Republic* Plato, after depicting the man who squanders his wealth and lives on in the community as a useless element, proceeds thus (552c): "Are you agreeable, then, that we should say of him that just as a drone is bred in a honeycomb, a diseased spot in the hive, so such a man is bred as a drone in his house, a diseased spot in the city? . . . God has created the flying drones all stingless, but of these walking drones he has made

---

[1] Grégoire (p. 112, n. 1), objecting to so odd an interruption of the argument believes this passage to have been interpolated from some other Euripidean play at the time of a later production (perhaps in 411), when such ideas were especially in the air. Goossens ("Périclès et Thésée", *Bull. de l'Assoc. Budé* (avril 1929), p. 37), thinks that the "interpolation" was made by Euripides himself, when he adopted the ideas of Theramenes. Such tentative measures will never cope with the king's addiction to irrelevance.

[2] But some editors fail to quote the *Republic*, apparently because they assume he cannot have known that work.

Sophocles (fr. 683, Pearson) writes:

οὐ γάρ ποτ' ἂν γένοιτ' ἂν ἀσφαλὴς πόλις,
ἐν ᾗ τὰ μὲν δίκαια καὶ τὰ σώφρονα
λάγδην πατεῖται, κωτίλος δ' ἀνὴρ λαβὼν
πανοῦργα χερσὶν κέντρα κηδεύει πόλιν.

In his notes thereon Pearson remarks: "It is curious that κέντρα occurs, though with a different application, in the similar context of Eur. *Suppl.* 240 ff. . . . Wilamowitz assumes a direct reference to this passage: see Introductory Note." See also Philostratus, *Life of Apoll.* VI. xxxvi.

only some stingless while to others he has given terrible stings." This simile recurs throughout the book, and, near the close, explaining how the well-to-do are forced to become oligarchs, he writes (565C): "this evil that drone engenders by stinging them"; at one point (564E) he remarks that the most disciplined citizens become the richest and provide "most abundant honey for the drones". From these passages, especially the latter, Theseus' words are beyond question derived. It is no ordinary case of parallel passages, or of a quotation deliberately or unconsciously made by Plato. The language of the play *presupposes* that of Plato. It cannot rightly be understood by anyone unfamiliar with the *Republic*: so familiar with it is the poet himself that he does not notice the *prima facie* obscurity of his own words.[1]

Exactly the same kind of reminiscence occurs in Iphis' lament (1108 ff.):

ὦ δυσπάλαιστον γῆρας, ὡς μισῶ σ' ἔχων,
μισῶ δ' ὅσοι χρῄζουσιν ἐκτείνειν βίον,
βρωτοῖσι καὶ ποτοῖσι καὶ μαγεύμασι
παρεκτρέποντες ὀχετὸν ὥστε μὴ θανεῖν.

"Ah, old age, thou dire wrestler, how sorely do I hate thee! Those too I hate who would prolong their life, seeking by dishes and potions and quackeries to divert the conduit and escape death." The last line shows the same obscurity as that just noted. The idea intended is very simple; why talk of diverting a channel or watercourse? There can be no thought of death as an overwhelming torrent: ὀχετός is far milder than (e.g.) χειμάρρους, meaning only an irrigation channel, as in Homer's simile of the gardener.[2] But what has irrigation to do with Iphis' fierce gibe at senile valetudinarians? He, or rather his poet, has in mind Plato's witty and trenchant satire,[3] which gives the irrigation metaphor[4] in language not only vigorous but clear: ἐπιχειρεῖν διαίταις κατὰ σμικρὸν ἀπαντλοῦντα καὶ ἐπιχέοντα μακρὸν καὶ κακὸν βίον ἀνθρώπῳ ποιεῖν, καὶ ἔκγονα αὐτῶν, ὡς τὸ εἰκός, ἕτερα τοιαῦτα φυτεύειν—"to attempt, by a regimen of pumping out a little here and pouring over their patients a little there, to make human life long and evil, and give them an upgrowth of children who will naturally show the same quality." Here again the play uses language

---

[1] Such sentences or "tags" are naturally frequent in times when literate people abound, e.g.: "My report, Mr. Chairman, is like Caesar's Gaul."

[2] *Il.* XXI. 257 ff. (The explanation in L. and S., "to make a side channel or means of escape", cannot stand: no one travels by ὀχετός.)

[3] *Rep.* III. 405C–408C.

[4] *Ibid.* 407D.

that can be understood only as a direct reference to another, and fully intelligible, passage.¹

(d) *The Cabal*

Theseus, in his rejection of Adrastus' appeal, condemns him for blasphemous presumption (216 ff.). "But reason seeks to be stronger than Heaven: pride invades the heart, and we think ourselves wiser than the gods. Thou too art found among that band [δεκάς], no wise man thou, who didst...." This word *decas* should of itself arouse doubt as to the traditional date of our play. It has neither of its usual senses, "a company of ten"² or "the number ten", but a "gang" (not definitely numbered). That meaning is found here only in the extant literature. How comes our author to use it? No other explanation seems available except that he has in mind the δεκαρχίαι or δεκαδαρχίαι, the boards set up by Sparta in Greek cities after the fall of Athens and later by Philip II, those cabals of tyrants and their hangers-on reviled by Athenian fourth-century writers³ as a leading cause of misery in Greece and of Spartan unpopularity.

(e) *The Suttee*

The scene (980–1113) in which Euadne, the widow of Capaneus, abruptly appears upon a rock that overhangs his blazing pyre, and flings herself down to join him in death, has again and again been condemned as "episodic" or obtruded (which is correct),⁴ occasionally praised as relieving the monotony of the normal obsequies. But rarely has it been noted that the scene is a replica of an Indian suttee.⁵ Not only does Euadne display passionate grief, utter devotion, and courage, as did the

---

¹ It may be well to subjoin other such passages, though they are less cogent instances.
(i) vv. 545–8: cp. *Rep.* III. 414D: ἦσαν δέ τότε τῇ ἀληθείᾳ ὑπὸ γῆς κτέ.
(ii) vv. 875–7: cp. *Rep.* III. 417A: μεταχειρίζεσθαι καὶ ἅπτεσθαι χρυσοῦ καὶ ἀργυροῦ οὐ θέμις, οὐδ' ὑπὸ τὸν αὐτὸν ὄροφον ἰέναι κτέ.
G. Feugère (*De Socraticae doctrinae vestigiis apud Euripidem*, pp. 60–62) remarks that in *Supp.* 195 ff. Theseus uses exactly the same proofs of a benevolent Providence as Socrates in Xenophon. He discusses the three points ἐνθεὶς σύνεσιν, ἄγγελον γλῶσσαν λόγων δούς, and μαντική, pointing to *Mem.* IV. iii and I. iv.

² That, and no more, is plainly the meaning in *Il.* II. 123–8. Ammendola (*ad loc.* in his *Supplici*) says "Il sost. 'decuria' è propriamente termine militare (cfr. Esichio: δεκάδες· οἱ ἐκ τῆς τάξεως τῶν δέκα στρατηγῶν συνεστῶτες)." But what Hesychius means he fails to explain: the words read like a slovenly condensation of an intelligible definition.

³ Xen. *Hell.* III. v. 13; Isoc. *Paneg.* 63d, *Phil.* 101c, *Panath.* 246d; Dem. *Phil.* II. 71. 12 (where see Sandys).

⁴ For the opposite view see Kitto, pp. 222 f., 226.

⁵ Paley (vol. I, p. 393) writes: "It may even be surmised that... the scene was taken from some account of an Indian *suttee*...."

Hindu widow—so much might well have been independently conceived by a Greek dramatist: there are two details corresponding exactly to the Indian custom. Euadne is not arrayed as a mourner, but wears gala dress in sign of glory.[1] Moreover, her death is "a victory over all[2] women in virtue, for I shall lie in death that I share with my husband" (1059–63).

Can we resist the conviction that this passage, which has no earlier Greek parallel, even in Herodotus,[3] must have been written not earlier than the time when Alexander's conquests had brought to Greeks a flood of information about the Far East?

C. THE FUNERAL SPEECH

When Theseus and his troops return after defeating the Thebans and so assuring burial for the Argive dead, he invites Adrastus to make an oration over the slain champions (841–3): "How came it that these men were conspicuous among mortals for courage? Speak (for thou knowest) to the younger of these citizens, as being wiser than they." When Adrastus has given a brief account of the merits shown by Capaneus, Eteoclus, Hippomedon, Parthenopaeus, and Tydeus, the Athenian speaks (925–32) of the two others whose bodies are not present, Amphiaraus and Polynices.

The five panegyrics uttered by Adrastus compose perhaps the most startling passage in the whole Euripidean *corpus*.[4] Each paragraph reads absurdly —except indeed the fifth, on Tydeus, which in our manuscripts is so doubtful textually, so obscure and ungrammatical, that Dr. Murray's edition leaves but two lines of seven, and even them many will think impossible: "Ambitious nature rich, and spirit equal in deeds, not words". The other

---

[1] Vv. 1054 ff.

[2] The Hindu widow triumphed over the dead man's other wives, who had in vain sought the honour of suttee. That detail is impossible here. Paley (*ad loc.*) well quotes Propertius III. xiii. 15–22; note especially *certamen habent leti*.

[3] In V. 5 he does indeed tell of a Thracian tribe that has the suttee-idea, but the widow is not burnt. Pomponius Mela (II. 2) gives precisely the same account; see also Solinus X. 3. The death of Laodamia in Euripides' *Protesilaus* is no exact parallel: cp. Hyginus, *Fab.* 103 f. The earliest case of Indian suttee mentioned by Western writers (Diod. XIX. 33 f.) happened in 317 B.C.: the rivals were the two wives of Ceteus, leader of the Indian contingent in Eumenes' army.

[4] All who have written a reasonably full account of the play have dwelt on this difficulty. Hartung, determined to defend everything through thick and thin, discusses Adrastus' encomia at length (*Euripides Restitutus*, vol. II, pp. 97–99), beginning with the untrue statement that Theseus inquires after the civic (not the martial) virtues of the slain, insisting that the poet's intention was to edify a grown-up audience, and ending: "Haec efficere pluris erat, quam mores heroum ab aliis poetis traditos, ad hanc fabulam nihil pertinentes, servare." That is the only tolerable excuse, but (as we shall see) it fails, because on any showing Adrastus talks rubbish.

four passages are only too intelligible: they name scarcely anything but solid humdrum virtues that are almost laughable when attributed to these fiery paladins, concerning whose warlike valour Theseus has wished his young citizens to be instructed. Of Eteoclus, for instance, it is said (873 ff.): "A young man he, whose livelihood was meagre, but who won many honours in the Argive land. Though friends pressed gold often upon him, he received it not into his house, lest he should enslave his character to the yoke of money. Those who sinned, not the city, he hated: for a city (be sure) is not to blame when it incurs evil repute through an evil statesman."[1] This staggering irrelevance marks all the paragraphs. But the first paragraph, that on Capaneus![2] Here is a man known to everyone in the audience as the wildest, most reckless, of blasphemers, who had proclaimed that he would sack Thebes "whether God willed it or no" and who had therefore been hurled down from the ramparts by the thunderbolt of Zeus. On this matter, at least, Aeschylus,[3] Sophocles,[4] and Euripides[5] himself are at one. The Theban Herald has used language (496 ff.) closely resembling, indeed modelled on, the passage in Aeschylus: "Is it then no longer just that Capaneus' body smokes, blasted by the thunderbolt: who thrust his ladders upright against the gates and swore to sack the town, God willing or unwilling?" What, then, says Adrastus concerning this devilish swashbuckler who would have made Marlowe's Tamburlaine think twice?

"This is Capaneus, who had plenteous livelihood but was no whit puffed up by wealth and had no more pride than a poor man, shunning whoever was excessively swollen by the table, despising sufficiency; for he said that goodness was not in the belly's food, and that moderate fare sufficed. He was a true friend to his friends, both present and not present; the number of whom is not

---

[1] In v. 879 the καί of κοὐδέν is impossible: see Murray and Wecklein. Like the γ' of L and P, it seems an attempt to mend the scansion of τοι οὐδέν. No satisfactory emendation appears to have been proposed, and one may suggest, *faute de mieux*, πᾶσ' οὐδέν, assuming that π has been miswritten as τ and α as οι—both simple errors; σ could originate the κ of κοὐδέν, C and IC being confused. The resultant ἐπεὶ πᾶσ' οὐδέν αἰτία πόλις gives good sense together with poor style, a combination frequent in this play.

[2] Grégoire (pp. 99 f.) suggests that he is thus described "pour rendre moins surprenant et plus humain le dévouement de l'admirable Évadné". This suggestion would be convincing as well as pleasant had our poet taken the obvious precaution of "preparing" for Euadne in his encomium.

[3] *Septem* 423–34.

[4] *Ant.* 126–35 (not actually naming Capaneus).

[5] *Phoen.* 1172–86. As for *Supp.* 496–9, it cannot of course be maintained that, since the Herald is highly "unsympathetic", his account may be rejected. It is pointless unless he can assume that Theseus, whatever he may think of it as argument, will instantly accept it as true to fact.

great. Truthful character, affable speech, keeping naught unfulfilled with respect to either slaves or citizens."[1]

Adrastus' lamentations would have been still more copious had he foreseen that he was to be thus brutally denied the "honeyed speech" wherewith Tyrtaeus[2] credits him, and exhibited as the worst judge of character since Zeus befriended Ixion. This presentation of him is incredible. Nevertheless, our poet, for all his faults of manner and matter, must have meant something. What can it have been?

One fairly obvious explanation is recommended both by Theseus' demand for an address that shall edify the young men and by the contents of the speech, which are almost entirely moral,[3] the residue being political. It has been set forth by Bengl: "The poet here wishes to show how a member of each social class in the ideal democratic state may be a fine and good citizen: he therefore retains little more of the Argive chieftains than the names, in other respects giving moral descriptions and seeing in each of the fallen chieftains an ideal embodiment of an Athenian citizen-type."[4] This looks convincing: it points to the rich and the poor citizen dwelling in town, the citizen who lives on a country estate, and the resident alien;[5] Tydeus being, however, extremely vague. But in the details given we miss (not to mention Euripidean pungency of thought and crispness of style) politics almost entirely—an astonishing weakness. Again, why does the poet attach "Capaneus", of all labels, to the type so emphatically acquitted of pride? And why is nothing said about that middle class so highly praised by Theseus (238–45)?

A second explanation seeks to identify the men here described with prominent Athenian citizens of Euripides' day. This was first briefly suggested by Musgrave,[6] and worked out fully by Giles,[7] who maintained that Capaneus stands for Nicias, Eteoclus for Lamachus, Hippomedon for Demosthenes, Parthenopaeus for Alcibiades, and Tydeus for Laches. Later students have rejected these identifications: it is impossible to

[1] Vv. 861–71. I have done my best to reproduce the clumsy and maundering style of the original. The last few words are no doubt an effort to render the simple thought, "he kept his word".   [2] Fr. 9. 8 (Diehl).
[3] Vv. 899 f. are applicable to the young only.
[4] *Staatstheoretische Probleme in Rahmen der attischen, vornehmlich euripideischen Tragödie*, pp. 44 f. Cp. Hartung (p. 126 above).
[5] Bengl quotes Pseudo-Xen. *Constitution of Athens* 1. 10 ff.: τῶν δούλων δ' αὖ καὶ τῶν μετοίκων πλείστη ἐστὶν Ἀθήνησιν ἀκολασία.
[6] "Puto poetam in ducibus Argivis laudandis nobilium quorundam Atheniensium vitam et mores effinxisse. Quare non est adeo mirandum si receptam de veteribus illis opinionem non anxie ubique secutus est." Quoted by Giles—see next note.
[7] P. Giles, "Political Allusions in the *Supplices* of Euripides", *Class. Rev.*, vol. IV (1890), pp. 95–98.

believe that any writer, however inept, would have expected a normal audience to recognize the notoriously pious Nicias in the wild blasphemer merely because wealth, for which the former was famous, is attributed to the latter; it is no less surprising that Alcibiades should be described as an immigrant when everyone knew that he belonged to a great old Athenian family, the Alcmaeonidae.

Thirdly, Wecklein[1] sees in this sensational divergence from tradition "a certain humour" and "a kind of satire on the pretty colours of funeral orations". This pleases at first sight: it is what Euripides might well have done. But we must reject it. For, first, can we believe that he wrote "humorous satire" in the blundering and at times barely grammatical verse delivered by Adrastus; secondly, would not satire be out of key with the simple manner and the conventional ideas that set this work apart?

What, then, are we to make of Theseus' attempt to "improve the occasion"? At present, nothing. We must leave this farrago alone until we discover some theory of the whole *Supplices* that may explain its presence.

D. POLITICS

Despite all that we have said about the five or seven mothers and sons, their seven, five, or two funeral-pyres, many will find even more startling the irrelevance and folly wherewith political history and doctrine are dragged in at the faintest opportunity. Some, it is true, have implied that politics are the very subject of the play. Not so: the play treats a chivalrous exploit of Theseus and his citizens, its reasons and its result. Politics certainly might be mentioned by any Athenian dramatist who took that exploit in hand: half a dozen lines from the king near the beginning and another half-dozen from Athena at the close. But for what we find here no excuse exists.

When Adrastus appeals to Theseus for aid in a matter of fundamental decency, the latter prefaces his refusal with a smug sermon (195-249): first an irrelevant testimonial to the Almighty, then an insufferable lecture to his unhappy guest, describing his folly in neglecting omens, the political danger caused by headstrong and self-seeking young militarists, and (finally) the salutary merits of the middle class. To all this Adrastus,

---

[1] On v. 858. Similarly Grégoire writes (p. 100): "Il n'est pas impossible qu'il se soit permis une légère satire des oraisons funèbres dont la loi fut toujours le *de mortuis nil nisi bene*, et qu'il ait visé — et atteint — le double but d'intéresser less imples par la nouveauté, et de faire sourire les esprits avertis et critiques."

who may have been a fool, but is not so bereft of discretion as his loquacious host, replies like a gentleman in unrhetorical words of dignified rebuke, marked most adroitly by one hint of irony:

> οὔτοι δικαστήν σ' εἱλόμην ἐμῶν κακῶν
> οὐδ', εἴ τι πράξας μὴ καλῶς εὑρίσκομαι,
> τούτων κολαστὴν κἀπιτιμητήν, ἄναξ,
> ἀλλ' ὡς ὀναίμην.[1]

"Not as a justicer of my sorrows did I choose you, Sir King, nor as a chastiser and appraiser if I am found in aught to have acted ill; nay, it was a boon that I asked." He goes on, with equal dignity, to bid the Mothers quit their suppliant attitude and depart.

A still more repellent scene is Theseus' altercation (399–466) with the Theban Herald, who enters asking the natural and normal question: "Who is tyrant of this land? To whom should I announce a message from Creon, master of Cadmus' country?" He means (of course) only that he seeks the person to whom his message should be delivered, certainly not "the tyrant" in any offensive, or even emphatic, sense. But to Theseus, as to stupidly suspicious democrats in Aristophanes,[2] the word *tyrannos* is like a red rag to a bull. He leaps at his visitor with promptitude and gusto, brandishing (as it were) a handful of leaflets, the first of which—"Democracy: What It Is, and How It Works"—he presents on the spot; later he will offer "The Dangers of Autocracy", "Wealth, Poverty, and Free Speech", "The Tyrant a Crowned Homicide", "Protect Your Homes!" Compared with this ill-timed and unseemly rhetoric, the corresponding moment in the *Heracleidae*[3] becomes downright laughable in its simplicity:

Herald: And who is king of this land and city?
Chorus-Leader: Demophon, sprung from a noble father: Theseus.

But we discover with joyful surprise that the king seems to have met his match. This Theban is no staid old-fashioned person like poor Adrastus, but as soon as he sees Theseus' mood interrupts him at the close of his first paragraph,[4] quite in the spirit of Sir Toby Belch's "Nay, if you be an undertaker, I am for you." This, he feels, is to be a battle of wits—

---

[1] Notice the -τής termination, thrice in three lines. So repeated, it gently implies that Theseus has talked like a professional censor.

[2] E.g. in *Wasps* 486–507, especially the delightful οὗτος ὀψωνεῖν ἔοιχ' ἄνθρωπος ἐπὶ τυραννίδι.

[3] Vv. 114 f. The Chorus-Leader has used τύραννος just before (v. 111) in precisely the same uncoloured sense as the Herald in our play.

[4] πρῶτον μέν (v. 403) makes one fear that Theseus intends to recite all his tracts in unbroken flow.

"advantage number one you give me there, as if we were playing chess"—and develops "The Merits of Monarchy"; which prove, however, to be rather "The Demerits of Democracy". He knows more about late fifth-century Athenian public life than a Theban of the heroic age has any business to know, and delivers a damaging attack, to which Theseus offers no genuine rebuttal at any point of his vehement counter-blast. This omission the Herald ignores with a courteous formula meaning "Let us agree to differ." He then delivers his long-postponed message from Creon, with an elaborate comment which does not at the moment concern us.[1]

On the manner of this debate nothing more need be said save to point out a touch of quiet fun. At the close of his harangue Theseus finds the hardihood to blame his opponent for irrelevance and loquacity, though the score so far is: Thebes 17 lines, Athens 37 lines! "To thy sorrow wouldst thou have come with this superfluous talk, had not thy city sent thee: a messenger should speak according to his commission and return with speed. For the future, let Creon send to my city some messenger less talkative than thou."

But if we pass on to the allied topic of political history we encounter a miracle of silliness rivalling the treatment of the chorus. Our poet believes heartily in the Athenian democratic constitution, as he has been at some pains to show; moreover, his theatrical and aesthetic tastes, and possibly[2] his concern with later history, have led him to select as his theme an exploit headed by the most renowned Athenian king. Can he combine these two enthusiasms and identify a completely democratic Athens with an Athens living under a monarch of the heroic age? "Impossible!" we answer. But he achieves this impossibility by alleging that Theseus founded the democratic constitution under which Athenians lived during the late fifth and the fourth centuries. Can we imagine an English playwright sending on an actor to announce "I am King Alfred the Great, and I have just instituted Female Suffrage"? There are some absurdities that the most foolish and ignorant audience will not allow, except in confessedly wild farces. It is true that gross falsifications of history have been committed by fine dramatists, but they always incur censure. Schiller is rightly condemned for depicting Joan of Arc as dying in the moment of victory: but that St. Joan should so die was in itself possible enough. Shaw's Britannus, who voices the prejudices of a nineteenth-century Englishman, is a stroke of irresponsible buffoonery that jars our

---

[1] The condemnation of war; see p. 118 above.
[2] For the relevance of Delium see pp. 150, 162–5 below.

taste, though we should not say that no ancient Briton could cherish such prejudices. Our poet goes beyond the bounds not only of history but of the possible.

For we are not to suppose that Theseus gave up despotic power and instituted limited monarchy, himself retaining the crown but accepting an elected "government". It is true that a half-hearted attempt is made to depict such an arrangement.[1] At v. 346 he first defies Thebes on his own authority, using the normal tone of a tragic king: "This will I do. I shall go and release the dead, by words of suasion: if these fail, straightway it shall be done by armed force, without the jealousy of Heaven." Then at once he recollects himself and dutifully recites a more republican formula: "But I would have the whole city also approve this. Approve she will, since I desire it; yet by granting the people a voice I shall find them better disposed." This light-hearted procedure may suit the microscopic affairs orchestrated by the official who assures us that "I think I may answer for my committee"; but as a method of "wielding at will that fierce Democratie" it strikes one as precarious. Yet Theseus is justified (393 f.): "Behold! Willing and glad the city undertook this task, when she saw my desire."[2]

But the conception of the Athenian polity offered by this whole play is hopelessly muddled. Beside the passages just cited others are found of different tenor. The first, indeed, presents a little internal muddle of its own (352 f.):

καὶ γὰρ κατέστησ' αὐτὸν [sc. τὸν δῆμον] εἰς μοναρχίαν
ἐλευθερώσας τήνδ' ἰσόψηφον πόλιν.

---

[1] Theseus would thus approximate to Pericles. Cp. Schmid, Müller's *Handbuch der Altertumswissenschaft*, Abt. VII, Teil 1, vol. 3 (Munich, 1940), pp. 726, 729. That the king here definitely stands for Pericles is the thesis of Goossens (*ut sup.*, pp. 8–40) who makes out an excellent case, without, however, facing the initial absurdities.

Grégoire, after saying that "on voyait en lui comme une préfiguration de Solon" (p. 90), later writes (p. 91): "Les Grecs du Ve et du IVe siècle n'avaient aucune peine à se figurer la royauté primitive associée aux institutions de la démocratie. Ils la concevaient sous la forme de la royauté constitutionelle." But his instance for the fifth century, a decree of Halicarnassus (Michel, no. 451; Hicks–Hill, no. 27) gives him very weak support, if indeed any (cp. Hicks–Hill *ad loc.*). His other example—three decrees of Mylasa in Mausolus' satrapy (Michel, no. 47; Hicks–Hill, no. 133)—plainly implies the political condition that he describes. But the decrees are certainly dated 367/6, 361/0, 355/4: their time, like their place, makes them irrelevant to the ideas of Euripides and his Athenian contemporaries.

[2] So far, Theseus takes exactly the same attitude, and with the same success, as the Argive king in Aeschylus' *Supplices*. All that follows is utterly un-Aeschylean. Bengl is not justified in saying (p. 26): "Was das Staatstheoretische anlangt, so hat er sich in seinen Hik. die des Aeschylus, mit dem er in der Auffassung von Monarchie und Demokratie durchaus übereinstimmt, bis in Einzelheiten zum Vorbild genommen."

"For, moreover, I have formed it into monarchy, giving freedom to this city by equality of votes." This immediately follows Theseus' words, quoted above, about giving the people a voice in public affairs, a very different thing from making the people "sole ruler". The natural meaning of the first line is "I have made Athens a monarchy", which plainly is not a republic. Moreover, the kingship existed before Theseus. All we can say at present about this jumble[1] is that its author has the *synoecismos* at the back of his mind and struggles to pretend that this "concentration" of the Attic communities means the birth of democracy.[2] Later, Theseus becomes lucid enough when addressing the Herald (403 ff.): "In the first place, stranger, thou hast begun thy speech falsely, seeking a tyrant here; for the city is not ruled by one man, but is free. The people is sovereign in yearly successions, turn by turn." He clearly denies his kingship. Where then in the state is his place? One can but answer: "He must be an ordinary citizen so far as rank goes, but of vast personal prestige"—which suggests someone like Pericles, an idea contradicted by all the rest of the play. If our author really means Pericles, he might at least have avoided such things as Adrastus' address (113), "O victorious king of the Athenian land", leaving only the next line or something like it: "Theseus, I come as thy suppliant and thy city's."

Observe, moreover, that his mysterious feat of statecraft is not merely liberation of the common folk. This constitution is later than that of Solon, who instituted or recognized four classes according to income, making only members of the wealthiest class eligible as archons. Here we find the Periclean system, which opened that office to all,

---

[1] Nauck, not unnaturally, felt that it should be rewritten: καὶ γὰρ κατέστησ' αὐτός ἐκ μοναρχίας . . .. He was followed by Kirchhoff and Wilamowitz. "For I myself established this city as ἰσόψηφος ('democratic'?), changing it from a monarchy." This *tour de force* means nothing less than the abdication of Theseus.

Murray retains the manuscript reading, with the remark "omnia sana: sc. τὸν δῆμον μόναρχον κατέστησα" (see above). Bengl, however, insists: "Von einer μοναρχία des δῆμος kann keine Rede sein (cf. Hik. 349 f. δόξαι δὲ χρῄζω καὶ πόλει πάσῃ τόδε· δόξει δ' ἐμοῦ θέλοντος). . . . Eine Stütze für die genannte Konjektur [Nauck's, as above] scheinen mir auch folgende Plutarch- und Isokrates-stellen zu bieten: Plut. Conv. Septem Sap. 152 A . . . μάλιστ' ἂν ἔνδοξος γενέσθαι καὶ βασιλεὺς καὶ τύραννος, εἰ δημοκρατίαν ἐκ μοναρχίας κατασκευάσειε τοῖς πολίταις, vgl. auch Isokr. Helena 35 über Theseus und Ps.-Dem. ἐπιτάφιος 28 . . . Θησέα τὸν Αἰγέως πρῶτον ἰσηγορίαν καταστησάμενον τῇ πόλει." But there is no end to the discussion of incurable nonsense.

[2] Theophrastus, writing about 320 B.C., drops a useful hint as to the way in which the συνοικισμός may have been interpreted by the uncritical as the beginning of democracy (*Char.* XXVI. 6): . . . καὶ ὡς μισητὸν τὸ τῶν δημαγωγῶν γένος, τὸν Θησέα πρῶτον φήσας τῶν κακῶν τῇ πόλει γεγονέναι αἴτιον, τοῦτον γὰρ ἐκ δώδεκα πόλεων εἰς μίαν καταγαγόντα λῦσαι τὰς βασιλείας. The last phrase looks important, but can mean only suppression of local magnates.

including the lowest income-class.[1] The passage translated above proceeds:

οὐχὶ τῷ πλούτῳ διδοὺς
τὸ πλεῖστον, ἀλλὰ χὠ πένης ἔχων ἴσον

"not giving preponderance to wealth, but the poor man too has equality".[2] Dr. Goossens's contention,[3] that Theseus is intended as the archetype of Pericles, must be accepted as an aid to appreciating the *Supplices*. It does nothing, however, to acquit the writer of deplorable bungling.

Shall we attribute these statements to his own fancy, or can we find endorsement of them, or explanation or excuse, in ancient literature? The well-known account of Theseus in Thucydides[4] describes his *synoecismos* only, and numbers him among the "first kings", with no hint of democracy or even of checks upon the monarchy. Nothing to our purpose survives in the fragments of the Atthidographers.[5] Indeed, we are almost completely justified in assuming that they never so reported of Theseus. Their remains give a good deal about his heroic feats; and this, set beside the fact that later authors never quote from them reports or comments concerning him as a statesman (of whatever kind), suggests strongly that for them he was nothing more or less than an Attic Heracles.[6]

But in Aristotle's *Constitution of Athens* we find a definite though very meagre statement. That part of the treatise which discussed Theseus is lost, like the other early chapters; but in his forty-second Aristotle luckily summarizes the historical portion of his book, noting the eleven "changes" that followed the first constitution. After mentioning Ion and the organization of the Four Tribes, he writes: "the second change—the

[1] The archonship was thrown open to the *zeugitae* in 457 B.C., a change perhaps brought in by Pericles himself. The *thetes* were never legally admitted, but actually could hold the office (cp. Aristotle, *Ath. Pol.* 7 *ad fin.*).

[2] For the bad syntax see p. 145 below.

[3] See above, p. 132, n.1.

[4] II. 15. 1 f.

[5] Fourth and (Philochorus) third centuries. They appear to have been, within their self-imposed limits, excellent researchers. Later writers and students certainly so regarded them, and at times quote them in preference to Thucydides: e.g., schol. on Ar. *Peace* 665, about a detail of the affair at Pylos.

[6] Wilamowitz (*Aristoteles und Athen*, vol. I, pp. 260–80) discusses the Atthidographers with his usual blend of vast learning and energetic imagination. If we accept all that flows from the latter source, we discover the authority from whom Aristotle, and the other writers named below, drew their ideas of Theseus' relation to the Athenian polity. On p. 279 he says that Solon and Cleisthenes are the great names of the Atthis, and also "in der Vorzeit der demokratenkönig Theseus". This latter statement, apparently (pp. 284–6), occurred in the first genuinely Attic chronicle, which he dates at 394–380 B.C. (As was said above, our fragments contain nothing about Theseus as democrat-king.)

first after Ion's to involve an adjustment of the constitution—was that occurring in Theseus' time, which diverged a little from monarchy".[1] How great was this divergence? We find, and in this summary can expect, no details; but the passage certainly does not support what we read in our play, for a moment later he writes: "The third came after the civil strife—Solon's change, which was the beginning of democracy."[2]

Can we learn anything positive about this lost "divergence" passage? Plutarch, no doubt,[3] quotes from it: "That he [Theseus] was the first to lean towards the mob, as Aristotle says, and relinquished monarchy, Homer also seems to testify, using in the Catalogue of Ships the word 'people' [*demos*] of the Athenians alone." Relinquishment of monarchy must be Plutarch's own comment on Aristotle's words: as we have just seen, it is impossible that the latter thus contradicted himself. We possess also an epitome of Aristotle's work made by one Heraclides,[4] which contains this entry: "And these men were continuously engaged in civil strife. Theseus made proclamation and brought these men together on equal and like terms."[5] That is fumbling as well as curt. "These men" may not be the Athenian people at all, but the sons of King Erechtheus, mentioned in the preceding passage as dividing his kingdom. If, however, they are the Athenian people, we may indeed understand "democracy" (Heraclides in that case misrepresenting Aristotle), but just as well equal rights under Theseus' sovereignty. To sum up, all Aristotle has to tell us is that Theseus allowed the commons some influence on, or share in, the government. But he clearly remained king of Athens: the "sovereign people" (*Supp.* 406) is out of the question.

---

[1] 41. 2: δευτέρα δὲ καὶ πρώτη μετὰ ταύτην ἔχουσα πολιτείας τάξιν, ἡ ἐπὶ Θησέως γενομένη, μικρὸν παρεγκλίνουσα τῆς βασιλικῆς. The phrase πρώτη ... τάξιν means that Theseus' change can be regarded as a development in the constitution, and that changes had occurred between Ion and Theseus which did not. Thus in the next sentence he mentions ἡ ἐπὶ Δράκωνος, Draco's change, which also was not constitutional—for next comes Solon's, called the third, not the fourth.

[2] Τρίτη δὲ ἡ μετὰ τὴν στάσιν ἡ ἐπὶ Σόλωνος, ἀφ' ἧς ἀρχὴ δημοκρατίας ἐγένετο. See the account of Solon's legislation in chapters 5–12, especially 6. 1: κύριος δὲ γενόμενος τῶν πραγμάτων Σόλων τόν τε δῆμον ἠλευθέρωσε καὶ ἐν τῷ παρόντι καὶ εἰς τὸ μέλλον κτέ. ἠλευθέρωσε contradicts Theseus' boast (*Supp.* 353) ἐλευθερώσας.

[3] Sandys assumes this (ed. of Ἀθ. Πολ., p. 157a). It is possible, however, that Plutarch has in mind not the full passage but the summary 41. 2 (quoted above): ὅτι δὲ πρῶτος ἀπέκλινε πρὸς τὸν ὄχλον, ὡς Ἀριστοτέλης φησί, καὶ ἀφῆκε τὸ μοναρχεῖν, ἔοικε μαρτυρεῖν καὶ Ὅμηρος ἐν νεῶν καταλόγῳ [*Il.* II. 547], μόνους Ἀθηναίους δῆμον προσαγορεύσας (*Theseus* 25).

[4] For this man, otherwise unknown, see Sandys (*ut sup.*, p. xxxvi) and Wilamowitz, *Aristoteles und Athen*, vol. I, pp. 292 f.

[5] Καὶ διετέλουν οὗτοι στασιάζοντες. Θησεὺς δὲ ἐκήρυξε καὶ συνεβίβασε τούτους ἐπ' ἴσῃ καὶ ὁμοίᾳ.

So much for Aristotle. The doctrine, naturally unsupported by him, that made Theseus the founder of democracy, appears not only in the *Supplices*, but in six other works of the fourth or later centuries.[1] These are:

(i) Isocrates, *Encomium Helenae*, 370 B.C.
(ii) Isocrates, *Panathenaicus*, 339 B.C.
(iii) Pseudo-Demosthenes, *Contra Neaeram*, c. 340 B.C.
(iv) Plutarch, *Theseus*, c. A.D. 100.
(v) Plutarch(?), *Septem Sapientium Convivium*, c. A.D. 100.
(vi) Pseudo-Demosthenes, *Epitaphios*, c. A.D. 130?

They shall now be described in chronological[2] order.

Isocrates devotes no less than a third of his *Helen* to Theseus, one of her suitors, celebrating that hero's manifold glories with such abundance of handsome rhetoric that he is fain to apologize for it. On politics, as on most[3] other themes, he strikes a rich vein.[4] First he relates that Theseus took to heart the lessons provided by the lives of commonplace tyrants and "proved that it is easy to be a despot and at the same time no worse off than those living under a constitution where all are equals". The methods and expedients of this *roi soleil* are recounted with the familiar Isocratean brilliance, further embellished by an engaging, if rather droll, adroitness in dovetailing ideas that less nimble fingers would have found hopelessly recalcitrant. After describing the *synoecismos* he proceeds: "Next, having established the fatherland as common to all and freed the

---

[1] It was presented also in a famous painting by Euphranor (*fl.* 360 B.C.) on a wall of the Ἐλευθέριος Στοά in Athens. The earliest account of the picture is given by Pausanias (I. 3. 3), who adds a rebuke of those ignorant enough to believe the story : . . . ἐπὶ δὲ τῷ τοίχῳ τῷ πέραν Θησεύς ἐστι γεγραμμένος καὶ Δημοκρατία τε καὶ Δῆμος. δηλοῖ δὲ ἡ γραφὴ Θησέα εἶναι τὸν καταστήσαντα Ἀθηναίους ἐξ ἴσου πολιτεύεσθαι· κεχώρηκε δὲ φήμη καὶ ἄλλως ἐς τοὺς πολλοὺς ὡς Θησεὺς παραδοίη τὰ πράγματα τῷ δήμῳ καὶ ὡς ἐξ ἐκείνου δημοκρατούμενοι διαμείναιεν, πρὶν ἢ Πεισίστρατος ἐτυράννησεν ἐπαναστάς. λέγεται μὲν δὴ καὶ ἄλλα οὐκ ἀληθῆ παρὰ τοῖς πολλοῖς οἷα ἱστορίας ἀνηκόοις οὖσι καὶ ὁπόσα ἤκουον εὐθὺς ἐκ παίδων ἔν τε χοροῖς καὶ τραγῳδίαις πιστὰ ἡγουμένοις κτέ.

[2] The first three dates may be regarded as certain; the fourth is roughly correct, falling in Plutarch's lifetime; the *Convivium* may be Plutarch's, and (even if it is not) probably belongs to his period; the sixth date is conjectural: the speech is certainly spurious, and I have tentatively assigned it to the reign of Hadrian, when the manufacture of forgeries flourished.

[3] About the rescue of the corpses, however, he is brief (214b): τῷ [sc. Ἀδράστῳ] δὲ τοὺς ὑπὸ τῇ Καδμείᾳ τελευτήσαντας βίᾳ Θηβαίων θάψαι παρέδωκε. Note his agreement with the play as to Theseus' employment of force, not persuasion as in the normal account.

[4] *Helen* 214c–e: ὁρῶν γὰρ τοὺς βίᾳ τῶν πολιτῶν ζητοῦντας ἄρχειν ἑτέροις δουλεύοντας κτέ. in the normal manner, ending with the less hackneyed remark: ἐπέδειξεν ὅτι ῥᾴδιόν ἐστιν ἅμα τυραννεύειν καὶ μηδὲν χεῖρον διακεῖσθαι τῶν ἐξ ἴσου πολιτευομένων.

souls of fellow-citizens,[1] he placed their rivalry in virtue on an equal footing, confident that he would surpass them no less if they practised virtue than if they neglected it, and knowing that honours bestowed by gallant men are sweeter than those received from slaves. So averse was he from courses lacking public approval that he on his side was for establishing the people as masters of the commonwealth; while they on theirs insisted that he should rule alone, believing monarchy held by him more trustworthy and co-operative than democracy administered by themselves."[2]

In his *Panathenaicus* Isocrates is more cautious, though he spoils his effect (for critical minds) by a broad hint that the story is his own invention.[3] Theseus, he says, in the prime of life handed over the government to the people and went off on a career of adventure.[4] Nevertheless, he attributes the foundation of democracy not to Theseus, but to certain "successors in the administration", whose identity and status are left undescribed. These founded democracy—of an austere form, which "used aristocracy".[5] If we choose to take this dim verbiage seriously, we shall call it a description of Solon's regime, not of that pictured in the *Supplices*.

The *Speech against Neaera* is considered un-Demosthenic by nearly all ancient and modern critics. That interests us little: its date falls early in the second half of the fourth century, so that it provides testimony about political doctrine or political fancy in the period with which we are concerned. We read that "when Theseus drew them together [the *synoecismos*] and created democracy, and the city became populous, the people [*demos*] none the less appointed the king by vote from persons selected for their manly excellence".[6] This election of Theseus' royal successors seems to be vaguely described in *Heracleidae* 35 ff.:

πεδία γὰρ τῆσδε χθονὸς
δισσοὺς κατοικεῖν Θησέως παῖδας λόγος,
κλήρῳ λαχόντας ἐκ γένους Πανδίονος.

---

[1] τῶν συμπολιτευομένων. Does he wish to leave it doubtful whether he means "the citizens thus concentrated" or "those who shared citizenship with Theseus"?

[2] *Helen* 215a, b.

[3] *Panath.* 259a: μιᾶς δὲ μόνον μνησθήσομαι πράξεως, ᾗ συμβέβηκε μήτ' εἰρῆσθαι πρότερον . . . .

[4] *Ibid.* 259c: ἀκμάζων, ὡς λέγεται, τὴν μὲν πόλιν διοικεῖν τῷ πλήθει παρέδωκεν, αὐτὸς δ' ὑπὲρ ταύτης τε καὶ τῶν ἄλλων Ἑλλήνων διετέλει κινδυνεύων.

[5] *Ibid.* 259d: . . . κατεστήσαντο γὰρ δημοκρατίαν οὐ τὴν εἰκῇ πολιτευομένην καὶ νομίζουσαν τὴν μὲν ἀκολασίαν ἐλευθερίαν εἶναι, τὴν δ' ἐξουσίαν ὅ τι βούλεταί τις ποιεῖν εὐδαιμονίαν, ἀλλὰ τὴν τοῖς τοιούτοις μὲν ἐπιτιμῶσαν ἀριστοκρατίᾳ δὲ χρωμένην. Cp. Pliny, *Nat. Hist.* VII. 200: *Fabricam ferrariam invenerunt Cyclopes, . . . regiam civitatem Aegyptii, popularem Attici post Theseum.*

[6] *Contra Neaeram* 1370.

"They say that Theseus' two sons inhabit the plains of this land, appointed by lot from Pandion's family."

Plutarch, four centuries later, writes with a notable air of precision about Thesean democracy, just before the passage (given above) that quotes Aristotle's remark on Theseus' "divergence towards the mob". "Wishing to expand the city still more, he summoned all upon equal terms; and they report that the cry 'Come hither, all ye peoples!' was Theseus' proclamation when founding what may be termed a union of parishes. Nevertheless, he did not permit the influx of a miscellaneous crowd to turn the democracy into a disorganized medley, but was the first to separate them into 'nobles', 'countrymen', and 'artisans'."[1] A little later[2] he says that Theseus found a ready hearing from private individuals and the poor, "but the powerful he tempted with a kingless constitution—a democracy that should use him as no more than warlord and as guardian of the laws, but in other matters should give equality to all".

In *The Banquet of the Seven Sages* Solon is made to remark: "My own view is that a king or a tyrant would be most likely to win glory if he set up democracy for his citizens."[3]

Finally, the pseudo-Demosthenic *Epitaphios* touches our theme at only one point: "Men of the Aegeid tribe were not ignorant that Theseus, Aegeus' son, was the first to establish the right of equal speech in their city."[4] This recalls, and may be a direct borrowing from, *Supplices* 438 ff. But it has small value: the whole speech is spurious and very late.

During the fourth and earlier centuries, so far as appears, prevailing—or, at least, instructed—opinion looked on Theseus as a heroic king who was not to be counted among Athenian statesmen; further, it attributed the birth of democracy definitely and solely to the Solonian legislation. That view is contradicted by a belief (found in the *Supplices* and the six prose passages set out above[5]) that Theseus was both a monarch and the actual or potential founder of democracy—under which, moreover, according to the *Supplices*, he lived. If we consider what Athens under-

---

[1] *Theseus* 23.
[2] *Ibid.* 24.
[3] *Conviv. Sept. Sap.* 152A.
[4] *Epitaph.* 1397.
[5] Not in the Aristotelian *Constitution of Athens*, as it now survives. It cannot be denied that Aristotle in the missing chapters described a change of the constitution that occurred in Theseus' time; but the "divergence" as summarized later can refer to a slight increase in the people's power, and an increase forced upon the king, not initiated by him. The vital fact is that the treatise unequivocally names Solon as the founder of democracy. See above, pp. 134 f.

stood by democracy and monarchy, we must condemn that belief as self-contradictory. Why, then, did these authors state it?

On the three latest passages we need not dwell. Plutarch's first refers entirely to the "concentration" (*synoecismos*) and concerns us only on the strength of the single word "democracy", for which, it seems, he could have substituted "people". In the *Convivium*, though Theseus is not named, we must surely assume that he is meant by the speaker (Solon) who can have heard of no other "king or tyrant" to whom this action was ever attributed. Similarly, the *Epitaphios*-writer has no doubt democracy in mind. All three, then, are (as it were) contained in the fourth-century passages and the *Supplices*, and must be supposed to draw either on those four works or on their authorities, whatever these may have been.

Reverting to the three prose passages of the fourth century, we find that one far transcends the others. Pseudo-Demosthenes gives but a few words on our theme. This brevity has some importance, for it suggests that the idea was already familiar. In his *Panathenaicus*, Isocrates is plainly offering a revised form of what he gave in his *Encomium on Helen*: it is far less absurd, and its fumbling suggests quaintly that some candid friend has begged him to give an account of Theseus that will at least make sense. Certainly it makes more sense than the story in his *Helen*; but its lameness hints broadly at mere invention, as indeed he half confesses.[1]

That earlier statement, though even less convincing, is more significant for our purpose. Isocrates lived five centuries nearer than Plutarch to the political and literary events that we are studying. His trickiness in manipulation can escape no reader: the reason for it is hardly less obvious. He would prefer to say that Theseus was both the perfect king and the perfect democrat—precisely what we find in the *Supplices*. Seeing, however, as well he may, that this will not do, since it contradicts not only itself but also the current attribution of democracy's genesis to Solon, he airily alleges that the king was indeed its founder so far as his own opinions and intention could go, but was thwarted by the amiable insistence of the citizens that a hero who slew murderous brigands and monsters was more to be trusted in politics than all his subjects taken together. But why this *tour de force*? Why seek to combine monarch and democrat? If anyone ever knew how to present a convincing case, it was Isocrates. He realized that even if one depicts a perfect man, one still must not hang

---

[1] See above, p. 137. In what precedes he owns to regret that he has already written about Theseus in the *Encomium*.

every excellence round his neck: it is impossible to be both a perfect jockey and a perfect heavyweight boxer. His business plainly was to portray the ideal king and leave democracy out of sight altogether. The clear implication is that, when he wrote, this notion of a democratic Theseus was in the air, well enough known to convince him that he must take account of it, whatever the cost to verisimilitude.

One passage in the *Supplices*, as we have seen, offers an unequivocal statement of this view, marred by no apology or misgiving. Theseus founds the democracy, and the people is sovereign; nevertheless, when he decides to plunge his country into war, he speaks unmistakably as head of the state, whose will is practically decisive, but who (nevertheless, again) gives his citizens "a share in the discussion" so as to keep them in good humour. Is it not plain that both the playwright and the essayist have the same absurdity in mind? But whereas the latter, being an adroit rhetorician, contrives to make nonsense plausible for a moment, the former suggests a half-witted conjurer whose rabbits play him false, and produces a bungle perhaps unparalleled in European drama.

What conclusions are we to draw from all this? First we must note that the whole discussion belongs to a period later than Euripides. In the fifth century, Athenians had not yet begun to study the history of their political constitution.[1] Even Thucydides says practically nothing of it: when he digresses to correct his countrymen's notions about their own history, it is hardly such matters that he handles, but personal details concerning the fall of Peisistratid tyranny.[2] Euripides, though noted as a student and as the first Athenian to possess a library, confined his researches to other fields, such as Attic myths, genealogies, and festivals. Only later did study of constitutions arise: the fourth and later centuries pursued it with enthusiasm, often with diligence and scientific method whereof Aristotle was but one, though the most illustrious, exemplar. Side by side with these researches appeared not only such imaginative theoretical constructions as Plato's *Republic* and *Laws*, but also the foolish and showy daub of Theseus flaunted before us by Isocrates and the rest, including our play. This latter must be set down confidently as a by-product of that age to which the Atthidographers belonged, and the great Peripatetic collection whereof Aristotle's *Athenian Constitution* is the only survivor.

[1] Solon was a very possible, and natural, exception: see p. 141 below.
[2] I. 202, VI. 54–58. The latter and far longer passage does allude to constitutional matters, but briefly (54. 6): τὰ δὲ ἄλλα αὐτὴ ἡ πόλις τοῖς πρὶν κειμένοις νόμοις ἐχρῆτο, πλὴν καθ' ὅσον αἰεί τινα ἐπεμέλοντο σφῶν αὐτῶν ἐν ταῖς ἀρχαῖς εἶναι.

THE *SUPPLICES* 141

Three[1] descriptions of Theseus' connexion with constitutional change lie before us.

The first is that he was king of Athens and remained king of Athens, but that in his time the commons obtained some voice in public affairs. It is Aristotle's account, and must be accepted without question on the strength of his unsurpassed qualifications and merits as a researcher, of its inherent probability, and of the numerous parallels that world history affords.

The second is that he was both king of Athens and also the founder of complete Periclean democracy. It is the account given in the *Supplices* and apparently supported by a very brief statement in the pseudo-Demosthenic *Neaera*. This must be rejected on the ground of its utter stupidity, not to mention its contradiction of Aristotle.

The third is that he was king of Athens, but wished to found democracy, being however led to acquiesce in a postponement thereof to a period indicated with extreme vagueness. It is Isocrates' revised account, which must be rejected because it ignores Solon, and because it is clearly an invention devised to secure an impossible reconciliation of the first and second accounts just described.

Whence came these doctrines? The Isocratean (we have seen) is a fabrication; but as regards the other two we are reduced to conjecture. It may seem easy and attractive to suggest[2] that Aristotle drew on one of the Atthidographers, perhaps Cleidemus; but, when we reflect that their numerous fragments include nothing on our problem and—vastly more important—nothing on the whole theme of constitutional history, we must look on that solution, such as it is,[3] with suspicion. We are to note by the way that Isocrates' statements possess, after all, indirect value: they prove that the *Supplices*-doctrine, or something rather like it, had a considerable vogue in the fourth century. It is a natural conclusion that both Aristotle and the playwright followed the same authority; but that, whereas the former used it with common sense, the latter garbled it absurdly.[4] What that authority was, we can only guess: it may have been one of Solon's poems.[5]

---

[1] It has been already pointed out that the passages later than the fourth century have no independent value.

[2] As does Wilamowitz: see above, p. 134.

[3] For Cleidemus was a contemporary of Aristotle, and we should have to look for his sources in their turn.

[4] Such garbling is easier to credit than stupidity frolicking *in vacuo*. Moreover, the "vogue" mentioned above suggests some fairly convincing authority rather than the unsupported nonsense of our poet.

[5] Beyond the fact that he is the single earlier writer who was in the least likely to

E. MISCELLANEOUS ABSURDITIES

(i) In 250 f. the Chorus-Leader thus excuses Adrastus:

ἥμαρτεν· ἐν νέοισι δ' ἀνθρώπων τόδε
ἔνεστι· συγγνώμην δ' τῷδ' ἔχειν χρεών.

"He erred. But that is natural to youthful men: he must be pardoned." Elsewhere his elderliness is clearly implied, and he calls himself in 166 "a hoary man" (πολιὸς ἀνήρ). Why this gratuitous silliness or blindness of the Chorus-Leader?[1]

(ii) In 465–510 the Theban Herald makes a long speech that contains a good deal of wisdom, but also much arrogance. The scene goes on:

> *Chorus-Leader*: God was sufficient as our chastiser! You ought not to have wreaked such outrage.
> *Adrastus*: Thou utter villain—
> *Theseus*: Silence, Adrastus! Check thy tongue, and set not thy words before mine. Not to thee has he come with his message, but to me: and me it behoves to answer him.

That Theseus should rebuke another for anticipating him with comment on the Herald's offensive speech was no doubt to be expected; but to fall upon his royal and unhappy guest with gross discourtesy, and yet to leave the Chorus-Leader unsnubbed, is ludicrous. To be sure, nothing occurs oftener in Greek tragedy than the insertion of two or three lines by the Chorus-Leader between two long speeches of contestants, the second of whom disregards the insertion. But here to ignore it and nevertheless object so brutally to the words of Adrastus is a stupidity without parallel.[2] Still, the king is not so much stupid as nervous. He cannot assume that Adrastus means to utter, like the Chorus-Leader, only a line or so: he has taken part in too many tragedies to make that mistake. His idea is: 'The Herald has delivered his long speech, and the Chorus-Leader his usual unimportant couple of lines. Now the second

---

mention Theseus and the "divergence", only one excuse for naming him appears. In *Supplices* 589 f. Theseus says that he will go to Thebes himself in arms, αὐτός τε κῆρυξ. This last phrase recalls Solon's verse (fr. 2. 1 Diehl): αὐτὸς κῆρυξ ἦλθον ἀφ' ἱμερτῆς Σαλαμῖνος.

[1] Grégoire's translation seems impossible: "Il a failli: les jeunes gens en sont la cause. . . ." Surely ἔνεστι cannot mean "is caused by". Grube (p. 232) makes Theseus the person who ἥμαρτεν. But (to mention nothing else) in that case the verb would be in the present tense.

[2] *El.* 213 ff. are odd, indeed, but not in the least stupid. We must remember the sort of woman Electra is in that play: she was prepared to keep up her lament till dusk.

oration is due. Your two words, Adrastus, mean that you propose to steal the big speech from me. Hold your tongue!"[1]

(iii) When Theseus, wishing Adrastus to make an edifying speech to the younger citizens of Athens, compliments him (841 ff.) on his wisdom and knowledge, he sharply contradicts his own earlier censure (161, 219–25, 248).

(iv) During the antiphonal lament of the Mothers and their grandsons, these lines occur (1139 ff.):

Boys: Gone! They are no more. Alas, father! They are gone.
Chorus: Heaven has them now, consumed by the ash of fire; on wings have they departed to Hades.

Two theories were in vogue concerning what follows death: that the soul ascends into the upper air,[2] and that it descends to Hades. Being, as we have seen, a broad-minded eclectic, the poet affirms that these particular spirits have succeeded in reaching both places at once. Or perhaps his nimble brain supposes that, since "Hades" is often used as a synonym for "death" and since some aver that the souls of the departed go up into the aether, there can be no objection to his placing Hades in the sky. For once his folly can be paralleled. Some kindred spirit placed in the parish church at Stratford-on-Avon a bust of Shakespeare and inscribed thereunder the incredible legend:

Judicio Pylium, genio Socratem, arte Maronem
Terra tegit, populus maeret, *Olympus habet.*

(v) Athena's intervention at the close has often been censured as an anticlimax. It is far worse. She rejects, with the weight of divine authority, the doctrine (repeatedly voiced earlier)[3] that war is a madness, and urges these children to renew the bloodshed. Equally repellent, and perhaps more astonishing, is her insistence that the chivalrous king blackmail the Argives by conduct like that of the very Thebans against whom he has just championed them.

(vi) Finally, this is perhaps the best place in which to consider Theseus'

---

[1] Contrast what happens in the similar situation of *Heracleidae* 181 ff. The Argive Herald speaks at length to Theseus' son, King Demophon, the Chorus-Leader delivers two lines, and Iolaus the suppliant utters a long reply; only after another four lines from the Chorus-Leader does the king speak.

[2] Cp. the inscription (*C.I.G.*, vol. I, pp. 197 f., no. 442) on the Athenians who fell at Potidaea in 432–1 B.C.: αἰθὴρ μὲν ψυχὰς ὑπεδέξατο . . . . Theseus, it must be noted, is on this point more sensible than the Chorus. He voices the Potidaea conception (533 f.).

[3] To the more elaborate passages might be added that brief outcry of the Chorus (1147 ff.) in reply to their grandsons' wish for vengeance: οὔπω κακὸν τόδ' εὕδει κτέ.

proclamation (195–215) of his optimism, in the true sense of that word: he believes that human life is good and ruled by gods who have led it to happiness.

"With others have I struggled hard before now in such an argument as this. One said that the evils of mankind are more numerous than their blessings. But I hold an opinion contrary to this: good things outnumber bad for mankind; were it not so, we should not be alive. I praise whatever god organized life for us out of a brutish chaos. First he bestowed intelligence, then gave a tongue to utter words so that we should perceive speech; he caused nurture of fruit and for that nurture sent watery drops from Heaven, to nourish Earth's produce and irrigate her womb. Besides all this, he gave protection against winter, to repel the sky's chill air, and voyages overseas, that we might receive by barter those things in which our land was poor. And obscurities, matters which we do not plainly comprehend, soothsayers foretell by gazing at fire and into the folds of entrails, and from birds. Then are we not spoiled children, if not content that God has thus furnished our life?"

It would be irrelevant here to discuss Theseus' doctrine,[1] or even whether Euripides himself held it;[2] we are now concerned with ineptitude, which is found neither in the matter nor in the language here. But the whole topic is thrust at us with a suddenness and inconsequence startling even in Theseus: why the square brackets were not long ago clamped round these lines it is hard to say. We must not refer to equally intrusive passages in the other plays; for even Hecuba's "earth's chariot" outburst[3] and Theonoe's words[4] on the life after death are very short, whereas Theseus' much longer address reads like the summary of a whole sermon. And further—though we cannot fairly talk of artistic failure here, as the speech is not out of Theseus' character—we must not fail to remark that its tone is so astonishingly un-Euripidean that it cannot be matched in the whole *corpus*. Perhaps the most important feature of Euripides' thought is not that he believes or rejects this or the other doctrine, but that he accepts none, however attractive or apparently edifying, until both his restless probing intelligence and his emotional alertness have played freely upon it from every side, so that in any statement of it which he at length offers may be seen the impress of his pecu-

---

[1] Especially as he flatly contradicts it later—ἀλλ', ὦ μάταιοι, γνῶτε τἀνθρώπων κακά and the rest (549–55). Is there any other play that falls so hopelessly to pieces the moment one handles it? (Murray would remove the contradiction by making 549–57 follow 170.)

[2] Nowhere else (save for a single word in *Ion* 1190) does he speak with unequivocal praise of soothsaying, and of course nowhere else with such unreserved optimism.

[3] *Tro.* 884–8.   [4] *Helen* 1014–16.

THE SUPPLICES

liar and vivid personality. But Theseus' preachment bears the mark of no personality at all: it is machine-made, smug, and glib: the report of a committee, not the voice of a soul.

F. FAULTS OF LANGUAGE OR STYLE

To impugn authenticity by condemning details of vocabulary, grammar, idiom, or style is notoriously inconclusive; but we shall complete our case by adding here whatever items of that kind have not been noted earlier.

(i) Intolerable flatness. We have seen that this pervades much of the play: little remains to be mentioned.

(*a*) v. 590: αὐτὸς σίδηρον ὀξὺν ἐν χεροῖν ἔχων.

(*b*) vv. 913 ff.:

ἡ δ' εὐανδρία
διδακτός, εἴπερ καὶ βρέφος διδάσκεται
λέγειν ἀκούειν θ' ὧν μάθησιν οὐκ ἔχει.
ἃ δ' ἂν μάθῃ τις, ταῦτα σῴζεσθαι φιλεῖ
πρὸς γῆρας. οὕτω παῖδας εὖ παιδεύετε.

The final sentence closes Adrastus' speech with a lump of banality that is made no more welcome by reading παιδεύσετε (Hermann) or ἐκπαιδεύετε (Markland).

(*c*) v. 1165: γυναῖκες Ἀργεῖαι γένος. Why drag in their nationality? Moreover, as we have said, three of them are not Argives.[1]

(ii) Ugly anacoluthon or asyndeton.

(*a*) vv. 406 ff.:

δῆμος δ' ἀνάσσει διαδοχαῖσιν ἐν μέρει
ἐνιαυσίαισιν, οὐχὶ τῷ πλούτῳ διδοὺς
τὸ πλεῖστον, ἀλλὰ χὠ πένης ἔχων ἴσον.[2]

(*b*) vv. 440 f.:

καὶ ταῦθ' ὁ χρῄζων λαμπρός ἐσθ', ὁ μὴ θέλων
σιγᾷ.

(*c*) vv. 528 f.:

εἰ γάρ τι καὶ πεπόνθατ' Ἀργείων ὕπο,
τεθνᾶσιν, ἠμύνασθε πολεμίους καλῶς.

---

[1] See p. 115 above.
[2] ἴσον σθένει, Herwerden; ἔχει μέρος, Holzner. For other attempts see Wecklein's Appendix.

(iii) Late or prosaic words.

(a) v. 186: ἐγὼ δίκαιός εἰμ' ἀφηγεῖσθαι τάδε. Under ἀφηγέομαι L. and S. remark: "A prose word, also found in Pseudo-Eur. Supp. 186."

(b) v. 209:

πόντου τε ναυστολήμαθ', ὡς διαλλαγὰς
ἔχοιμεν ἀλλήλοισιν ὧν πένοιτο γῆ.

διαλλαγή seems nowhere else to mean "interchange".

(c) v. 442: ὅπου γε δῆμος αὐθέντης χθονός. αὐθέντης clearly means κύριος, a sense never found in fifth-century Greek, where it always means "doing an act oneself", usually a deed of bloodshed.[1]

(d) v. 561: οὐ γάρ ποτ' εἰς Ἕλληνας ἐξοισθήσεται. οἰσθήσομαι is not found till the fourth century: Ar. *Phys.* 205^{a}13, 214^{b}18, 21; Dem. *Leochares* 1094. 8.

(e) v. 661: πρὸς κρασπέδοισι στρατοπέδου τεταγμένον. This metaphorical use of κράσπεδον is found only here and in Xen. *Hell.* III. ii. 16.

(f) v. 871: Ἐτέοκλον, ἄλλην χρηστότητ' ἠσκηκότα. χρηστότης is otherwise fourth century or later: it is most unlikely that any fifth-century poet would coin the word in place of the obvious ἀρετή.

(iv) Obscurities.

(a) vv. 452 ff.:

... ἢ παρθενεύειν παῖδας ἐν δόμοις καλῶς
τερπνὰς τυράννοις ἡδονάς, ὅταν θέλῃ,
δάκρυα δ' ἑτοιμάζουσι;

Such is the manuscript reading, printed by Wecklein. No one has been able to make sense of v. 453. In the next line ἑτοιμάζουσι is supposed to stand for τοῖς ἑτοιμάζουσι with the sense "(but bringing tears) to those who prepare them for the tyrant's embrace"!

(b) vv. 476 ff.:

σκέψαι δὲ καὶ μὴ ...
σφριγῶντ' ἀμείψῃ μῦθον ἐκ βραχιόνων.

The last line is badly written. Are we to take βραχιόνων as comparative of βραχύς or as a part of βραχίων? The former will mean "(give a lusty answer) though your strength is insufficient"; but βραχιόνων is then obscurely brief. The latter will mean (as Grégoire translates it) "ne va

---

[1] Markland would substitute εὐθυντής, which in itself is excellent. But why was so good a word ousted by so bad a word as αὐθέντης? The conclusion must be that the latter is "correct".

point . . . mettre la force de ton bras dans ta réponse!" That makes very harsh Greek; still, we must allow that σφριγῶντα suggests muscles. Both explanations suit the context, but only after a struggle.

(c) vv. 494 f.:

σὺ δ' ἄνδρας ἐχθροὺς θεοῖς θανόντας ὠφελεῖς,
θάπτων κομίζων θ' ὕβρις οὓς ἀπώλεσεν.

οἰκεία or its equivalent is indispensable with ὕβρις: the natural meaning, as the sentence stands, is that insolence of others destroyed the Argives.

(d) vv. 508 f.:

σφαλερὸν ἡγεμὼν θρασύς·
νεώς τε ναύτης ἥσυχος, καιρῷ σοφός.

The Herald is warning Theseus: "Do not rush heedlessly into war." V. 508 fits this idea. But what of v. 509? Apparently it is intended to mean "the cautious navigator is the best navigator". This can, indeed, be extracted from the Greek: "A navigator can be quiet (i.e., easy in mind, i.e. out of danger), if he shows wisdom in a crisis." But the effort is considerable. Moreover, why is the very odd phrase νεὼς ναύτης used for κυβερνήτης?

(e) vv. 899 f.:

πολλοὺς δ' ἐραστάς, κἀπὸ θηλειῶν ὅσας
ἔχων ἐφρούρει μηδὲν ἐξαμαρτάνειν.

Not only is ὅσας impossible; not only has no acceptable emendation for it been suggested:[1] even if we did put that phrase right, the first line as a whole would be bad. We need to say 'Many men and many women offered him love'; and to contrast the single word ἐραστάς (instead of, e.g., πολλοὺς ἀπ' ἀνδρῶν) with the emphatic ἀπὸ θηλειῶν is very poor style. Of course πολλοὺς δ' ἀπ' ἀνδρῶν would not fit the remainder of the clause, which (it seems) must be given up as hopelessly bungled.

(f) v. 1219: συσκιάζοντας γένυν.[2] "Shadowing your jaws", without, for example, θριξί must be condemned as slovenly.[3]

---

[1] No one appears to have proposed τόσας, which (so far) seems quite satisfactory: it answers πολλοὺς—"many men and as many from among women". κἀπὸ θηλειῶν is clumsy, to be sure: but that is another matter.

[2] For the rest of the passage see below.

[3] It is true that practically the same words occur in Phoen. 63: τέκνων γένυς ἐμῶν σκιάζεται. But that prologue contains much poor writing that cannot be Euripides' work.

(v) Remarks dubious in style or silly in content. (Many have been already noted.)

(*a*) v. 674: ποιμένες ὄχων.
(*b*) vv. 714–17: Theseus knocks head off with his club.
(*c*) v. 764: ἠγάπα νεκρούς.
(*d*) v. 888: ὁ τῆς κυναγοῦ δ' ἄλλος Ἀταλάντης γόνος.

(vi) Rhetorical or idiomatic blunders.

(*a*) vv. 774 ff.:

> ... φίλους προσαυδῶν, ὧν λελειμμένος τάλας
> ἔρημα κλαίω· τοῦτο γὰρ μόνον βροτοῖς
> οὐκ ἔστι τἀνάλωμ' ἀναλωθὲν λαβεῖν,
> ψυχὴν βροτείαν· χρημάτων δ' εἰσὶν πόροι.

The last clause is a masterpiece of futility. In Greek, as in English, the usual form of expression puts the less important clause first: "You may recover lost wealth; but life, once lost, can never be recovered." A famous example[1] (if example is needed) happens to treat this same idea, and may indeed have suggested our mumbling passage:

> ληϊστοὶ μὲν γάρ τε βόες καὶ ἴφια μῆλα,
> κτητοὶ δὲ τρίποδές τε καὶ ἵππων ξανθὰ κάρηνα·
> ἀνδρὸς δὲ ψυχὴ πάλιν ἐλθεῖν οὔτε λεϊστὴ
> οὔθ' ἑλετή, ἐπεὶ ἄρ κεν ἀμείψεται ἕρκος ὀδόντων.

But Greek writers sometimes use a development of this form, the simple *ab* order being replaced by *bab*: first the main idea, then the minor, after which the main idea returns. So in *Heracles* 633 ff.:

> πάντα τἀνθρώπων ἴσα·
> φιλοῦσι παῖδας οἵ τ' ἀμείνονες βροτῶν
> οἵ τ' οὐδὲν ὄντες· χρήμασιν δὲ διάφοροι·
> ἔχουσιν, οἱ δ' οὔ· πᾶν δὲ φιλότεκνον γένος.[2]

That final πᾶν κτέ. is vital to the rhetorical form. Our poet has written *ba*—and stopped dead.

(*b*) v. 1219:

> ἀλλ' οὐ φθάνειν χρὴ συσκιάζοντες γένυν
> καὶ χαλκοπληθῆ Δαναϊδῶν ὁρμᾶν στρατόν. ...

So Murray, following the manuscripts, except for Brodeau's certain

---

[1] *Il.* XI. 406 ff.   [2] *Med.* 1228 ff. is another instance.

THE *SUPPLICES*

alteration of φθονεῖν to φθάνειν.[1] Surely the intention must be: 'Lose no time in growing up and (thus at the earliest possible moment) lead the Argives against Thebes.' It is rather silly, making Athena sound like an arch maiden aunt; still, the root idea is important—"make this enterprise your ambition". But someone has blundered over the idiom of φθάνω and what she says really means "You must not be in time", "You must let someone else outstrip you in the race for early beards".

G. ARGUMENTS FOR EURIPIDEAN AUTHORSHIP

The following seems to be a complete list.

(i) The *Supplices* appears in two manuscripts of Euripides, the Laurentian and the Palatine.[2]
(ii) It appears also in a list[3] of plays inscribed on the base of a statue of Euripides.
(iii) Passages from our text are quoted by later Greek writers.[4]
(iv) Modern scholars almost unanimously assert that the play was suggested by events that occurred in Euripides' lifetime.[5]
(v) Some find allusion to two of his most distinguished contemporaries, Pericles and Alcibiades.
(vi) Parts of the play are written with unmistakably Euripidean eloquence.

The first three arguments prove only that ancient scholarship recognized a Euripidean *Supplices*.[6] So much will not be denied here: on the

---

[1] Wecklein, baffled (as well he may be) by the above reading, prefers ἀλλὰ φθάνειν . . . ἢ (*vel* πρίν) χαλκοπληθῇ. . . . This gives correct idiom, but the resultant sense is unlikely: "Grow up quickly, so that the second expedition against Thebes may not start without you." But they *were* the expedition. It suffices to substitute ἀλλὰ for ἀλλ' οὐ.

[2] See Wilamowitz's *Analecta Euripidea* and Murray's *Praefatio* to his text of Euripides.

[3] *C.I.G.*, vol. III, no. 6047.

[4] For example, Polybius V. 5 and 9 (quoting 860); Plutarch *Cons. ad Apoll.* 110C (1109–14), *De Ei Delphico* 394B (974–6), *Pelop.* I. 13 (860 f.); Athenaeus IV. 158F, 159A (861–6).

[5] See Schmid, p. 455, n. 2, for the fullest account.

[6] The earliest quotation is to be dated 218 B.C. Polybius (IV. 62) tells us that Scopas the Aetolian destroyed the Macedonian town Dium, in revenge for which (V. 8 f.) Philip V took revenge upon the Aetolian city of Thermum (218 B.C.): κατέγραφον δὲ εἰς τοὺς τοίχους καὶ τὸν περιφερόμενον στίχον, ἤδη τότε τῆς ἐπιδεξιότητος τῆς Σάμου φυομένης, ὃς ἦν υἱὸς μὲν Χρυσογόνου σύντροφος δὲ τοῦ βασιλέως· ὁ δὲ στίχος ἦν

ὁρᾷς τὸ δῖον οὗ βέλος διέπτατο; [*Supp.* 860.]

This pun must be held to correct the reading ὁρᾷς τὸν ἁβρόν of our MSS. Not only does ἁβρόν make no sense (see the context): unless δῖον already occurred in the line, Samus showed very poor "smartness".

contrary, that he wrote *a Supplices* is part of our thesis. The arguments cast no light on the question: Who wrote our existing text? Even if we asserted that it is entirely non-Euripidean, they would not be decisive. The presence of *Rhesus* in the Euripidean *corpus* has not deterred scholars from assigning it to a period much later than Euripides' death; and the objections to it are trivial compared with those now brought against the *Supplices*. Again, a *Constitution of Athens* appears in seven manuscripts of Xenophon, but today no one accepts it as his work. The fact is, of course, that when a composition of unknown or doubtful origin exists side by side with a body of similar writings by a well-known hand, these latter exercise a powerful attraction upon the former, which is (so to put it) sucked into the vortex. This happened to *Minos*, *Cleitophon*, the second *Alcibiades*, and other pseudo-Platonic pieces; to the *Fourth Philippic* and some other writings that figure in the manuscripts of Demosthenes; to the quasi-Theocritean Fisher-Idyll; to the Fifth *Olympian Ode* and (as has been recently asserted)[1] the Third and Fourth *Isthmians*; this, finally, happened to our *Supplices*, because of its unmistakable, though scattered, resemblances to Euripidean work.

The fourth point refers to the behaviour of the Boeotians[2] after their victory over the invading Athenian force at Delium in 424 B.C. When the latter asked the usual facilities for collecting the bodies of their dead, the Thebans made it a condition that the Athenians should evacuate Boeotia.[3] This ruffianly conduct and the resentment it caused in Athens are thought to have prompted Euripides. Further, the alliance with Argos that closes the *Supplices* is held to point at the alliance of Athens and Argos engineered by Alcibiades in 420 B.C.[4] These arguments, at first sight impressive, by no means necessarily date the play.[5] The refusal of obsequies is the single feature common to it and Thucydides' narrative, Thebans being not the only opponents of Athens at Delium; and we shall observe later that a similar situation can be found in the fourth century. The Argive treaty is still less convincing: the fourth century as well as the fifth has its treaties. But we postpone discussion of the battle and the treaty.[6]

[1] See my *Pindar*, pp. 172-5.
[2] Not the Thebans only, which would give a more striking parallel to our play. Still, Thebans formed the most important element in the Boeotian army, and Pagondas the Boeotarch was himself a Theban (Thuc. IV. 91). [3] Thuc. IV. 97-99.
[4] See Thuc. V. 43-47 and Decharme, *Euripide et l'esprit de son théâtre* (1893), pp. 200 ff.
[5] Murray is one of the very few who doubt that it does: "Actam esse circa tempora Nicianae pacis (A.C. 421) fortasse arguit historia; scriptam magna ex parte aliquot ante annos mihi persuadet stylus." [6] See below, pp. 162-5.

As for the fifth item—allusion to Euripides' contemporaries—there is a great difference between the case for Pericles and that for Alcibiades. Dr. Goossens has adduced strong evidence that Theseus is intended for Pericles,[1] remarking for instance on the similarity of what is here said about the king and what Thucydides writes of the statesman. But there is probably nothing to support the notion that Alcibiades is indicated by the Messenger's advice (726 ff.) to choose a general, such as Theseus, who blends valour in war with moderation in peace. This may or may not be a snatch of election propaganda: in any case Theseus as here depicted bears no resemblance to Alcibiades. Both the Delium argument and the alleged hint at Alcibiades[2] tend to show that the *Supplices* belongs to the fifth century, not that it was written by Euripides.

So far, the evidence has little weight. The sixth point, however, is far more cogent. Our attack on the matter and manner of this play must assuredly not blind us to the fact that some passages, hitherto ignored by us, exhibit the full power of Euripides. Wilamowitz strangely asserts that our poet laid the scene at Eleusis purely because Aeschylus had done so in a play of similar theme, *The Men of Eleusis*: an imitation that involved him in gratuitous difficulties.[3] This remark ignores an admirable dramatic effect—indeed more than one. It would have been simple enough to make Theseus act like his son in the *Heracleidae*, accepting the refugees as soon as their case was laid before him. Our poet causes him to refuse:[4] obviously (one would have thought) to give occasion for Aethra's magnificent admonishment of her son. The whole scene is modelled to this end: nor are we to overlook the sad beauty of the lines preceding Theseus' entrance—mothers appealing to a mother. But if we are to see the queen before her son arrives, Athenian convention demands that some important reason be offered for her appearance in public. That need explains the setting at Eleusis: she has come from her house in Athens to offer sacrifice in the shrine of Demeter and the Maiden, goddesses especially

---

[1] Cp. p. 132. Grégoire, less happily, sees in him a "préfiguration de Solon".

[2] Not the Theseus-Pericles idea: Pericles could perfectly well be regarded much later as hero of the Golden Age of Athenian democracy. On Alcibiades see p. 165 below.

[3] *Der Mütter Bittgang*, pp. 11 f.: "Der Chor kann nicht fort gehn, daher muß Theseus das Heer nach Eleusis bescheiden: am Schlusse aber geht der Chor ab, gleich als ob er nicht in Eleusis schwören könnte. Wie wenig auf den Ort der Handlung ankommt, zeigt sich darin, das der Tempel, der auf der Bühne ist, keine Bedeutung hat: die Hinterwand bleibt geschlossen. Auch die eleusinische Religion kommt nur obenhin vor."

[4] Had he done so in ten lines (at most) of dignified, if severe, explanation, the whole scene would have been perfect.

revered by Athenian women, as the Thesmophorian and other festivals witness.[1]

Her address to Theseus is beyond compare the play's finest passage:[2] it shows the familiar Euripidean eloquence; the athletic diction, lithe and buoyant without glibness, beautifully adroit but just on the right side of mere cleverness.

> ἐρεῖ δὲ δή τις ὡς ἀνανδρίᾳ χερῶν
> πόλει παρόν σοι στέφανον εὐκλείας λαβεῖν,
> δείσας ἀπέστης, καὶ συὸς μὲν ἀγρίου
> ἀγῶνος ἦψω φαῦλον ἀθλήσας πόνον,
> οὗ δ' ἐς κράνος βλέψαντα καὶ λόγχης ἀκμὴν
> χρῆν ἐκπονῆσαι, δειλὸς ὢν ἐφηυρέθης.[3]

Nor must other excellent parts go unacknowledged, such as the *stichomythia*[4] between the two kings and the moving lament (955 ff.) sung by the Mothers as the bodies of their sons are borne away.

H. WHO WROTE OUR SUPPLICES?

No one. Were this merely a bad play, we could without misgiving attribute it, if not to some known member of the Alexandrian Pleiad, then to some anonymous poetaster of that or any other suitable period. But it is far more complex, containing excellent matter, bad matter and—what is vastly harder to interpret—matter that in itself or in its context or both is nonsense. We must not take the usual method of dealing with ill-written or irrelevant passages, and suppose that this play has undergone nothing worse than ordinary interpolation:[5] the absurdities are too

---

[1] So in New Comedy and the novels, etc. "heroines" are regularly first seen by "heroes" in church (as we say).

[2] Grégoire (pp. 86 f.) admirably remarks: "Aethra, prenant la place d'Adraste sert en quelque sorte à élever le débat; et de plus ce rôle athénien achève de *nationaliser* la vieille légende." (His italics.)

[3] Vv. 314 ff. I shall not attempt a translation.

[4] Vv. 115 ff. Milton's imitation (*P.L.* II. 992 ff.) of two lines seems to have passed unnoted:

> ΑΔ. οἶσθ' ἣν στρατείαν ἐστράτευσ' ὀλεθρίαν.
> ΘΗ οὐ γάρ τι σιγῇ διεπέρασας Ἑλλάδα.
>
> I saw and heard, for such a numerous host
> Fled not in silence through the frighted deep
> With ruin upon ruin.

[5] So Wilamowitz, *Einleitung in die griechische Tragödie*, p. 218: "Die Hiketiden enthalten eine partie durch erweiternde interpolation entstellt, welche noch um 250 v. Chr. in Athen unverdorben geläufig war." (He proceeds to discuss 901 ff.) Then why does our text contain only 1234 lines—a good deal less than the average Euripidean play

THE SUPPLICES

pervasive. Our *Supplices* is not a "work" at all, but a heap of lumps thrown together by some meddling dullard.

Two facts, at least, have emerged from the preceding sections. First, a good deal is Euripides' work: so much is proved by its excellence of matter and manner. Secondly, other portions were written several generations later. We have therefore a combination of two plays by two dramatists: that is the foundation whereon study of our text must base itself. Let us first attempt, then, with the aid of our earlier investigations, to disentangle these two plays, or what remains of them.

Vv. 1–70. *Euripidean.* An admirable and thoroughly typical opening—as regards its language: but we must note what may be briefly called the curtain-problem.[1]

Vv. 71–86. *Anonymous.* This passage consists of two lyrical stanzas sung by handmaids, who have been foisted upon the Euripidean play by someone who wished to complete the number of its chorus.[2] As to that, we are compelled (however disconcerting the results) to believe what we are repeatedly[3] told: Euripides' chorus contained seven people, and seven only—the mothers of the Seven Champions.

Vv. 87–194. *Euripidean.* The close is uncertain, but most reasonably placed at v. 194: vv. 184–92 are excellent;[4] and the startling 'hymn-writer' passage[5]

(see above, pp. 32 f.) whereas the *Phoenissae*, which underwent the process described, has 1766?

[1] Cp. pp. 116, 162.

[2] Cp. p. 113. Vv. 171 f. imply that the Mothers have no attendants, though at vv. 275 f. they suddenly imagine they have some, and call out for them, unluckily in the wrong metre (see below, p. 155). The Anonymous works them in better at vv. 1115 ff.

[3] Cp. pp. 112–15.

[4] Save that v. 186 is objectionable, partly for its pomposity, partly for ἀφηγεῖσθαι (cp. p. 146).

[5] Vv. 180–3. Murray (on 179) retains this, believing (with Kirchhoff) that some lines have been lost after v. 179. Their content he supposes to have led up to the ὑμνοποιός passage: ". . . nam debet, qui ceteris persuadere velit, ipse se felicem ac sapientem praebuisse."

Grégoire makes an ingenious attempt to show these four lines relevant. The lacuna, he suggests, ran somewhat thus. 'Do not be surprised that I cannot show the eloquence with which fame credits me: I am but a vanquished wretch, who can do no more than beg your pity. An orator must be in good spirits. . . .' Unfortunately, Adrastus goes on at once to speak with notable skill and vigour.

The attempt to force this passage into relevance seems hopeless. Dindorf remarks *ad loc.*: "Ineptissima haec est praecedentium sententiarum amplificatio, quam eiciendam esse bene intellexit Reiskius, falsus tamen quod ex alia tragici fabula illatos hos versus esse credidit, quos ipsum dicendi genus prodit non a poeta Attico, sed a grammatico esse confictos." But nothing seems wrong with the diction or style. These lines look like a note of some reader as tired of "sufferings" as the valet in *John Bull's Other Island*: he no doubt took them from another play of Euripides, as Reiske thought.

could be taken as a normal interpolation unrelated to the special problems of this tragedy.[1]

Vv. 195–252. *Anonymous*. The first part, Theseus' sermon about Divine Providence, is utterly un-Euripidean.[2] It has nothing to do with the matter in hand; begins with no apology for, or explanation of, its irrelevance; has no marks of Euripides' peculiar ferreting manner in such discussions; contains the only praise of divination to be found in the nineteen dramas; and, above all, blandly ignores[3] those agonies and deep-rooted misgivings so often described elsewhere. The second part, to be sure, is nearly all concerned with the situation, being joined to its predecessor by the (unfair) statement that Adrastus has shown himself like the ungodly and conceited people just described. But it begins with the word *decas*[4] and continues with a muddle-headed insistence that Adrastus has "wounded his house" by marrying his daughters as he did, though in the funeral speeches (for what they are worth) both suitors are eulogized, one of them by this very moralist.[5] Further, though Euripides himself is prone enough to digress on such themes as politics, the passage not only contains a reminiscence of Plato:[6] it makes a ridiculous[7] prelude to Theseus' rejection of Adrastus' appeal—"There are three classes of citizen: the rich useless and selfish; the poor led by demagogues to assail the rich; the middle class, which saves the country by its discipline. *And after that*, you expect me to help you? Begone!" The Chorus adds its mite to this foolish collection, pleading (250) for Adrastus as misled by his youthfulness, though we have heard that he is aged.[8]

Theseus' refusal is of course needed by the Euripidean play. Whether we should extract vv. 246–9 from this part and add it to our collection of Euripidean passages, or suppose that what Theseus said (naturally in similar words) has been obliterated, matters little.[9]

---

[1] It should be added that this section contains one of the "little snags" discussed in the first essay (pp. 37 f.). Theseus (91 f.) gives a reason for his arrival different from that stated by his mother (36 ff.).

[2] It may be asked: "Why, in the name of dramatic art, should Euripides not make a character talk in a non-Euripidean way?" The best brief answer is that a great painter signs every picture by his brush-work.

[3] Masqueray dwells on this omission with disgust. "Nous croit-il stupides? Est-il inconscient? Est-il aveugle?" *Euripide et ses idées* (1908), p. 123.

[4] Cp. p. 125.   [5] Or so he says (see p. 157).

[6] Cp. pp. 122 ff.

[7] κἄπειτα (246), which should indicate a climax as usual, emphasizes the absurdity. It would come vastly better after 231.

[8] Cp. p. 142. Note that πολιὸς ἀνήρ (166) belongs to a Euripidean passage. I am at a loss to account for this remark of the Anonymous.

[9] See, however, p. 123, n. 1.

THE *SUPPLICES*

Vv. 253-62. *Euripidean*.

Vv. 263-70. *Anonymous*. This ascription should be accepted for two reasons. First, the admirable vv. 267-9 have a strong fourth-century tone.[1] Secondly, that the Chorus-Leader should deliver some ten iambic lines before the lyrical passage, is unparalleled[2] in extant Greek tragedy, and somewhat odd in itself.

Vv. 271-398. *Euripidean*. Though this portion is on the whole remarkably fine, we are arrested by three passages:

(i) Vv. 275 f. This brief outcry was undoubtedly thrust in to give the alleged handmaids something to do for a moment. It is metrically objectionable, and should be looked on as an ordinary interpolation.

(ii) Vv. 349-53. After announcing that he will espouse the Suppliants' cause, Theseus explains—or apparently thinks that he explains—his position in the Athenian polity; at this moment the situation is precisely the same as in Aeschylus' *Supplices*: the king after strong reluctance decides on aiding the strangers, and departs to persuade his people, taking the Suppliants' leader with him as "object-lesson" or "evidence". There is no difficulty save in vv. 352 f., καὶ γὰρ . . . ἰσόψηφον πόλιν, a passage hopelessly muddled, as we have seen.[3] The most satisfactory view is that these two lines are inserted[4] from the anonymous play, which contained also the later nonsense about Theseus' relation to Athenian democracy. We have then no trouble with the preceding remark about consulting the populace:[5] it is natural for any leader or king, except the traditional despot.

(iii) Vv. 359-64. An affectionate and respectful dismissal of Aethra is of course appropriate, indeed necessary. But is not the passage too elaborate?[6] Beck deletes the two last lines,[7] and many will applaud him. Still, the point has small importance.

Vv. 399-597. *Anonymous*. They contain the badly composed description (404-8) of the archonship[8] and a ludicrous blend of complete democracy with heroic kingship.[9] Later occurs weak or bad writing (432, 440 f.,

---

[1] Cp. pp. 118-21.
[2] In *Heracles* 252-74 we find a still larger number; but they are followed by no lyrics.
[3] Pp. 132 f. [4] They were deleted by Schenkl.
[5] There is no need to postulate what would be a fourth-century feature—the "divergence" mentioned by Aristotle: see above, p. 135.
[6] See however Grégoire, p. 87.
[7] Possibly the speech was extended by someone who recalled Thales' remark (Diog. Laert. I. 37): οὓς ἂν ἐράνους εἰσενέγκῃς τοῖς γονεῦσι, τοὺς αὐτοὺς προσδέχου καὶ παρὰ τῶν τέκνων.
[8] Cp. p. 145. [9] See pp. 131-41.

454 f., 478, 487, 508 f.); a long passage (476–93) on the evils of war that strongly suggests post-Euripidean feeling;[1] some lines (531–6) that Stobaeus[2] attributes to Moschion; and (545 f.) a reminiscence of Plato's *Republic*.[3] Nor must we overlook the foolish snubbing (513 ff.) of Adrastus by Theseus.[4] Much more striking is the passage (543 ff.) where he scornfully asks whether the Thebans fear vengeance of the buried dead. In itself an excellent point, it strongly contradicts the statements or spirit of many other places in Euripides.[5] The remainder (548–97) is less objectionable,[6] but contains a shocking sentiment[7] uttered by the hero-king; a poor bit of padding (569 f.); the Herald's abrupt departure, unremarked by any words of Theseus,[8] in the middle of a line (584); a bungling sentence (594 f.) in which the king appears to imply that some gods have little respect for justice; and a colloquial phrase[9] of his that comes with particular oddity at the scene's end.

Vv. 598–633. *Euripidean*.

Vv. 634–777. *Anonymous*. This scene, concerning Theseus' victory and its immediate sequel, is on the whole not un-Euripidean in subject-matter and treatment. But a later poet could have written it, for there are no unmistakably distinctive thoughts or turns of idiom or rhetoric. Therefore we seem justified in giving full weight to the non-Euripidean features. These are:

(i) In v. 682 διεφύλασσον for "commanded" is odd—a tiny point, confessedly.

(ii) Vv. 714–17, an absurdly boisterous and impossible picture of Theseus' beheading his opponents with a club. This wild nonsense is out

---

[1] See pp. 118–21.
[2] *Flor*. 123. 3: see below, p. 169.
[3] See p. 125, n. 1.
[4] Pp. 142 f. See below, pp. 173 f.
[5] I owe this remark to Schmid (p. 721, n. 20) who quotes *Hec*. 534 ff., *Tro*. 1305 ff., *El*. 677 ff., *I.T*. 170 ff., *Helen* 959 ff., 1009 ff., 1028 f., *Or*. 1225 ff., 1231 ff., *Hec*. 833 ff., *Heracles* 490, *Or*. 580 f., *Alc*. 1127 f., fr. 912, *Helen* 914 f., *Or*. 675 f.

[6] It scarcely needs to be said that by "objectionable" or "non-Euripidean" here and elsewhere is not meant that nothing in the whole passage could have been written by Euripides; for instance, 481–5 are fine: Murray gives prominence to 484 f. in his admirable article "Reactions to the Peloponnesian War in Greek Thought and Practice", *J.H.S.*, vol. LXIV, pp. 1–9. Again, something very like Theseus' "To arms!" speech (584 ff.) must have appeared in the Euripidean play.

[7] V. 557: ἀδικεῖν τε τοιαῦθ᾽ οἷα μὴ βλάψαι πόλιν.

[8] His son does better in the *Heracleidae* (284 ff.): φθείρου· τὸ σὸν γὰρ Ἄργος οὐ δέδοικ᾽ ἐγώ.

[9] Vv. 596 f.: ἀρετὴ δ᾽ οὐδὲν λέγει βροτοῖσιν. But whereas λέγεις τι ("you are right") is good dignified Attic (cp., e.g., Soph. *O.T*. 1475 f.), surely οὐδὲν λέγεις ("Nonsense!") is colloquial, as in Murray's example, Ar. *Knights* 334: νῦν δεῖξον ὡς οὐδὲν λέγει τὸ σωφρόνως τραφῆναι ("Show up all this humbug about gentle breeding"). But there is some evidence in the manuscripts for the far better φέρει which makes sense of βροτοῖσιν.

of the question for Euripides. To equal it one must turn to such Cambyses-vein stuff as *Phoen.* 1183–5.[1]

(iii) Vv. 744–9. This outburst against the murderous folly of mankind we have seen to express the spirit of the fourth, not of the fifth, century.[2] And, for all its excellence, it flies in the face of what the speaker has just said (734–6): if mortals act merely according to the will of Zeus, why round on them as fools?

(iv) The inept χρημάτων δ' εἰσὶν πόροι passage, 775–7.[3] It cannot be successfully deleted; unless, indeed, we end at δακρυρρόους. That makes an abrupt close of the whole scene, not in the least objectionable to modern taste, but nearly impossible for a Greek tragedian, whose final bit of moralizing seems indispensable.

Vv. 778–837. *Euripidean.*

Vv. 838–954. *Anonymous.* This passage opens with an unmistakable suture. Theseus enters speaking to some unidentified person three lines which have indeed a crisp business-like air, but of which no one has been able to make head or tail.[4] He alludes (we must surmise) to something that has happened in the anonymous, not the Euripidean, play. Then he jerkily breaks off, remarking "but now I see Adrastus", and at once invites him to address the youthful men among "these citizens", whom, apparently, he has brought along with him—for the surprise of their lives. Adrastus then delivers those five panegyrics the stupidity of which we have examined.[5] Since he leaves unnoticed the two Champions whose bodies are necessarily absent, Theseus offers to fill the gap. Amphiaraus, he remarks, has received manifest praise from the gods who carried him off alive into the earth's recesses. So far, well. But what has he to say of the other? "And Oedipus' son, even Polynices, I shall praise without falsehood. He was my guest-friend before he quitted Cadmus' town and removed to Argos in self-chosen exile." That is all! Where is the praise? "Call you this backing of your friends?" He turns to Adrastus without a pause: "But do you know what I wish to do concerning these (other corpses)?"

Two further aspects of Theseus' opening lines are to be noted here. First, after his suggestion that Adrastus should expound the virtues of the Champions, he proceeds (844 f.): "For I[6] saw their bold deeds, mightier

[1] Naturally bracketed by Murray after Nauck.
[2] See pp. 118–21.
[3] See p. 148.
[4] See the rewritings in Wecklein's Appendix, and p. 167 below.
[5] Pp. 126–9.
[6] To understand εἶδον as plural, referring to the νέοι just mentioned, is no help: they

than words can tell, wherewith they hoped to capture the city." This contradicts everything that we have heard of the attack on Thebes. It cannot belong to Euripides' account of that affair, and is in itself quite enough to damn at least the speech that contains it. Secondly, he adds a lengthy sarcasm (846–56) directed against the Choosing of the Champions in Aeschylus' *Septem*. This (it may be urged) is anything rather than evidence that Euripides did not write the passage: similar gibes of his are too well known to be cited. But this sneer differs from the others in its length: Euripides would have ended at 852; moreover, the remaining lines are very weak.

To the residue (933–54) of this scene there are three objections, the first slight, the second serious, the third overwhelming.

(i) The allusion to Capaneus' obsequies (934–9) reads like preparation for Euadne's episode, which we are about to condemn as non-Euripidean. There seems no other need to emphasize Capaneus.

(ii) Vv. 949–54 are fourth-century in feeling[1] and therefore (excellent as they are) belong to the Anonymous.

(iii) After the discussion (934 f.) of Capaneus we read:

Thes.: These others are my care. On with the funeral procession!
Adras.: Come, unhappy mothers, close to your children.
Thes.: That is a most unfitting speech, Adrastus.
Adras.: How so? Should not they who bare them touch their children?
Thes.: It would kill them to see their sons thus altered.[2]
Adras.: Aye, bitter is the sight of bloody-wounded corpses. [? *See below.*]
Thes.: Why then wouldst thou add to their sorrow?
Adras.: I yield. [*To the Mothers*] Ye must be patient and stay here: Theseus is right. But after we have given these bodies to the fire, ye shall embrace the bones.

Taken by itself, this passage is perfectly sound, in feeling and in dramatic technique also: it gives an admirable excuse for keeping the Chorus in

are Athenians, and cannot have watched the assault on Thebes. See further, below, p. 167, n. 1.

Grégoire (p. 135) writes: "Thésée a lui-même relevé les corps, et des positions où il les a trouvés, il peut conclure à la vaillance extraordinaire des Sept." This would in any case be doubtful, and is almost certainly contradicted by 665, which seems to show that the corpses have been collected by the Thebans before Theseus saw them.

[1] Cp. pp. 118–21.

[2] ἠλλοιωμένους. This gentle word of course points to something grimmer than the blood and wounds that some find in the next line: αἷμα κὠτειλαὶ νεκρῶν (so Murray, following Toup). But the MSS. L and P give κᾆμα (or καὶ ἅμα) τῷ τέλει νεκρῷ. See Wecklein *ad loc.* and Appendix. Probably we should read χἄμα τῷ τέλει νεκρῶν, with the sense: "Aye, bitter is the sight of a corpse, even when newly dead (much more, then, later)."

the orchestra, as the tragedians nearly always do. But what of the preceding Euripidean passage (798–836), where the Chorus not only utter lament over the dead, but actually embrace them, with the heart-broken approval of Adrastus, whom we now hear agreeing with Theseus and unmistakably implying that the Mothers have not earlier approached the bodies? These two passages cannot belong to the same play.

Vv. 955–79. *Euripidean.* Note especially 961 f.:

$$\pi\lambda\alpha\gamma\kappa\tau\grave{\alpha} \; \delta' \; \dot{\omega}\sigma\epsilon\acute{\iota} \; \tau\iota\varsigma \; \nu\epsilon\phi\acute{\epsilon}\lambda\alpha$$
$$\pi\nu\epsilon\upsilon\mu\acute{\alpha}\tau\omega\nu \; \dot{\upsilon}\pi\grave{o} \; \delta\upsilon\sigma\chi\acute{\iota}\mu\omega\nu \; \dot{\alpha}\acute{\iota}\sigma\sigma\omega.$$

Vv. 980–1164. *Anonymous.* This long portion, containing Euadne's scene and the Urn-Bearing, though excellent "theatre" and written, if not with distinction, yet with competence, must be judged non-Euripidean. Here and there from beginning to end it presents difficulties both grave and various, which (as it were) drag the whole fabric down.

(i) Euadne's scene violates all that we know concerning the facts of Athenian "stage"-presentation. Even if we suggest (very boldly) that the pyre of Capaneus and his widow's "towering rock" stand ready before the action begins,[1] we are contradicted by the Chorus, whose καί μὴν (980) should imply that something is noticed of a sudden—which is surely too ridiculous to postulate. Shall we, then, assume that while they sing the preceding lyric, facing the audience, sundry slaves have been erecting the pyre?[2] If such activities were admitted here, why was their usefulness ignored in other plays? Consider how great the increase in "modern realism" this freedom would have conferred on *Medea*,[3] *Heracles*,[4] or *Ion*,[5] to mention the first examples that come to mind.

Is it possible to resist the conclusion that this portion (if nothing else) was written by one of those dramatists mentioned by Aristotle,[6] who composed plays to be read, not acted? He could have erected both pyre and

---

[1] As in the medieval mystery-plays, where the Temple, Pilate's house, and other needed backgrounds stood ready in a long line, all but one being ignored during the visit of the Magi, the trial of Jesus, etc.

[2] We need not trouble (though the plural is strange after 936) about the ἀναθήματα of the other corpses which they tell us they see (982 f.). These are supposed invisible to the spectators (ἐκτὸς μελάθρων) and of course do not physically exist at all. Hartung, however, says (*Euripides Restitutus*, p. 99) that the pyres of both Capaneus and the rest were built up "in ipsa scena" and visibly blazing.

[3] Set up a throne, etc. to present Creon's house, and show his daughter's reception of the fatal gifts.

[4] Bring in a column or so, and depict more of Heracles' outbreak.

[5] The sensational banquet-scene would need a few tables and couches—very little compared with a pyre, and a burning pyre into the bargain.

[6] See p. 118.

rock with a stroke of his pen. But can he have been Euripides? None of our authorities, beginning with his contemporary Aristophanes, gives a hint of such "closet-plays"[1] for the fifth century.

(ii) Euadne's death is not merely a spectacular suicide, like that of Ajax, but an imitation of the Indian suttee, unknown to Greeks before the age of Alexander.[2]

(iii) After his daughter's death, Iphis laments (1080–1103) his own *deserted* wretchedness without a word of or to his wife, who stands listening as one of the Chorus.

(iv) We may glance, without undue rancour, at the ill-written vv. 1089 ff., into which Dr. Murray plunges two well-deserved daggers:

> εἰ δ' ἐς τόδ' ἦλθον κἀξεπειράθην τέκνων
> οἷον στέρεσθαι πατέρα γίγνεται τέκνων,
> οὐκ ἄν ποτ' ἐς τόδ' ἦλθον εἰς ὃ νῦν κακόν.

The repetitions are very bad as they stand, but they can be removed.[3]

(v) His final bitter remark (1109 ff.) about valetudinarianism could not have been so worded by anyone unread in Plato's *Republic*.[4]

(vi) In vv. 1115 f. the handmaids, whom we have banished from the Euripidean play, are suddenly remembered and asked for their very intermittent help.

(vii) The *commos* between the mothers and young sons of the Champions contains several oddities. Here occurs (1140–2) the assertion that the dead have departed both to Heaven and to Hades.[5] Moreover, although this Urn-Bearing[6] is full of the pathos that Euripides loved, we must note that it has been anticipated in the shorter Euripidean scene (798–836) where Adrastus brings the bodies for lamentation and embraces of the Mothers. Secondly, as we have seen,[7] five boys must confront seven grandmothers: again we think of Aristotle's closet-dramatist. Further, Theseus begins the next scene with words strongly suggesting that no Urn-Bearing *commos* has preceded (1166–7): "Adrastus and ye women of Argive race, behold these boys carrying in their hands the bodies of their noble fathers." This cannot but mean that he has just led them in. Finally, if it be maintained that we need this *commos* as preparation for

---

[1] Plays were certainly read then (cp. for instance *Frogs* 1109–14), but these were texts published after performance.
[2] See pp. 125 f.   [3] Cp. Wecklein's Appendix.
[4] See pp. 124 f.   [5] See p. 143.
[6] Since all but Capaneus are cremated on the same pyre (936) one does not see how the various sets of bones were distinguished and placed each in its appropriate urn. But this question occurred, perhaps, less easily to a spectator than to a reader.
[7] Pp. 114 f.

the importance that Athena's address is to give the sons, it may be replied that Theseus' words just quoted, and (still more) what he next says to them are enough.

Vv. 1165–1231. *Euripidean*, in all its parts and aspects.[1] Athena's exhortation to the boys, that they grow up and continue the vendetta, though put to shame by the humaner sentiments repeatedly uttered in the anonymous portions, is very like the barren senseless remarks that Euripides again and again allots to his epilogizing deities; nor is the blackmail plan impossible to such persons.[2]

Vv. 1232–4. *Anonymous*, if we are to take these words quite seriously.[3] It is, however, possible that they are careless writing of Euripides himself: "Let us take the oath" might (perhaps) mean "We will accompany you to the place where you will take the oath". The Chorus must be got out of the orchestra somehow.

This sorting-out[4] has given us eight passages from a Euripidean *Supplices*, which together make rather more than one-third (526 lines) of the average length. They offer the same plot[5] as our full text, and the plot which we should expect from Euripides on this theme; but with the omission of four elements (ousted by anonymous portions) that may fairly be called indispensable—something like 300 lines—and possibly[6] other passages, at whose contents it would be presumptuous to guess. The four elements (replaced in our text by anonymous work) are (i) Theseus' refusal to help the Suppliants; (ii) his altercation with the Theban Herald; (iii) his call to arms; (iv) a Messenger's narrative of the battle. The first and third would no doubt be brief; and, if we do not shrink from increasing the scissors-work, we may well take over into the Euripidean portion relevant passages from those assigned above to the Anonymous. Nor is it impossible to deal in some such way with the altercation and the Messenger's speech. In the former, we might cut away the objectionable

---

[1] Even 1219 need not trouble us if we emend as proposed in p. 149, n. 1.

[2] Her "mistake" about the number of pyres (p. 115) is now easily explained. The two pyres (934–6) belong to an anonymous portion.

[3] Cp. pp. 116 f.

[4] Is the stitchery too complex? Those who can credit Euripides with more dubious work than we have found it possible to attribute to him may perhaps contrive a simpler scheme, conceivably no more than two great masses, one by him, one by another poet: it would be interesting to study their results.

[5] A slight plot, but the story is simple. Its *peripeteia* occurs unusually near the beginning: Aethra's great speech of intervention (297–331). The remainder is a presentation of what ensues therefrom.

[6] Possibly: for this work may well have been abnormally brief.

matter (that is, nearly all) of our text and pick out bits for our purpose: but that will strike many as too reminiscent of Mrs. Todgers' method with the "collation" in *Martin Chuzzlewit*. In the Messenger's speech, to delete a few insertions (at any rate Theseus' impossible feats with his club) is an easier and more highly esteemed procedure.

The drama which thus begins to take shape before us is in structure, matter, and language *ex hypothesi* perfectly Euripidean. Nevertheless, it offers two grave difficulties already described.[1] The opening tableau apparently needs a curtain, which was unknown in the fifth century. The chorus consisted of seven persons only, a number incredible for the Dionysiac theatre of that period. We must meet these objections by assuming that Euripides did not compose his play with such a performance in mind—that he addressed a private audience.[2] In this way both our problems are solved. The tableau could be made ready before the guests entered the room or courtyard. None of these would be scandalized by a miniature chorus.[3] The hitherto overwhelming objections[4] to the belief that all seven Mothers were present now vanish. Euripides conceived the excellent and natural idea of making "the bereaved mothers" —simply as such, and with no particularity—appeal to Athens, supporting Adrastus as a chorus. That is all. It was not he who wrote those absurd speeches about the dead heroes, dragging in the name of Polynices and so turning all eyes to seek Iocasta among the choristers, or the Urn-Bearing in which five boys approach seven grandmothers. He left the members of his chorus as undifferentiated as his bacchants or Trojan women, and quietly unifies[5] them in the phrase uttered by Theseus (1165): "ye women of Argive race", as most of them actually were.[6]

Here let us turn back[7] and examine the current opinion that Euripides

[1] See pp. 112-15, 116-18.

[2] Cp. pp. 33-35, 118.

[3] It seems likely that for non-official displays seven was even the regular number: the story in Diodorus (see above, p. 117, n. 3.) implies as much.

[4] See pp. 115 f.

[5] This statement does not really endorse Lesky and Wilamowitz (see above, pp. 112, 116), for they have in mind the whole composite *Supplices*, which contains clashes between the number seven and situations that make seven absurd. In the Euripidean passages there is no difficulty—not even in vv. 811-17, where the Mothers embrace the corpses. The corpses also are seven. It must be clearly realized that the Euripidean text presents us with nothing more definite than certain Argives (cp. 957, 965) who are seven mothers and their seven sons, not further described or identified. This, it must be owned, is suddenly contradicted (as regards the sons) at the close (1217 f.), when Athena both names Tydeus and implies (what everyone knew) that he was no Argive. But such "snags" must be endured from epilogizing deities in Euripides.

[6] Nevertheless, this is a bold distortion, as was noted on pp. 115, 145.

[7] See p. 150.

was led to write this drama by the conduct of the Boeotians, who after Delium (424 B.C.) refused to let the Athenians take up their dead for burial unless they quitted Boeotian soil; and that Athena's advice to Theseus was inspired by the alliance made with Argos in 420 B.C.

Apart altogether from the strong evidence that a good deal of our text was written much later than Delium (evidence that would probably have been recognized at once had not scholars been obsessed by that battle and that treaty), even the miniature play that is all we are leaving to Euripides need not refer to those events. Certainly it may so refer, but we cannot affirm it with any confidence. Aeschylus' *Eleusinians* dealt with the same theme, but he knew nothing of Delium and its consequences: why insist that his successor had them in mind? Still less need we so insist concerning the Anonymous.

Thucydides' account of the Boeotian refusal reads strangely. It is hesitating and indeed muddled—through the fault of the Boeotians, no doubt. First, they charged the invaders "to quit the temple if they would bring off their own".[1] That is the nearest they come to refusing unconditional consent. Moreover, the Athenians have not yet asked for it,[2] though, of course, the request would be in all minds: nevertheless, they interpret the obscure phrase, neuter gender included, with complete precision,[3] and call upon the enemy not to demand evacuation of Boeotia as the price of their consent. The Boeotian answer is woefully involved, but they apparently[4] insist on their improper demand. Then comes the attack on the fortified temple and the expulsion of the Athenian remnant. After this, when an Athenian herald arrived again[5] about the dead, "the Boeotians gave them up and no longer made the same reply".[6] Why should they? Boeotia was now rid of Athenian troops. The whole story falters and mumbles. When we note, further, that Diodorus,[7] who gives a full account of the battle, says no word about the dispute, we begin to suspect that (for whatever reason) this affair made little noise in Athens even at the time. Thus Euripides' genuine work may have had

---

[1] IV. 97. 4: ἐκ τοῦ ἱεροῦ ἀπιόντας ἀποφέρεσθαι τὰ σφέτερα αὐτῶν.

[2] Cp. IV. 97. 2.

[3] IV. 98. 7: τούς τε νεκροὺς πολὺ μειζόνως ἐκείνους ἀντὶ ἱερῶν ἀξιοῦντας ἀποδιδόναι ἀσεβεῖν ἢ τοὺς μὴ ἐθέλοντας ἱεροῖς τὰ πρέποντα κομίζεσθαι. The Boeotian disingenuousness is branded in the word wherewith they begin their next sentence: σαφῶς τε ἐκέλευον σφίσιν εἰπεῖν κτέ.

[4] IV. 99. They adhere to their absurdly evasive neuter, never mentioning the corpses. (ἐν ᾗ τοὺς νεκροὺς ... συνέβη is of course Thucydides' own "footnote".)

[5] On his first attempt he had been turned back by a Boeotian herald (97. 2).

[6] IV. 101. 1.

[7] XII. 69 f.

no connexion at all with the historical Boeotian demand;[1] possibly he never heard of it.

To pursue (for what it is worth) this topic of allusions to contemporary events: we can find other[2] such refusals in the period between Euripides and the Anonymous. In his speech against Eratosthenes (403 B.C.), Lysias says that the Athenian oligarchs denied burial to the corpses of their democratic enemies "from the Piraeus".[3] A few years later (395 B.C.), the celebrated Lysander, with a thousand others, died fighting against a Theban force at Haliartus in Boeotia. King Pausanias came upon the scene just too late for the battle. Xenophon[4] relates that on reflection he preferred not to renew the fight. "So for all these reasons they decided to take up the dead under a truce. But the Thebans announced that they would not surrender the dead, save on condition that [Pausanias and his troops] quitted the country...." Except that the invaders were Spartans,

---

[1] Some have held that the Messenger's speech—which has been assigned above to the Anonymous, not to Euripides—more or less closely describes the Battle of Delium. So Goossens (pp. 12 ff.), who says, moreover, that Euripides criticizes the Athenian tactics (p. 12): "C'est donc bien un récit de la bataille de Délion, mais la bataille refaite par Euripide, et gagnée." This appears baseless. To mention nothing else, no four-horse chariots (*Suppl.* 667, 674–9) were used in the historical engagement. Diodorus, it is true, says (*ut sup.*): προεμάχοντο δὲ πάντων οἱ παρ' ἐκείνοις [sc. τοῖς Βοιωτοῖς] ἡνίοχοι καὶ παραβάται καλούμενοι, ἄνδρες ἐπίλεκτοι τριακόσιοι. (These names may have suggested the lines of the *Supplices* just mentioned.) But Giles (*ut sup.*, p. 98) writes: "The names ... show that the band was really a survival from a time when the heroic methods of fighting were still in vogue and might therefore be attributed by Euripides without difficulty to the heroic period." That is, the names ἡνίοχοι and παραβάται were anachronisms in 424 B.C.; and for no period do they imply *four*-horse chariots.

[2] We must not, however, seek a parallel among the atrocities committed by Alexander of Pherae. There seems to be no authority for Meineke's idea (see below, p. 172): note the silence of Diodorus (XV. 75. 1), Plutarch (*Pelop.* 29), Pausanias (VI. v. 2), and Aelian (*V.H.* 40). Nor does it appear wise to accept the statement (in, e.g., *The Cambridge Ancient History*, vol. VI, p. 264) that Philip of Macedon after Chaeronea at first refused to let the Thebans take up their dead. Of all ancient writers who discuss the battle, only Justin (IX. 4) seems to have heard this story. His account (written probably in the Antonine Age) is so muddled as to be incredible. After telling us that Philip behaved with extreme decorum—*quantum in illo fuit, ita vicit ut victorem nemo sentiret*—he goes on: *Thebanorum porro non solum captivos, verum etiam interfectorum sepulturam vendidit*. The last words obviously imply that Philip at first refused the burial and had to be bribed before he would change his mind. But Justin does not mean them so: he clearly (*porro*) intends them as an instance of magnanimity. He has no doubt misunderstood Pompeius Trogus, of whose history (written under Augustus and now lost) his work is an abridgement. Diodorus (XVI. 86) practically denies that Philip made such a refusal: μετὰ δὲ τὴν μάχην ὁ Φίλιππος τρόπαιον στήσας καὶ τοὺς νεκροὺς εἰς ταφὴν συγχωρήσας κτέ.

[3] *Contra Eratosth.* 129: οὐδὲ ταφῆς τῆς νομιζομένης εἴασαν τυχεῖν. Lysias of course had personal knowledge of all these events, and addressed an audience equally well informed.

[4] *Hell.* III. v. 23 f.

THE *SUPPLICES* 165

not Athenians, this situation exactly repeats what followed the Battle of Delium. If a play needs the stimulus of actual events, here was an adequate[1] stimulus to compose our post-Euripidean *Supplices*.

Nor need the epilogue be so firmly tied to the treaty of 420 B.C. Alliances that meet the case well enough were made between Athens and Argos in the fourth century. About 343 B.C. "the Athenians... succeeded in... securing at least the nominal alliance of... the Argives"[2] when they squared up to Philip. Twenty years later Argos engaged in the Lamian War (323–321 B.C.) together with Athens and other states.

Even less value attaches to the idea that our *Supplices* contains a vigorous recommendation of Alcibiades.[3] It is of course likely that when Adrastus says (190 ff.) to Theseus concerning Athens: "In thee she hath a young man as her excellent shepherd, in need whereof many cities have perished, lacking a general", the poet is thinking of some contemporary young soldier and statesman. But why should that be Alcibiades? If we know anything about Euripides, it is that he hated selfish, cynical cleverness, and that he put his faith in the middle class, from which Alcibiades was utterly and naturally alien. The story that Euripides wrote a dithyramb to celebrate his chariot-victory (420/419 B.C.) at Olympia has but dubious authority.[4] Here again we may doubt if research is worth while. In 421 there were surely more young men than one whom the cap would fit, and in the days of the Anonymous lived the greatest exemplar of combined youth, statesmanship, and soldiership whom the world had seen or was to see. That Alexander is the real subject of our passage we need not affirm; but we must have far less confidence in asserting that it is Alcibiades.

Finally, we should look at a passage of Aristotle that (relevant or not) was almost certainly written before the anonymous play, for Aristotle died in 322. "In such democracies each man lives as he chooses—'according to his fancy', in Euripides' words."[5] Some have taken the phrase εἰς

[1] Many years old, it is true; but of course the author needed no such incentive for a play about the obsequies of the Seven.

[2] *Cambridge Ancient History*, vol. VI, p. 249.

[3] Held, for example, by Nestle (*Euripides, der Dichter der griechischen Aufklärung* (1901), p. 15). "Wilamowitz and others consider it practically a party pamphlet in the interest of Alcibiades" (Giles, *ut sup.*, p. 95). But the one argument for Alcibiades worth a moment's attention is this, that in Thucydides VI. xviii. 6 he mentions the three classes, as does Theseus (238–45): νομίσατε... ὁμοῦ δὲ τό τε φαῦλον καὶ τὸ μέσον καὶ τὸ πάνυ ἀκριβὲς ἂν ξυγκραθὲν μάλιστ' ἂν ἰσχύειν. Even this is of little use, for Theseus says that the middle class alone saves the state.

[4] Plutarch, *Demosth.* 1, says only ὡς ὁ πολὺς λόγος κρατεῖ.

[5] *Politics* 1310ᵃ32 ff.: ὥστε ζῇ ἐν ταῖς τοιαύταις δημοκρατίαις ἕκαστος ὡς βούλεται, καὶ εἰς ὃ χρῄζων, ὥς φησιν Εὐριπίδης. "According to his fancy" is Jowett's translation. The

ὁ χρῄζων for a (corrupt) reminiscence of *Supplices* 440. That is part of an anonymous passage where Theseus, in his description of the complete Athenian democracy, mentions freedom of debate and says that the man who wishes to give counsel wins glory. No likeness exists between that passage and the irresponsible freedom to which alone—however we emend the corrupt words—Aristotle unmistakably alludes; and therefore we cannot regard it as evidence about the *Supplices*.[1]

After this long digression, let us return to our two tragedies. We have described the Euripidean: the anonymous remains.

At the outset we must note that it contains a great deal of competent, and a certain amount of excellent, verse. Its theme of course is that of the Euripidean play: we find Theseus' refusal to aid the Suppliants; a brief passage (263–70) that corresponds dramatically to Aethra's appeal, and may have been originally much longer than our clearly incomplete address;[2] the Herald's message forbidding Athenian interference, Theseus' defiant reply and call to arms; the Messenger's account of the battle and some ensuing comment; the Funeral Speeches and the Urn-Bearing. In addition, it contains a good deal that is the reverse of obligatory: the intrusive handmaids (71–86, 1115 ff.); Theseus' "theodicy" (195–218); the muddle about political institutions (403–55); and Euadne's suttee (980–1103).

This anonymous play—perhaps named *Hiketides*, quite possibly not—thus appears to have resembled the Euripidean in its outline, but with additions entirely its own: some *in themselves* entirely or almost entirely respectable, such as the "theodicy", the battle, and the Urn-Bearing; others utterly absurd, such as the Funeral Speech.

The next question, however, is : May not this "anonymous play" have been in fact no play at all, but only a series of addenda to the Euripidean? Two peculiarities have been noted in the latter. First, it was probably

---

grammar of χρῄζων must be explained (if at all) with Newman (*ad loc.*) by understanding τυγχάνει! Even so εἶς ὁ is very hard: Susemihl's *apparatus* (p. 554) shows how it has puzzled editors. εἶς ὁ χρῄζων is far better Greek, but makes no sense in the context.

[1] Nauck places the Aristotelian passage among the fragments of "uncertain" plays (ed. 1, fr. 883; ed. 2, fr. 891).

[2] It begins in the middle of a sentence, ὃς Πέλοπος. . . . The six lines with which it ends are a fine piece of fourth-century comment, precisely in Adrastus' vein (cp. 184 ff., 744 ff., 949 ff.), found nowhere else in the words of chorus or coryphaeus. It is extremely probable that these lines originally belonged to Adrastus (though of course they do not suit what he has just said in the Euripidean play) and that he made yet another long appeal, now almost obliterated by the queen's.

THE *SUPPLICES* 167

much briefer than the average: the Anonymous may have wished to give it normal length? Secondly, its chorus contains but seven persons: perhaps he invented the handmaids (eight in that case) merely to secure the official number? Did some later dramatist take it in hand to render the Euripidean work literally "presentable"? This idea, at first sight tempting, is disproved by what then become clashes between the two writings: the appeal (263 ff.) of Adrastus (or the Coryphaeus?) side by side with Aethra's (297 ff.); Theseus' assertion (844 f.) that he witnessed the prowess of the Seven Champions, which contradicts the implications of his first talk[1] with Adrastus; and other inconsistencies.

Thirdly: in any case, why does the anonymous play contain what we have called rubbish? That is much easier to answer than it may seem at the first glance: for the anonymous play, *taken by itself*, contains (after all) few absurdities. Most of the stumbling-blocks that astonish us are faults of our existing play when assumed to be homogeneous: passages where (as we now view these twelve hundred-odd lines) the Anonymous contradicts Euripides, or writes far less well than he, or voices ideas, emotions, or knowledge that belong to a later age. Our "received" text again and again stultifies itself; but this merely shows that it is not "a text" at all in the normal meaning of that term. There remains but one[2] foolish passage that cannot (so far as we have come at present) be accepted with little misgiving or none if attributed to another and inferior dramatist: Adrastus' Funeral Speech. To discuss which Athenian citizens are pointed at in this farrago, without asking what archon and what audience would tolerate it, is to distort critical perspective.

No archon, no judge in the theatre of Dionysus, was invited to "give a chorus" or the official prize to a drama containing this monster: of that we may be sure. Our anonymous drama must have been one of the closet-

---

[1] He there speaks throughout as if his knowledge of the campaign were drawn from hearsay. Dobree banished the difficulty by reading ἰδὼν τὰ τούτων (ἰδών referring to Adrastus: cp. ἐπιστήμων γὰρ εἶ just before), Schenkl by reading εἶδες γὰρ αὐτῶν. But whence came the *difficilior lectio*? It seems much better to assume that the Anonymous in his earlier scenes made Theseus somehow directly cognizant of the campaign.

We can obviously take εἶδον as plural (though εἴσομαι κτέ. in 845 f. is rather strongly against this); but that makes no difference to the argument (cp. p. 157). Schmid (p. 458, n. 6) seeks to mend our text by (quite legitimately) reading ἱστορῶ for εἰσορῶ and by two incredible statements: that ἐκεῖ is temporal in opposition to νῦν and that σε means the Mothers.

[2] Certain others are on a different plane: vv. 714–17, Theseus' club; vv. 744–9 contradict 734–6; vv. 928 f. are not encomium; vv. 1140 ff., the identification of Aether and Hades. Foolish they are, beyond question, but of tiny scope and utterly unlike those products of what might seem constructive idiocy whereby our composite text is defaced: they can be set down to pure carelessness. (But see further p. 154, n. 8.)

plays already mentioned.[1] When a man writes for the delectation[2] only of himself and those indulgent friends or "amateurs of the curious" to whom he feels he can hand copies "without fear of being misunderstood", he may permit himself esoteric references and outrageous whimsies on which even Aristophanes would not have ventured when writing for the public. Beyond doubt, the Anonymous was aiming at contemporary Athenians, and we can easily believe that his coterie relished sundry "exquisite" strokes of portraiture. But who were the originals, and who the coterie-members, we cannot know.

Only thus shall we make sense (such as it is) of this astonishing scene. No other passage so unmistakably demands that explanation, but we of course ask whether any others, though less odd, become more interesting, perhaps more intelligible, in the light of it. Less odd indeed, but odd enough in all conscience, is the assertion that Theseus founded the complete democracy which in fact was created by Pericles. Its absurdity grows more intelligible if we suppose it propounded to some pretentious but ignorant clique.[3] Theseus' theodicy, or disquisition on a benevolent Providence, is, strictly in itself, quite beyond censure. But it is ludicrously intrusive. Moreover, the king devotes three lines to stating that he speaks in opposition to some unnamed pessimist thinker.[4] This sounds very like an echo from a discussion circle.[5] We can now solve those grave difficulties of stage-management, the need for a curtain[6] and the presentation of Euadne's scene.[7] This writer, being one of the "anagnostic" dramatists mentioned by Aristotle,[8] would have no trouble at all. Moreover, he could imagine as many handmaids as he chose.

Can we identify the Anonymous? It has been shown that he wrote his play in the fourth century at the earliest. Next, a *terminus post quem* is

---

[1] See pp. 118, 159.

[2] This writer increases it by his choice of poor Adrastus as orator. Like Euripides (161), he thinks Adrastus a fool (219–25, 248), but now suddenly dubs him a man of wisdom and knowledge (841–3). Cp. p. 143.

[3] Such ideas were in the air, as we have seen. This interest in politics may explain also why the three classes are dragged in (238–45) with such irrelevance.

[4] Nestle (*Euripides*, pp. 66–72) discusses the "Theodicee" at length. He identifies the pessimist with Prodicus (so Welcker, *Rhein. Mus.* vol. I, p. 622), "dessen düstere Lebensauffassung aus dem pseudo-platonischen *Axiochos* (Kap. 4–9 pp. 366c–369c; *Fr.* 2 Mullach) bekannt ist". (In n. 42 Nestle says: "Daß die Theodicee des Theseus nicht ernst zu nehmen ist, zeigen schon seine gänzlich widersprechenden Worte 549 ff.") Bengl (*ut sup.*, pp. 7 f.) has much interesting matter on theories of the origin of culture.

[5] It is not over-fanciful to paraphrase ἄλλοισι δὴ 'πόνησ' ἁμιλληθεὶς λόγῳ τοιῷδε thus: "Let me offer a summary of a speech I made the other day before our debating society." [6] See pp. 116 f.

[7] See pp. 159 f. [8] See p. 118.

THE *SUPPLICES* 169

given by the suttee-passage: Alexander entered India in 326; and the *terminus ante quem* is 218, the year of the Dium incident and the quotation from our text. It is reasonable to date that text early in the period 326–218, the fourth-century tone being still marked: we may suggest the year 300. Can we point to a known dramatist who was probably or possibly working then and who unquestionably wrote a play or plays concerned with refusal of obsequies and an appeal against it?

The obvious answer is "Moschion".[1] To him Stobaeus (late in the fifth century after Christ) in his anthology attributes the lines, insisting on burial of the slain warriors, that appear in the Euripidean *corpus* as *Supplices* 531–6.[2] This of course by no means settles the matter: Stobaeus may have blundered, though that is a weak explanation; or the Moschion passage which Stobaeus quoted may have fallen out, together with the name 'Euripides' prefixed to the ἐάσατ' ἤδη extract[3]—again not a strong argument; or these verses may indeed be Moschion's, but may have crept into our *Supplices* from the margin where they at first stood as an illustrative note: that is better, for such accretions are of course frequent.[4] Nevertheless, Stobaeus provides at least a good excuse for examining more closely Moschion's right to identification with our Anonymous.

All that we know of him for certain is that he was an Athenian and that his reputation as a dramatist stood high.[5] No ancient authority gives

[1] In addition to the general histories of Greek tragedy see the monographs of F. G. Wagner (*De Moschionis poetae tragici vita ac fabularum reliquiis commentatio*, Breslau, 1846) and of Meineke ("Der tragische Dichter Moschion," *Monatsber. d. Berl. Ak.*, 1855, pp. 102–11), and Ribbeck's article "Ueber einige historische Dramen der Griechen" (*Rhein. Mus.*, N.F., vol. XXX, pp. 147 ff.). F. Schramm (*Tragicorum Graecorum hellenisticae, quae dicitur, aetatis fragmenta* (Münster, 1929), pp. 63–83) gives an excellent report on more recent work (with useful contributions of his own) concerning details of Greek usage, emendations, and the like; for his discussion of Moschion's date, see below.

[2] *Flor.* 123. 3.

[3] Meineke, pp. 113 f. His suggestion springs from his belief that this passage cannot be Moschion's because of the resolved foot in its penultimate line: nowhere else in the fragments (all iambic) do we find resolution. Wilamowitz (*Analecta Euripidea*, p. 101) follows Meineke. See below, pp. 177 f.

[4] Excise 531–6, and our text runs with perfect smoothness.

[5] So much is proved by the silver goblet discovered at Boscoreale near Pompeii in 1925: cp. Michaelis (*Preuβ. Jahrb.* (1896), pp. 41, etc.), and de Villefosse (*Monuments et mémoires de l'Acad. des Inscrr. et Belles-Lettres*, vol. V, 1899). He appears thereon with Sophocles, and is named Μοσχίων Ἀθηναῖος.

The statuette that Meineke adduces (p. 111) by no means certainly commemorates our Moschion, for the name was common; and the Attic coin (Wagner, p. 8) which also bears that name is certainly too late for this purpose, because the "new style" coins with magistrates' names began to be issued only in 229 B.C. (if not much later: see M. B. Thompson, *Hesperia*, vol. X (1941), pp. 199–236).

him a date. Some modern scholars place him in the fourth century, some in the third: the year 300 B.C. to which we assigned the work of our Anonymous agrees well enough with dates[1] suggested by more than one of them.

About his tragedies[2] our knowledge is fuller, but still meagre; Stobaeus gives three titles: *Themistocles* (one fragment of two and a half lines), *Telephus* (four lines), *Pheraeans*[3] (one line). In addition we have nine fragments from unnamed[4] plays, all from Stobaeus except fr. 12, two lines quoted by Clement of Alexandria.[5] By far the longest remnant is fr. 7 (from an unnamed tragedy), which in thirty-three lines sketches the rise of civilization,[6] leading in the last four verses to a very particular feature thereof, the custom of interring the dead:

> κἀκ τοῦδε τοὺς θανόντας ὥρισεν νόμος
> τύμβοις καλύπτειν κἀπιμοιρᾶσθαι κόνιν

---

[1] Moschion's *floruit* is placed about 393 by Kayser (*Historia critica tragoediae Graecae*, pp. 298 f.); about 328 by Wagner (p. 9); by Ribbeck (p. 152) in "the latter half of the fourth century"; about 370 by Meineke (p. 111)—if, as he remarks, his idea concerning Xenophon *Hell.* VI. iv. 33 ff. (see below, p. 172) is right: in any case "long before Alexander". Their chief reason is that a Moschion was often derided by comic dramatists of that century. The first to set him in the third century was R. J. Walker (*Addenda Scenica* (1923), pp. 221 ff.) who thinks his metrical technique reminiscent of Sositheus, a member of the "Pleiad" under Ptolemy Philadelphus (283–246 B.C.). He was followed by Wilamowitz (with some hesitation, *Hellenistische Dichtung in der Zeit des Kallimachos* (1924), vol. II, p. 149), by Körte (*Die hellenistische Dichtung* (1925), p. 216) and by Schramm (pp. 66 f., 82 f.) who is approved by Diehl (*s.v.* in Pauly–Wissowa). Schramm offers arguments (of little weight) for placing Moschion in the Hellenistic Age—from the death of Alexander (323) to Actium (31); this, it will be noticed, does not exclude our year 300.

[2] It has been found most convenient to keep the numeration of Moschion's fragments given in Nauck's first edition. That followed by him later, and by others, combines 3 (κενὸν... σκιάν) and 4 (ζῶντας... εὐσεβές) into 3: thus the old 5 becomes 4, etc.; but 11 (ἐάσατ'... λαβεῖν) is omitted, and 12 (κεῖνος... βίον) becomes 10.

[3] *Men of Pherae* or *Women of Pherae*? Stobaeus gives the genitive as Φεραιῶν (fem.); Meineke (p. 102), followed by Nauck, prefers Φεραίων (masc.). The name, whatever its gender, refers to the chorus.

[4] This of course does not mean that none of them belongs to one or another of the three plays whose names we have. See below.

[5] *Strom.* VI. 745: Μοσχίων ὁ κωμικὸς [sic] γράφει·

> κεῖνος δ' ἁπάντων ἐστὶ μακαριώτατος,
> ὃς διὰ τέλους ζῶν ὁμαλὸν ἤσκησεν βίον.

Meineke (p. 108) rejects this attribution on the ground of the three resolved feet: see pp. 177 f. below.

[6] This puts one in mind of Theseus' "sermon" (195 ff.), but the basic ideas are quite different. The Anonymous refers human benefits to the watchful kindness of "some deity", Moschion to Time (18) and a choice (20–2) between the "study" (μέριμνα) of Prometheus—whatever that means—, necessity, and the effect of experience (τριβή) on man's nature.

THE *SUPPLICES*

νεκροῖς ἀθάπτοις,[1] μηδ' ἐν ὀφθαλμοῖς ἐᾶν
τῆς πρόσθε θοίνης μνημόνευμα δυσσεβοῦς.[2]

"And thenceforth custom ordained that they should hide the dead in tombs, spreading dust upon unburied corpses, and not leave in sight a reminder of their former wicked banquets." This ending proves that Moschion's play was concerned wholly or largely with a refusal to grant obsequies and a vigorous condemnation of that refusal, precisely as in the *Supplices*. Moreover, the fact that a speech on human progress abruptly ends with a very precise moral recalls Theseus' behaviour in rounding on Adrastus (219 ff.) at the close of his own remarks on civilization.

Concerning *Telephus* nothing needs to be said here. *Themistocles* is naturally assumed to have dealt with Salamis,[3] especially as its one fragment is appropriate to that victory: "In the glens a great pine-branch is cloven by a little axe, and a scanty force conquers a myriad of spearmen."

The Pheraeans seems far more important for us. True, we have but one verse quoted as belonging to it: κενὸν θανόντος ἀνδρὸς αἰκίζειν σκιάν, "'tis folly to outrage a dead man's shadow". Still, our fragments from plays unnamed, few as they are, contain more on the subject. The close of the longest has already been quoted; to it must be added three others. Fr. 4 reads: ζῶντας κολάζειν, οὐ θανόντας, εὐσεβές, "piety bids us chastise not the dead, but the living". Fr. 8 says:

τί κέρδος οὐκέτ' ὄντας αἰκίζειν νεκρούς ;
τί τὴν ἄναυδον γαῖαν ὑβρίζειν πλέον ;
ἐπὴν γὰρ ἡ κρίνουσα καὶ τὰς ἡδονὰς
καὶ τἀνιαρὰ φροῦδος αἴσθησις φθαρῇ,
τὸ σῶμα κωφοῦ τάξιν εἴληφεν πέτρου.

"What profits it to outrage the dead that are no more? What boots it to insult the voiceless earth? For as soon as the sense that judges pleasure and pain has vanished in destruction, the body ranks no higher than a deaf stone".[4] Finally, fr. 11 (= *Supp.* 531-6), though of contested authorship, treats the same idea. Are we justified in adding all these fragments

---

[1] So Meineke for the MS. νεκρούς τ' ἀθάπτους (gov. by ἐᾶν).

[2] So Valckenaer for the MS. δυσσεβές.

[3] Ribbeck (pp. 147 ff.), however, prefers a portrayal of Themistocles as a suppliant in the house of King Admetus (cp. Thuc. I. 136), and offers an attractive sketch of such a play; he also suggests Themistocles' death and burial.

[4] The spongy composition of this passage reminds us of many places in our Anonymous. Its second line practicaly echoes the first; φροῦδος is unneeded with φθαρῇ; the long phrase ἡ κρίνουσα ... αἴσθησις means no more than the one word ψυχή.

to *The Pheraeans*?[1] To do so is natural, especially if we lay emphasis on the fewness of Moschion's plays[2] and argue that he was unlikely to devote two of them to this subject. But though we hear of only three titles, can we depend on our ignorance? Still it may be worth while to assume, if only for the moment, that all these passages belong to *The Pheraeans* and ask whether we can discover more about that work.

One piece of evidence offers itself: the title. This play concerned the Thessalian city of Pherae. Welcker,[3] who takes the name as *Women of Pherae*, thought that Moschion treated the same subject as Euripides in his *Alcestis*, the action of which passes in that town: the chorus was female, however, not male as in *Alcestis*. This guess is easily confuted by Wagner,[4] who rejects also Kayser's idea[5] that Moschion portrayed the sufferings inflicted on Pherae by Conon and Pharnabazus, adding that he himself declines to guess the subject of this tragedy. Meineke's theory is at first sight more attractive. He finds its basis in the career of Alexander, despot of Pherae (369–358 B.C.), and notorious for his atrocities. Pointing to Xenophon's account[6] of the family murders, he says that Alexander after slaying Polyphron refused him burial; whereupon the Athenians, who were friends of Alexander at the opening of his reign,[7] asked him to permit his victim's obsequies; the fragments quoted above belong to the plea addressed by an Athenian envoy to Alexander.[8] Unfortunately Meineke has to introduce the refusal itself with the words "so it seems"; nor does he say why the Athenians intervened.[9]

Such flimsy conjectures have no value.[10] So far as Moschion himself and his commentators go, nothing is known about this play save that it had a chorus of Pheraean men or women. Do our own earlier inquiries help? For of course we ask ourselves whether by any chance *The Pheraeans* can be that play of which we found large masses in the *Supplices*. Certainly

[1] So Meineke (102 f.) who would further add fr. 5 (ὅμως τό γ' ὀρθὸν ... παρρησίαν) and fr. 6 (μόνον σὺ θυμοῦ ... λεχθήσεται), followed immediately by the long fr. 7.

[2] As does Meineke.

[3] *Die griechischen Tragödien*, p. 1049.

[4] *Ut sup.*, p. 14: it is contradicted by the one unquestionable fragment (κενόν κτέ).

[5] *Ut sup.*, pp. 298 f. The suggestion is a mare's-nest. Both Kayser and Wagner, who discuss Xen. *Hell.* IV. viii. 7, confuse Pherae in Thessaly with Pharae in Laconia.

[6] *Hell.* VI. iv. 33 ff.

[7] Dem. XXIII (*Contra Aristocr.*) 660. See also my *Greek Comedy*, p. 51.

[8] Meineke, pp. 105 f.

[9] Ribbeck (p. 153) also makes this objection; but he accepts Meineke's idea as correct in the main and develops it at length, without (however) showing definite cause for thinking of Alexander's story in the first instance.

[10] I have not thought it worth while to discuss Iason of Pherae, the longest account of whose death was given by Conon (Photius, *Bibl.* 186).

THE *SUPPLICES*

not: *The Pheraeans*—this at least we learn from its title—dealt with Thessalian affairs, whereas the masses in question unmistakably treat the story of the Seven against Thebes. Must we not leave *The Pheraeans* to its fate with a solitary surviving line, and regard those other fragments that for the sake of argument we assigned to it as not after all belonging thereto but floating loose; and so heap them upon what we tore out of the *Supplices*, thus adding forty-five verses to our non-Euripidean matter? We then have on our hands two preachments about the progress of civilization; but (as we saw) they differ greatly.

At this point let us pause to realize exactly what we are discussing. The suggestions are: (*a*) Moschion wrote a normal tragedy (which may be tentatively named *Supplices*); (*b*) from this certain large portions, by us hitherto called anonymous, were extracted and imposed upon the brief but technically complete Euripidean play; some of them ousting Euripidean matter; (*c*) of the passages quoted by Stobaeus as fragments of Moschion some belonged, like the portions just mentioned, to Moschion's *Supplices*.

Our business at this moment, then, is to see whether the "burial" fragments of Moschion can with tolerable ease be fitted into our "anonymous" portions. They are four:[1] fr. 4 (ζῶντας κολάζειν . . ., one line), fr. 7 (πρῶτον δ' ἄνειμι . . ., 33 lines), fr. 8 (τί κέρδος . . ., 5 lines), fr. 11 (ἐάσατ' ἤδη . . ., 6 lines). The last we shall leave where it stands (531–6) in our text.[2] The other three also, because of their contents, must be placed rather early: at latest before Theseus' call to arms (586 ff.). Two of them, frr. 4 and 8, can hardly be addressed to anyone save the Theban Herald, being not only argument, but reproof. We cannot well assign them to Theseus, who has already a long and vigorous passage (531–58) of the same tenor; but they suit Adrastus excellently. When does he thus address the Herald? Where but at v. 513, a place to which we have already[3] taken serious exception? His outburst, cut short not so ruthlessly soon, and fitted with a brief introduction, might then read somewhat like this:

ὦ παγκάκιστε, ⟨λῆξον αἰσχίστων ἐπῶν,
μέμνησο δ' ὧν ἄνθρωπος, ὥστε σωφρόνως

---

[1] Excluding fr. 3, κενὸν θανόντος ἀνδρὸς αἰκίζειν σκιάν, because Stobaeus quotes it from *The Pheraeans* by name. This exclusion means, apparently, that after all we must credit Moschion with two plays on a dispute about burial. Apparently: for we cannot with confidence describe a whole drama on the strength of a single line.

[2] Nauck is not justified in calling its position "locus incommodus"; but he is trying to discover some reason for accepting Stobaeus' attribution of it to Moschion.

[3] Pp. 142 f.

> τἀγαθὰ φέρεσθαι μηδὲ μωρίᾳ πεσεῖν.⟩
> τί κέρδος οὐκέτ' ὄντας αἰκίζειν νεκρούς;
> τί τὴν ἄναυδον γαῖαν ὑβρίζειν πλέον;
> ἐπὴν γὰρ ἡ κρίνουσα καὶ τὰς ἡδονὰς
> καὶ τἀνιαρὰ φροῦδος αἴσθησις φθαρῇ,
> τὸ σῶμα κωφοῦ τάξιν εἴληφεν πέτρου.
> ζῶντας κολάζειν, οὐ θανόντας, εὐσεβές.

Theseus is now less worthy of blame for cutting his guest short. He allows Adrastus nine verses, ample space to show that he is less eloquent than tradition reports. The king, moreover, does not now interrupt in the middle of a line (another proof of self-restraint), beginning perhaps: ἔα τὰ λοιπά.

What of the thirty-three lines on human progress? There is no place for them between the "anonymous" portions. They are best set near the opening of Moschion's *Supplices*, some time before the Herald arrives: for, though the speech ends with the origin of funeral rites, it has no tinge of rebuke. Adrastus, one supposes, uttered an elaborate appeal to Theseus as part of an opening scene that is replaced in our text by the admirable composition of Euripides. Aethra's version (so to call it) of Adrastus' plea (not so full as Moschion's, because preceded by explanatory dialogue) naturally rendered superfluous that of Moschion. If anyone asks why Adrastus' speech is so irrelevant except in its abrupt moral at the close, he should reflect that this kind of writing seems to have been favoured by Moschion, who gives Theseus a passage showing precisely the same features.[1]

To this early portion of his tragedy we may with some confidence assign a fragment not yet mentioned. Stobaeus quotes (fr. 10) from Moschion without naming the play:

> σὺν αἷσι δόξῃ πρόσθε καὶ γένει μέγας
> Ἄργους δυνάστης, λιτὸς ἐκ τυραννικῶν
> θρόνων, προσίκτην θαλλὸν ἠγκαλισμένος
> ἔστειχεν, εἰς γῆν ὄμμα συμπαθὲς φέρων
> καὶ πᾶσι δεικνὺς ὡς τὰ λαμπρὰ τῆς τύχης
> τὴν κτῆσιν οὐ βέβαιον ἀνθρώποις νέμει.
> ὃν πᾶς μὲν ἀστῶν ἠλέησεν εἰσιδών,
> ἅπας δὲ χεῖρα καὶ προσήγορον φάτιν
> ὤρεξε κάνθους τ' ἐξέτηξε δακρύοις

---

[1] Vv. 195 ff. See above, p. 154 f.

THE SUPPLICES

τύχαις συναλγῶν· τἀξίωμα γὰρ νοσοῦν
τὸ πρόσθε πολλοῖς οἶκτον ἐμποιεῖ βροτῶν.[1]

"And with them paced he who aforetime was great in renown as in birth, the ruler of Argos, his princely throne exchanged for a lowly guise, embracing a suppliant's olive-bough, his sorrowful glance turned earthwards, and showing to all men that Fortune's glory bestows upon mankind no sureness of possession. Him the townsmen all pitied as they gazed; all offered hands and speech of greeting: their eyes melted to tears in sympathy with his disasters. For in many a human breast compassion is born when former greatness pines." The explanation of all this, especially its first word or two[2] and the Argive king's identity,[3] has baffled many. But looked at from our novel standpoint it grows clear, and deeply interesting. The king who has come to a city not his own as a suppliant, accompanied by certain women[4] (described in the lines that preceded our fragment, as the relative pronoun shows), and who at once receives popular sympathy, is surely[5] Adrastus, reaching Athens[6] with the mothers

---

[1] In v. 4 Nauck prefers συννεφές to συμπαθές. In v. 11 ἐμποιεῖ is Haupt's emendation of εὐπορεῖ, which Meineke (p. 110) accepts as one of Moschion's oddities, meaning "provides".

[2] σὺν αἷσι or σὺν αἴσσι is the reading of the Stobaeus MSS. Some editors have suggested συνέσει τε, which is awkward: it could mean only: "Great aforetime—as men thought—in wisdom as in birth." Wagner (pp. 17 f.) rejects sundry conjectures and himself proposes σύνες, ὡς ὁ δόξῃ ..., comparing Soph. Trach. 868 ff.: ξύνες δὲ τήνδ᾽ ὡς ... χωρεῖ πρὸς ἡμᾶς γραῖα. But σύνες does not suit the following imperfect ἔστειχεν (contrast Sophocles' χωρεῖ). No change is needed: αἷσι may be obscure to us, but that is not Moschion's fault.

[3] Wagner for instance says (p. 17) that it is hard to give him a name, "despite the lists to be got from Hyginus Fab. CXXIV and Apollodorus II, 2, 1. sq." However, "mihi sermo de Thyesta esse videtur, ut fabulae argumentum, ex qua hi versus fluxerint, non multum a Sophoclis Thyesta Sicyonio ... discrepuerit." There is nothing in the fragments of the Sophoclean play to support this. For a discussion of its argument (an intricate inquiry) see Pearson, The Fragments of Sophocles, vol. I, pp. 185-7. Hyginus (Fab. 88) does indeed say that Thyestes fled to King Thesprotus: but that helps little.

[4] This stands beyond doubt. αἷσι cannot refer to things with a feminine name (e.g. δύαι or ἀνίαι), for we read later a list of his woes. And ἔστειχεν of itself suggests that αἷσι refers to no abstractions. Schramm however (p. 78) says, with Meineke, that if we retain σὺν αἷσι we may suspect an antecedent ἀτιμίαι.

[5] No other such situation seems to have occurred in Greek legend. But there is one difficulty: λιτὸς ἐκ τυραννικῶν θρόνων almost certainly means that "Adrastus" has been dethroned—as he deserved; and nowhere else (I believe) is that reported. This may incline some to prefer the suggestion of Walker (p. 226) that the exile is Archelaus, Temenus' son, who was driven by his brothers from Argos and fled to King Cisseus of Macedonia (Hyginus Fab. 219). But what of σὺν αἷσι? Schramm (p. 79), noting Hyginus' words profugit ... capra duce, remarks that we might emend to σὺν αἰγί (Walker, p. 226, had suggested σὺν δ᾽ αἰγί) or αἰξί. This she-goat, however, was a late addition to the story.

[6] At any rate Attica: of course we need not suppose Eleusis.

of the Seven to implore Athenian aid.[1] We conclude that our fragment belongs to the very opening of Moschion's work. In Euripides the position is otherwise explained. Moschion gave the facts in a more picturesque prologue, followed by the entry of Adrastus and the Mothers. Who delivered this prologue it were idle to guess.

Two other fragments demand attention. Fr. 5 runs:

> ὅμως τό γ' ὀρθὸν καὶ δίκαιον οὔποτε
> σιγῇ παρήσω· τὴν γὰρ ἐντεθραμμένην
> ἀστοῖς Ἀθάνας τῇ τε Θησέως πόλει
> καλὸν φυλάξαι γνησίως παρρησίαν.

"But what is right and just never will I leave unspoken; for honour bids a true man guard the freedom of speech fostered in Athena's citizens and the town of Theseus." The third line tempts us to add this to Moschion's *Supplices*, and perhaps to place it immediately before the long fr. 7 which begins fitly enough with πρῶτον δέ. Still, it would suit a great many themes. In any case, it could hardly have been spoken by Adrastus, but surely belongs to an Athenian. Were it certain, and it is not even very probable, that the passage belongs to Moschion's *Supplices*, we should assign it to some citizen who expostulates with Theseus for refusing his aid. Fr. 6 runs thus:

> μόνον σὺ θυμοῦ χωρὶς ἔνδεξαι λόγους
> οὓς σοὶ κομίζω· τὸν κλύοντα γὰρ λαβὼν
> ὁ μῦθος εὔνουν οὐ μάτην λεχθήσεται.

"Only do thou receive unangered the words I bring to thee: for when speech has a kindly hearer it will be uttered not in vain." That is even more commonplace. But it might well be appended to fr. 5 (above) and so lead straight on, even better than that fragment alone, to the civilization-speech.[2] All this seems likely enough,[3] but must not be assumed.

Finally, do Moschion's fragments show any peculiarities of thought, dramatic technique, versification, style, or language that help us to decide for or against our two theories—that large portions of our *Supplices* originally belonged to a play by Moschion; and that some of his fragments, not incorporated in the Euripidean work, also belonged to this same play of Moschion?

In thought and technique we discover nothing of the kind. As for

---

[1] After writing this sentence I find welcome agreement in Ribbeck, pp. 154 f.
[2] So Meineke (p. 104).
[3] Except that Theseus' name in fr. 5 makes it less probable that he is directly addressed.

THE SUPPLICES

versification, Meineke asserts that Moschion avoids resolution in iambics (the metre of all his acknowledged fragments). He therefore rejects fr. 12,

κεῖνος δ' ἁπάντων ἐστὶ μακαριώτατος,
ὃς διὰ τέλους ζῶν ὁμαλὸν ἤσκησεν βίον,

which has no less than three resolutions in two lines; and regards the initial dactyl in the fifth verse of fr. 11 (= *Suppl.* 531–6) as another reason for disbelieving Stobaeus and retaining the passage as Euripidean.[1] He would have rejected our Moschionian elements in the extant *Supplices*, where the resolutions number 69[2] in 577 iambic verses, whereas they are but three in the "recognized" 73 verses: that is, the frequency in these latter is only one-third of the frequency in the former. On the face of it, we should infer that the recognized fragments and our "portions" were written by different hands. It is true that, so stated, the objection is not formidable: that 73 verses are too small a bulk for trustworthy statistics; and that in Euripides, to whom on this showing the "portions" must be restored, one can easily find passages as long as fr. 7 (33 lines) that have no resolution.[3] Statistics, then, have little weight here. But they do point towards a doubt based on versification in general. The fragments unmistakably flow more smoothly than the "portions". Not that the former are glib, or the latter rough: rather the difference is between nimbleness and sinewy force. This nimbleness is produced partly, indeed, by the absence of resolved feet; but also by the frequent absence of elision and— this perhaps is the most important cause—the large number of lines that form a syntactical whole. In fr. 7, for instance, vv. 4–10 show not even the slightest elision, and fr. 10 has nothing but τ' in all its eleven verses; the "self-contained" line is frequent in fr. 7. Nothing in our "portions" makes this effect so strongly, though Theseus' "sermon", the Funeral Speech, and Iphis' final outburst belong to the same class of writing: at its best lithe and quick, at its worst almost to be called scribble. Nevertheless, as we have so often agreed, much of the "portions" is admirable, to be dubbed non-Euripidean only because of very different matter from

---

[1] Schramm also (pp. 21–35) denies fr. 12 to a tragedy of Moschion because of its resolutions and ὁ κωμικός in the lemma, saying that we must assume (i) a comic dramatist of the same name, or (ii) a satyr-play of Moschion (so Walker, p. 227), or (iii) a mistake in attribution by Clement.

[2] Ignoring proper names, which are rather frequent and account for 23 resolutions out of 92.

[3] Examining the first place that comes to mind, Medea's opening speech (*Med.* 214 ff.), we find no resolution till v. 255, the forty-second line. The remaining ten also contain no resolved foot.

which it cannot be separated. On the whole, the versification tells against our theory, so far as it concerns Moschion.

Style and language remain to be considered. The items earlier[1] examined do not, as is natural, all find their analogues in the "recognized" fragments, which contain but seventy-three verses. Still, their quality is akin to the sponginess of texture[2] that pervades those fragments, their repetitiveness[3] and inept or strained phrasing. The late words or usages that we noted are paralleled[4] with a frequency remarkable in so small a number of lines.

Such, then, was the origin of our text: someone blended an Euripidean *Supplices* with a play by Moschion having the same theme.[5] If the reader feels that he would rather believe almost anything else in the world, he should consider two facts. First: our text has been shown to contain not only gross stupidities but also more than one element that no writer, not insane, would have admitted to his play. Secondly, most of these faults disappear suddenly and completely if we assume two dramatists instead of one, since they arise from the mere juxtaposition of statements or scenes in themselves unexceptionable.

But certain obvious questions still await answer. Can we believe that anyone, in any period, was so bereft of sense as to produce this repellent mixture? Who was he? Why did he produce it? And when?

The first can be met easily. Such eccentric surgery became in time not (as one might expect) the fantasy of a single ancient Dr. Moreau, but a thriving trade. The distinguished "grammarian" Phrynichus, a Bithynian scholar who wrote in the second century after Christ, tells us that "'putting on patches and heels' means renovating old goods, and is applied to those who refashion old dramas by sewing together pieces from two."[6] That last phrase is an attempt to render the one word

---

[1] Pp. 145–9. The obscurities and false idiom mark that decay of Atticism which Meineke (pp. 110 f.) observed in the "recognized" fragments.

[2] This quality, it is by no means forgotten, was noted earlier (p. 39) as marking the work of Euripides himself, but mostly in *Helen* for a special reason; if we can take these fragments as typical, it tinges everything that Moschion wrote.

[3] See, e.g., vv. 1–3 and 31 f. of fr. 7, and most of frr. 9 and 10. Compare with these especially *Suppl.* 1089 ff. (see above, p. 160).

[4] ὄμπνιος (7. 10), εὐιῶτις (7. 11), ζυγουλκός (7. 26), ἀροτρεύειν (7. 26), ἐπιμοιρᾶσθαι (7. 31), κάνθος (10. 9), εὐπορεῖν (10. 11, in the sense of "supply", but see p. 175, n. 1).

[5] That Moschion dealt somewhere with the obsequies of the Seven has been asserted before: Welcker (*Die griechischen Tragödien*, p. 1050) refers fr. 8 (τί κέρδος . . .) and fr. 7 (civilization) to an otherwise unknown tragedy on that subject written by him.

[6] Fragment in *Anecdota Bekkeri*, 31. 19: ἐπικαττύειν καὶ πτερνίζειν· τὰ παλαιὰ ἐπισκευάζειν, λέγουσι δ' ἐπὶ τῶν τὰ παλαιὰ τῶν δραμάτων μεταποιούντων καὶ μεταρραπτόντων. The

μεταρραπτόντων: a piece is taken from one old play and stitched into the fabric of another, so as to make a "new" play (μεταποιούντων). Phrynichus describes exactly the process which, we have asserted, resulted in our *Supplices*: not mere accretions, not even those longer additions by actors or their attendant versifiers.[1] The difference becomes plain if we compare what happened to the *Supplices* with what happened to the *Phoenissae*.[2] This latter now contains far more than the average number of lines, and is the longest of all extant Greek plays except *Oedipus Coloneus*—and *Christus Patiens*. It seems clear that originally it had about the normal length, and that actors (determined to give their public the whole Oedipus-story in one gigantic mass) distended it with the portions that now bring in Antigone and her father,[3] thereby distorting the focus of the whole and causing textual or stylistic[4] difficulties. Whereas the *Supplices* became a new play by receiving masses cut out of another independent drama, the *Phoenissae* remains what it was, but has lumps hanging upon its still undamaged structure, these lumps being not portions already existent as parts of another tragedy,[5] but matter specially written for insertion.[6]

That such stitchery as produced our *Supplices* was common we learn not only from the assertion of Phrynichus but also from the known history of certain other extant plays. Aristophanes, when the *Clouds* was defeated by works of Cratinus and Ameipsias, produced a second version that met still more decisive failure; our text is a combination of these two, and reveals its origin by sundry faults of structure.[7] Much the same thing happened to his *Peace*.[8] Another Greek play, *Christus Patiens*, traditionally but wrongly attributed to St. Gregory of Nazianzus (c. 329–c. 389), is a *cento* of extracts from Euripides, eked out by bad iambics of the compiler's

phrase is taken as a fragment of comedy by Meineke (fr. 46) and Kock (fr. 267): the words of course scan as an anapaestic dimeter.

[1] W. G. Rutherford (*History of Annotation* (1905), p. 60) suggests that a guild of players had acting editions of favourite dramas made by a "literary hack". See especially D. L. Page, *Actors' Interpolations in Greek Tragedy* (1934).

[2] Compare Powell's Introduction.

[3] Verrall's explanation, in defence of their authenticity ("Last Scene of All" in *Euripides the Rationalist* (1895), pp. 231–60), is hopelessly fantastic: Oedipus and Antigone, he says, are symbolic: Oedipus of the poet himself, Antigone of his plays.

[4] On all these matters see Powell's commentary.

[5] A. Balsamo, however, seeks to prove "contamination" of two drafts ("Sulla composizione delle Fenicie di Euripide", *Studi Ital. di fil. class.*, 9 (1901), pp. 241–90).

[6] The difference is well marked by the word προσέρραπται (not μετέρραπται) in the last lines of the Hypothesis: ὅ τε ἐπὶ πᾶσι μετ' ᾠδῆς ἀδολέσχου φυγαδευόμενος Οἰδίπους προσέρραπται διὰ κενῆς.

[7] Cp. my *Greek Comedy*, pp. 212–16.

[8] *Ibid.*, pp. 231–4.

own. More familiar is the *contaminatio* which Plautus and Terence[1] used in composing their comedies during a period that began only a century later than Moschion's play. *Contaminatio* meant using parts of Greek comedies (translated and remodelled much or little) to make a single Latin comedy. The achievements of Plautus should (by the way) reassure any who are incredulous of the feats that we have attributed to the bungling carpenter who bestowed our *Supplices* upon posterity. The *Poenulus*, for instance, is based on two Greek plays (now lost). Their action passed in Athens and Calydon respectively: Plautus, in consequence, by a miracle of careless stupidity, calls the unchanged scene of his own work now Athens, now Calydon.[2] Many generations later, Thomas Otway, author of those masterpieces *The Orphan* and *Venice Preserved*, did not disdain to embellish his *Caius Marius* with lavish verbatim borrowings from *Romeo and Juliet*. Nahum Tate, born in the same year (1652), though Poet Laureate and credited with two highly esteemed hymns,[3] was also a sinister collaborator of Shakespeare's,[4] and fitted *King Lear* with a happy ending: this compound, ousting the original version, held our stage well into the nineteenth century.

The first of our four questions—can we believe that so odd a feat was ever performed?—has now been answered. The others were: who performed it, and why and when?

His name we cannot give, nor is that any reason for regret. It was not Moschion, of course, who (however mediocre he might seem to us had we the materials for a verdict) was at least a playwright of some repute in his own day and for centuries not altogether forgotten. Our Unknown's qualification as a dramatic expert consisted in the power to see that two plays had the same theme and to force them into a single bulk by leaving out of each whatever would only repeat something in the other. So far his sense of fitness helped him, but no farther.

Why did he undertake his unseemly feat? Not for glory. He had the grace to omit his signature: otherwise we should not have found Euripides' name attached to the result, and Moschion's to the traditional fragments. Was it to satisfy a pure love for drama? Did he observe with pain that this miniature work, though written by the author of *Hippolytus* and the *Bacchae*, contained grave "faults": that seven was not the correct

---

[1] Also Naevius and Ennius; but the plays of neither survive.
[2] See my *Plautus and Terence*, pp. 89 f., and the rest of the chapter for other blunders, no less gross.
[3] *While shepherds watched* and *As pants the hart*.
[4] For *Macbeth*, see above, p. 33, n. 2.

number for a tragic chorus, and that the play itself was too brief? Such a theory is wrecked by the destructive bungling that he showed in remedying the supposed defects. Anyone with an alert, though vicarious, artistic conscience would by instinct avoid making what seemed bad so horribly worse. No: he was producing merchandise for a market.

That brings us at once to our last question: when did he concoct this text? The great and continued popularity of Euripides at length called forgers into being; the trade in spurious writings of his (as of other eminent authors) flourished during the second century after Christ.[1] To that period, or perhaps to the next century,[2] we may assign the compound text before us. It is not, of course, a forgery in the most usual sense;[3] its compiler lacked the requisite skill, and was content to choose a genuine but hitherto neglected Euripidean play that could be passed off, with lavish additions from another, as different from any then before the public.

Our long and complicated study of Moschion's contribution thereto should be placed in the right perspective. It was pursued because he seems the playwright whom we can most plausibly name as Euripides' fellow victim. The case for him appears on close examination to be strong. More important than this identification is the fact that we have proved our *Supplices* a collection of portions torn from two dramas, one composed by Euripides, the other by a much later poet. Possibly the reader finds himself after all more willing to believe our text Euripidean throughout than to accept so novel a view, and may cite what has been said earlier concerning eccentricities to which Euripides was beyond question prone. That position is untenable. Our text presents us, not with mere eccentricity, not even with ungoverned fantasy, but with self-contradiction wanton and ruinous.

[1] Galen, *In Hipp. de nat. hominis* 2, p. 57, 12, Mewaldt (cited by H. J. Rose, *Oxford Classical Dictionary*, p. 743 b).

[2] Wilamowitz (*Einleitung in die griechische Tragödie*, p. 163) assigns to that century the spurious works of Plato, Demosthenes, Lysias, and comic dramatists.

[3] But to this particular kind Phrynichus, also of the second century, is a sound witness (see pp. 178 f.).

INDEX

Achilles, 26 f., 42; (*Iph. Aul.*) 23, 47 n.
Actium, 170 n.
Adams, S. M., 102 n.
Admetus (*Alcestis*), 3, 12 f., 15 n., 35, 101 (K. of Molossi), 171 n.
Adonis, 98
Adrastus, 27, 114 n. (*bis*), 116 f., 118, 119, 122, 126 n., 128, 129 f., 133, 136 n., 142 f., 145, 153 n., 154, 156, 157, 158, 160, 165, 166 n., 167 (*bis*), 173 f., 175
Adriatic, the, 111
Aegeus, 34, 96 f., 97 n., 138
Aegialeus, 114 n.
Aegisthus (Soph. *El.*), 29; (Eur. *El.*), 23
Aegospotami, 119
Aelian, 164 n.
Aeschines, 120 n. (*bis*), 122 n.
Aeschylus: 1–5, 8 f., 10, 29, 30 f., 49, 85, 108 n.; chorus, use of, 31, 114 n.; on Delphic oracle, 16; recognition tokens, 15, 45
   Agamemnon, 5, 30 f.; vv. 160–83, 85 n.; v. 582, 95 n.; vv. 1407 ff., 67 n.
   Choephoroe, 13, 15, 31, 81 n.
   Danaides, 114 n.
   Edoni, 61 n.
   Eleusinians (*Men of Eleusis*), 163
   Eumenides, 9, 16, 20, 31, 45 n., 104 n.; vv. 517 ff., 49 n.
   Persae, 9, 31
   Prometheus Vinctus, 56 n., 116 n.
   Septem, 49, 158
   Supplices, 8, 11, 112, 113 f., 114 n., 132 n., 155
Aethra, 112, 116, 155; her great speech, 27, 151 f., 161 n., 166, 167, 174
Aetiological passages, 20
Agamemnon, 97 n.; (*Hecuba*), 35, 47 n.; (*Iph. Aul.*), 24, 101
Agamemnon. See Aeschylus
Agathon, 17 n., 31, 33
Agaue, 28 n., 55, 56 and n., 58, 62, 64, 65 n.
Aidôs. See Αἰδώς
Αἰδώς, 75 f., 78 n., 81 n., 85 n.
Ajax, 27, 160

Ajax. See Sophocles
Alcestis, 12 f., 35, 37, 94 n., 101
Alcestis. See Euripides
Alcibiades, 9 and n., 128 f., 149, 151, 165
Alcibiades (*Second*), 129
Alcmaeonidae, 129
Alcmena, 7 n., 22 n.
Alexander (the Great), 119, 126, 160, 165, 169, 170 n.
   (of Pherae), 164 n., 172
Alfred the Great, 131
Alliances of Athens in fourth century, 165
Amata (*Aeneid*), 92 n.
Amazon, 105
Ameipsias, 179
Ammendola, G., 125 n.
Amphiaraus, 45 n., 114 and n., 115 n., 126, 151, 157
Amphitryon, 56 n.
Amyclae, 104 n.
"Anagnostic" (Closet-) dramatists (ἀναγνωστικοί), 118, 159, 167 f.
Anaphora, 83 n.
Anaxagoras, 15 and n.
Anaximenes, 15
Andromache (*Androm.*), 46, 50; (*Troades*), 25, 43
Andromache. See Euripides
Andromeda. See Euripides
Anecdota Bekkeri, 52 f. n., 178 n.
Anonymous "Supplices", 166–8
Antigone, 36, 179
Antigone. See Sophocles
Antiphanes, 3 n.
ἀφηγεῖσθαι, 146, 153 n.
Aphrodite, 19, 28, 29, 38, 58, 66, 68, 74, 79 f., 83–85, 87, 98, 103–7, 109, 110. See also Cypris
Apollo, 42, 96; (*Alcestis*), 12; (*Ion*), 20, 28, 43; (*Iph. Taur.*), 23, 28; (*Orestes*), 22, 24, 29, 102; (*Winter's Tale, The*), 29
Apollodorus (comedian), 122 n.
   (mythologist), 175 n.
Apollonius Rhodius, 42 n., 107 n.
Apuleius, 104 n.
Archelaus, 175 n.
Archonship, 133 f.

Arginusae, 117 n.
Argives, 112; "Argive girls", 115
Argos, 3, 94, 102, 112, 114 n., 117, 119, 150, 157, 163, 165
Ariadne, 79
Ariel, 57
Aristocrates (Demosthenes), 172 n.
Aristophanes: 2, 8, 10, 11 n., 15, 18, 39, 44, 45, 56 n., 108 n., 110 n., 119, 179; criticizes Eur., 5 f., 13 f.
  Clouds, 179; vv. 1079 ff., 83 n.; v. 1415, 27
  Frogs, 56 n., 109 n., 119; v. 82, 5 n.; vv. 959–63, 13 and n.; vv. 907–50, 14; vv. 971–9, 14; vv. 1006–98, 78 n.
  Knights, 10, 109 n.; v. 334, 156 n.; vv. 537 ff., 11 n.
  Lysistrata, 8
  Peace, v. 665, schol. on, 134 n.; two versions of, 179
  Plutus, 45, 119
  Thesmophoriazusae, 44; v. 153, 78 n.; vv. 445 ff., 110 n.; v. 497, 78 n.; vv. 546 ff., 78 n.
  Wasps, 109 n.; vv. 486–507, 130 n.
Aristophanes of Byzantium, 35 n.
Aristotle: 3–5, 11, 12, 18 n., 42, 94, 140 f., 159, 168
  Constitution of Athens (*Ath. Pol.*), 138 n., 141; 7: 134 n.; 41. 2: 134 f.
  Metaphysics, 1090^{b}19, 6 n.
  Physics, 205^{a}13: 146; 214^{b}18, 21: 146
  Poetic (1449, etc. are entered as 49, &c.), 49^{a}9 ff.: 4 n.; 49^{a}14 f.: 4 n.; 51^{a}6–9: 32 n.; 51^b: 3 n.; 51^{b}19 ff.: 17 n.; 51^{b}33 ff.: 44 n.; 51^{b}37 ff.: 33 n.; 52^{a}12: 44 n.; 52^{b}19 f.: 18 n.; 53^{a}28 ff.: 5 n.; 54^{a}31 ff.: 4 n.; 54^{a}37 ff.: 20 f., 34 n.; 55^{a}22–9: 45 n.; 60^{b}33 f.: 14 n.; 61^{b}19–21: 34 n.
  Politics, 1310^{a}32 ff.: 165 f.
  Rhetoric, 413^b: 118 n.
Arms and the Man, 22, 26 n.
Arnold, Matthew, 8
Arnoldt, R., 114 n. (*bis*)
ἀροτρεύειν, 178 n.
Artemis (*Hipp.*), 19, 29, 37, 70, 74 ff., 76, 85 n., 87 n., 88 n., 89, 90 f., 96–103, 105, 106–9, 110 f.; (*Iph. Taur.*), 23
Arthurian legend, 3 n.

As pants the hart, 180 n.
Asceticism, 74 ff., 105
Asclepius, 28
Aspasia, 33
ἄστρωτος, 52 f. n.
Astyanax, 25, 43
Astydamas, 11
Atalanta, 115, 148
Athelstane (*Ivanhoe*), 48
Athena, 21, 96; (*Odyssey*), 57; (Aesch. *Eum.*), 104 n.; (*Heracles*), 57 n.; (*Ion*), 20, 102; (*Rhesus*), 44 n., 97 n.; (Eur. *Supp.*), 114 n., 115, 117 and n., 120 f., 129, 143, 149, 161, 162 n.; (*Troades*), 21
Athenaeus, 149 n.
ἀθράνευτος, 52 f. n.
Atreus, 97 n.
Atthidographers, 134, 141
Augustine, St., 83 n.
Aulis, 26, 38 n.
αὐθέντης, 146
Autonoe, 56 n.
Axiochus, 168 n.
Axt, C. A. M., 114 n., 115 n.

Bacchae. See Euripides
Bacchus. See Dionysus
Bacchylides, 11, 41, 97 n.
Balsamo, A., 179 n.
Banquo, 54
Beck, C. D., 155
Bee in *Hippolytus*, 75 f.
Bekker, I., 52 f. n., 178 n.
Bellerophon, 78 n.
Bengl, H., 128 n., 132 n., 133 n., 168 n.
Blaydes, F. H., 94 n.
Boeckh, A., 113 n., 114 n.
Boeotians, 150, 162–4. See also Delium
Boileau, 3, 11
Boscoreale, 169 n.
Bowra, Sir Maurice, 97 n.
Bradley, A. C., 3, 92 n.
Bremi, J. H., 18 n.
Britain, ancient, 3
Britannus (*Caesar and Cleop.*), 131
Brodeau, J., 148
Bruhn, E., 54 n.
Bull (*Bacchae*), 57 n., 59 n., 62; (*Hipp.*), 57 n., 91 f.
Burial, denial of, in fourth century, 164 f.
Burnet, J., 1, 3
Butcher, S. H., 19 n., 32 n.

INDEX

Butler (*Alcestis*), 13
Byron, 10, 23
Bywater, I., 32 n., 33 n.

Cabal (*decas*), 125
Cadmeia, 136 n.
Cadmus, 2, 22 n., 38, 55, 56 n., 67 n., 70, 130, 157
Caesar and Cleopatra, 101
Caius Marius, 180
Caliban, 9
Calydon, 115, 180
Can Grande della Scala, 21 n.
Capaneus, 114 n., 115, 116, 125, 126, 127 f., 128 (*bis*), 158, 159 n., 160 n.
Carcinus, 45 n.
Carthage, 38 n.
Cassandra, 47 n.
Catalogue of Ships, Homer's, 135
Cephalus, 82
Ceteus, 126 n.
Chaeronea, 119, 164 n.
Chalcis, 38 n.
Chance, 121 f.
Chansons, early French, 3
Characterization in Euripides, 6
Charition, 7 n.
Chaucer, 2
Choephoroe. See Aeschylus
Choerilus of Samos, 4
Chorus, in Aeschylus, Sophocles, Euripides, 31 f.; of *Bacchae*: see Eur. *Bacchae*; of *Supp.*, 112–18, 153, 162
Chorus, On the (Sophocles?), 10 n.
Χρηστότης, 146
Christ, W., 118 n.
Christus Patiens, 179
Chrysogonus, 149
Cicero, 84 n., 88 n.
Cimon, 119
Cisseus, 175 n.
Cleidemus, 141
Cleisthenes, 134 n.
Cleitophon (pseudo-Plato), 150
Clement of Alexandria, 170, 177 n.
Cleon, 17 n., 49
Closet-dramatists. *See* "Anagnostic" dramatists
Clouds. See Aristophanes
Clytemnestra, 102; (Soph. *El.*), 29; (Eur. *El.*), 23; (*Iph. Aul.*), 24, 40, 45
Coleridge, S. T., 10, 62

Comedies, comic or quasi-comic dramaturgy of Euripides, 21 ff.; different meanings of "comic", 21 n.; forgeries, 181 n.
Conon (general), 172
(mythographer), 172 n.
Constitutional history, study of, in Athens, 140
"Contamination" of plays, 35, 180
Cope, E. M., 118 n.
Corneille, 18
Cornford, F. M., 98 n.
Coward, Noel, 29, 33
Crates, 11 n.
Cratinus, 46, 179
Creon (*Medea*), 34, 37, 159 n.; (*Phoen.*), 27, 36; (Eur. *Supp.*), 130, 131
Crete, 79, 104
Creusa, 19, 27, 43
Croiset, M., 118 n.
Curtain-difficulty in *Supp.*, 116, 153, 162, 168
Cyclopes, 137 n.
Cyclops. See Euripides
Cymbeline, 3, 103
Cypris, 84 n., 85 n., 90, 97. *See also* Aphrodite
Cyprus, 68, 71 n.
Cyrano de Bergerac, 43
Cyrene, 117 n.

Danaides. See Aeschylus
Danaids, 112, 113 n.
D'Annunzio, 79 n., 88 n., 104 n., 114 n.
Dante, 10, 21 n., 92 n.
Darwinism, 10
Dawn-goddess, 82
De Corona (Demosth.), 263. 6 ff.: 120 n.; 311. 7–312. 10: 121 f.; 316. 24 ff.: 121 f.
Death-goblin (*Alcestis*), 13
Δεκαρχίαι or δεκαδαρχίαι, 125
Decas (δεκάς), 125, 154
Decharme, P., 102 n., 150 n.
Delium, battle of, 131 n., 150 f., 162–4, 165
Delphi, 38; oracle, 16, 34
Demeter, 42, 151
Democracy, Athenian, 120–41
Democrates, 50 n.
Δημοκρατία (in fresco), 136 n.
Demophon, 143 n.
Demos (Δῆμος), 135 n., 136 n., 137

Demosthenes (general), 128
    (orator), 39, 119, 120 n., 121 n., 121 f., 146, 150
    Pseudo-Dem., 133 n., 136, 137, 138, 139
Dénouement, 46
Desdemona, 102
Desire under the Elms, 12
Deus ex machina, 7, 19 ff., 102; *homo ex m.*, 21, 35
Diagoras, 15
Διαλλαγή, 146
Dickens, 48, 162
Dindorf, K. W., 94 n., 153 n.
Dio Chrysostom, 16
Diodorus, 92 n., 117 n., 126 n., 162 n., 163, 164 n. (*ter*)
Diogenes Laertius, 155 n.
Diomedes, 97 n., 114 n.
Dionysiac religion, 7, 71–73; festivals, 8, 30–33
Dionysus, 6 n., 21, 28, 38, 46, 52–73
Dioscuri (Twin Brethren), 108; Homeric *Hymn to Dioscuri*, 97 n.
Disciples, the Twelve, 112 f.
Dium, 149 n., 169
Divergence from monarchy under Theseus. *See* Monarchy
Dobree, P. P., 167 n.
Dodds, E. R., 6, 52 (*bis*), 55, 56 n. (*bis*), 58 n., 66 n., 67 n., 68, 70 n., 71 n., 78 n. (*bis*), 81 n.
Doll's House, A, 26 n.
Dolon, 27
δώματα, 52 n., 54, 62 n.
Draco, 135 n.
Dreiser, T., 5 n.
Dryden, 23

Eccyclema, 83 n.
Echion, 69
Eckermann, J. P., 1, 69 n.
Economy, dramatic, 6
Edoni. *See* Aeschylus
Egyptian expedition of Athens, 119
Egyptians, 137 n.
ἐκρυφθεν, 93 f., 95 n.
Electra. *See* Sophocles *and* Euripides
Eleusinians. *See* Aeschylus
Eleusis, 75, 151, 175 n.
Ἐλευθέριος Στοά, 136 n.
Elizabethanism, 37

Ellen Irwin, 17
Elmsley, P., 94 n., 113 n.
Emilia (*Othello*), 24
Ennius, 18, 180 n.
Epidauria, 94
ἐπιμοιρᾶσθαι, 178 n.
Episodic scenes. *See* Euripides
Epitaphios (pseudo-Demosth.), 133 n., 136, 138, 139
Erechtheus, 135
Eros, 42 n.
Eteocles, 27, 36
Eteoclus, 116 n., 126, 128, 146
Euadne, 44, 116, 125 f., 127 n., 158, 159 f., 166, 168
εὐιῶτις, 178 n.
Eumenes, 126 n.
Eumenides, 119
Eumenides. *See* Aeschylus
Euphranor, 136 n.
εὐπορεῖν, 175 n., 178 n.
Euripides: dangers of a subjective view, 2 f.; discussed by Aristophanes, 5 f., 13 f., 78; by Aristotle, 3–5, 20 f., 34, 165 f.; by Dio Chrysostom, 16; by Plato, 16; by Sophocles, 14, 94; divergence of modern opinions, 1 f.

    His conception of his business, 13 ff., 30 n.; criticizes Aeschylus, 15 f., 45; expanded his plays, 33–36; an experimenter, 11 f.; "great tragic period", 42; inconclusiveness, 49; inconsistency, 42–44; no law of Euripidean dramaturgy, 3, 6; licence in handling tradition, 16 f.; "man of the theatre", 29 f.; not classical but romantic, 49; private performances, 33, 118, 162; realism, 6 n.; relevance: its meaning for him, 14 f., 17; stumbling-blocks, 18–30; trained his audience, 13 f., 108–10

    Characterization, 6 n.: *see also* Admetus, &c.; chorus: *see* Chorus; *deus ex machina*: *see* D. *ex m.*; embellishments, 50 n.; "fillers", 31; lyrics, 40–42, 67–70, 71 n.; melodrama, 19 f., 23–30; messengers: *see* Messengers; prologues, 18 f., 28

    Feeble writing, 39–42; freakishness, 112 f.; magnificently readable, 49 f.; sometimes morbid or salacious? 78 n.; opinions on the basis

INDEX

of morals, 84 f.; opinions on theology, 70–73, 102–10; sardonic piquancy, 21 ff.; wit, 8, 21, 51; fun, 8, 21

Bad work, 30–91, external causes of, 30–70; episodic scenes, 6, 44 f.; faulty construction, 42–47; fissions of plot, 46 f.; little snags, 37 f., 154 n.; plots sometimes go awry, 45 f.; untimely messengers' speeches, 45

Summary, 48–51

Alcestis: 7 n., 12 f., 172; "Apollo with Admetus", 41; padded, 35; rescue in, 28 n.; a tragicomedy, 12 f., 18–27

Vv. 152–88, 35; vv. 280–325, 35; v. 608, 37; v. 691, 13 n.; v. 740, 37; v. 780, schol. on, 14 n.; v. 898, 37; vv. 903–10, 15 n.; vv. 995 ff., 41; vv. 1127 f., 156 n.

Andromache: 6, 7, 11, 21, 30, 42, 108; ascribed to Democrates, 50 n.; fission in, 3, 46 f.; rescues in, 28 n.; tirade against Sparta, 50; two time-schemes, 43

Vv. 732 ff., 43; vv. 1243 ff., 101 n.; vv. 1266 ff., 114 n.

Bacchae: 2, 6 n., 7, 12, 17, 24, 52–73; balance therein, 71; chorus, 28, 31, 52–58, 61–64, 65 n., 67–70; chorus-leader, 64 n.; conspiracy of Tiresias? 66 f.; Dionysiac religion, *see s.v.*; glamour, 56–58, 62 f., 65, 66; hypnotism, 57 f., 65; hypothesis, 53 n.; lyrics, 41, 67–70; magic, 57 n.; messenger (first), 54, 64 f., 66; (second), 54; palace-miracle, 52–64; other miracles, 64–66; palinode, 71; phantom, 57, 62; prologue, 28; prophecies, false, 46, 70; "Stranger", 52 n., 58; sympathizers with Dionysus, male, 64; Theban votaries, 59, 64. *See also* Agaue, Cadmus, Dionysus, Pentheus, Tiresias

Vv. 50 ff., 28; vv. 72–88, 67 n.; vv. 135–67, 67 n.; vv. 201–3, 70 n.; vv. 264–6, 64 n.; vv. 278–85, 66 n.; vv. 326 f., 66; v. 331, 67 n.; vv. 360 ff., 67 n.; vv. 370–86, 67 n.; vv. 402 ff., 38, 68; vv. 416–23, 67 n.; vv. 427–32, 67 n.; v. 431, 70 n.; v. 438, 38; v. 457, 38; vv. 587 f., 54; vv. 594 f., 54 n.; v. 602, 63 n.; vv. 605 f., 57 n.; v. 606, 60 n., 63 n.; v. 613, 55 n.; v. 614, 60 n.; vv. 615 ff., 57 n.; v. 624, 57 n.; vv. 632–4, 52, 63 n.; vv. 636 f., 57 n.; v. 647, 60 n.; vv. 712–21, 64 n.; v. 726, 61 n.; v. 733, 68 n.; vv. 775–7, 64 n.; vv. 810–61, 65 n.; v. 823, 38; v. 827, 65 n.; v. 843, 55; vv. 848–61, 66; vv. 862–901, 69; vv. 873–6, 67 n.; vv. 877–81, 67 n.; vv. 882–96, 67 n.; vv. 902–11, 67 n.; vv. 912 f., 65 n.; vv. 912–76, 65 n.; vv. 920 ff., 57 n.; vv. 923 f., 65 n.; vv. 976–96, 67 n.; vv. 1005–16, 69; vv. 1006–10, 67 n.; vv. 1153–64, 67 n.; vv. 1157 f., 66 n.; vv. 1212–15, 55 n.; vv. 1223 f., 38

Cyclops: 62; rescue in, 28 n.

V. 174, 37; v. 611, 37; vv. 624 ff., 37; v. 627, 37; v. 648, 37; v. 652, 37; vv. 688 f., 21 n.

Electra: 6, 22, 23, 45

Vv. 54–81, 22 n.; vv. 112–24, 41; vv. 213 ff., 142 n.; vv. 274–6, 23 n.; v. 355, 22 n.; vv. 418 f., 23 n.; vv. 432 ff., 42; vv. 524–6, 23 n.; vv. 677 ff., 156 n.; vv. 698 ff., 103; vv. 737 ff., 15 n.; v. 1287, 22 n.; vv. 1347–55, 9

Hecuba: 6, 9, 21, 31, 42, 93 n., 116 n., 120 n.; fission in, 35, 47; last scene, 26 n.; lyric of Troy's downfall, 41

V. 3, schol. on, 17 n.; v. 16, 40 n.; v. 254, schol. on, 14; vv. 499 f., 40 n.; vv. 534 ff., 156 n.; vv. 571 ff., 37; vv. 604 ff., 37; vv. 671 ff., 37; vv. 786–845, 47 n.; vv. 833 ff., 156 n.; vv. 894 ff., 37; v. 900, 37; vv. 1183 f., 77 n.; vv. 1289 f., 37

Helen: 7, 16 n., 23, 44, 108; *deus ex m.* in, 19; lyrics, 41; messenger's speech, 45; rescue in, 28 n.; spongy diction, 39, 178 n.; Verrall on, 33 n. *See also* Isocrates, Goethe

Vv. 27–36, 98 n.; vv. 528–45, 24; vv. 698–1106, 41 n.; vv. 777 f., 24; vv. 914 f., 156 n.; v. 932, 39; vv. 959 ff., 156 n.; vv. 1009 ff., 156 n.; vv. 1014–16, 144 n.; vv. 1028 f., 156 n.; vv. 1035–84, 39; v. 1056, 36 n.; vv. 1151–7, 120 n.; v. 1261, 114 n.; vv. 1301 ff., 42; vv. 1501 f., 39

Euripides (*cont.*)
  Heracleidae: 17, 21, 31, 35 f., 42, 43, 93 n., 116 n., 120 n., 151; bad structure, 46; last scene, 26 n.; rescue in, 28 n.
    Vv. 35 ff., 137; vv. 45 ff., 43; v. 111, 130 n.; vv. 114 f., 130 n.; vv. 181 ff., 143 n.; vv. 284 ff., 156 n.; vv. 539 ff., 94 n.; v. 588, 36 n.; vv. 646–59, 7 n.; vv. 847 f., 16 n.; vv. 855 f., 39; v. 856, 16 n.
  Heracles: 3, 6, 21, 30 n., 31, 42, 45, 53 n., 56 and n., 97, 116 n., 159; collapse of building, 56; *dénouement*, 16 f., 26 n.; Euripides' proclamation, 41; fission in, 46 f.; rescue in, 28 n.
    Vv. 65 f., 93 n.; vv. 240 ff., 37; vv. 252–74, 155 n.; v. 490, 156 n.; vv. 633 ff., 148; vv. 843 ff., 103 n.; vv. 1002 ff., 57 n.; v. 1056, 56 n.; v. 1386, 37
  Hippolytus: 5, 6 and n., 10, 24, 29, 31, 39, 40, 42, 43, 57 n., 58, 70, 74–111, 117; aetiological passages, 20; chorus, 32, 82, subsidiary chorus, 32, 113 n.; chorus-leader, 87; deities, 74, 91–110; *deus (dea) ex machina*, 19; gift of prayers, 87–89, 91–95, 97, 98–100; Homeric and Sophoclean features, 92–95; huntsman, 98; hypothesis, 93 n., 108 n.; lyrics, 41, 104, 111; messenger's speech therein, 92–95; prologue, 28; source of the action, 106–10
    Vv. 24 ff., 75 n., 79 n.; vv. 29–33, 80 n.; vv. 61–72, 32; v. 76, 95 n.; vv. 88–113, 76 n.; v. 113, 87 n.; vv. 135 ff., 80 n.; v. 155, 79 n.; vv. 166–9, 37; v. 244, 81 n.; vv. 250–66, 81 n.; v. 281, 80 n.; v. 317, 79 n.; v. 335, 81 n.; v. 340, 79 n.; v. 367, 95 n.; v. 372, 39 n.; vv. 373–430, 84; vv. 375 ff., 86; vv. 375–83, 84 n.; v. 384, 80 n.; vv. 385 ff., 81 n.; v. 401, 84 n.; vv. 415 ff., 84 n.; vv. 420–5, 85 n.; vv. 433–45, 83 n.; vv. 447–50, 83 n.; vv. 451 f., 83 n.; vv. 486 f., 96; vv. 490–7, 83 n.; vv. 503–5, 83; vv. 507–24, 80 n.; vv. 565–600, 80 n.; vv. 634–7, 76 n.; vv. 651 f., 77 n.; v. 659, 6; v. 672, 79 n.; vv. 688–92, 86 n.; v. 719, 79 n.; vv. 720 f., 85 n.; vv. 728 ff., 86 n.; vv. 752–75, 79 n., 104 n.; v. 776, schol. on, 83 n.; vv. 786 f., 83 n.; v. 810, 83 n.; vv. 828 f., 86; vv. 831 ff., 87; vv. 887 ff., 87, 88; v. 891, 100 n.; vv. 925–31, 105 n.; vv. 948 ff., 89 n.; vv. 948–55, 75 n.; v. 953, schol. on, 14 n.; vv. 967–9, 87 n.; vv. 983–1035, 89 n.; vv. 986 f., 76 n.
    Vv. 1034 f., 79 n., 89 n.; v. 1059, 87 n.; vv. 1102–10, 32 n.; vv. 1120–30, 32 n.; vv. 1153–70, 88 n.; v. 1167, 88 n.; vv. 1169 f., 96 n.; vv. 1175–81, 91 n.; v. 1189, 95 n.; vv. 1196 f., 94, 95 n.; v. 1201, 92; vv. 1206 f., 92 n.; v. 1212, 92 n., 95 n.; v. 1214, 92 n.; vv. 1216 f., 91 n., 92 n.; v. 1218, 95; vv. 1219 f., 95; vv. 1223 ff., 92 f.; vv. 1240 f., 92 n.; vv. 1243 f., 95 n.; v. 1245, 93 n.; v. 1247, 93, 95 n.; v. 1248, 91; vv. 1282 f., 96; v. 1304, 85 n.; vv. 1313–15, 97 n., 99; v. 1316, 88 n.; vv. 1320 ff., 87 n.; vv. 1325–7, 97 n., 98 n.; v. 1331, 98 n.; v. 1333, 90 n., 102 n.; vv. 1355 ff., 92 n.; v. 1396, 102 n.; v. 1398, 102 n.; vv. 1401–5, 90 n.; vv. 1411–13, 87 n.; vv. 1423–30, 101 n.; v. 1431, 101 n.
  Ion: 6, 17, 21, 159; banquet-scene, 159 n.; basket-scene, 27; *deus ex m.* 20; epilogue, 102; messenger's speech, 45; prologue, 28; tapestries, 50 n.; temple-reliefs, 50 n.
    Vv. 72 f., 28; vv. 336–58, 43 n.; vv. 499 ff., 41 n.; vv. 510 ff., 37 f.; vv. 651 ff., 43; vv. 859–922, 43 n.; vv. 934–65, 43 n.; vv. 1157 ff., 38; v. 1190, 144 n.; vv. 1364–1438, 38; vv. 1374 f., 38; v. 1397, 38; v. 1404, 38; v. 1406, 38; v. 1424, 38; vv. 1427 f., 38; vv. 1470–1500, 43 n.; vv. 1575 ff., 101 n.
  Iphigenia at Aulis: 4, 7, 23, 44 f., 60, 101, 120 n.; chorus, 32; two prologues, 18 f.
    V. 414, 24 n.; vv. 420–3, 45; vv. 590–7, 32; vv. 919–74, 23 n.; vv. 1054 f., 114 n.; v. 1078, 114 n.; vv. 1124 ff., 40; vv. 1129 ff., 24 n.; v. 1356, 94 n.; vv. 1429 ff., 23 n.; vv. 1568 f., 23 n.

INDEX

Iphigenia in Tauris: 6, 7 n., 19, 25, 26, 41, 45, 64 n.; rescue in, 28

Vv. 102 f., 23; vv. 123–235, 39; vv. 248–51, 27; vv. 374 ff., 22; vv. 499–504, 27; vv. 535 ff., 26; vv. 584–7, 25; vv. 660–71, 22 n.; vv. 711 ff., 23; vv. 915–22, 27; vv. 947–54, 17; v. 1172, 40; vv. 1204 f., 22 n.

Medea: 6, 11, 25, 33 ff., 42, 108 f., 117, 159; her chariot, 18, 34 n.; *deus ex m.*, 20 f.; messenger's speech, 45 n.; plot, 46; "Praise of Attica" lyric, 41; prologue, 18; rescue in, 28

Vv. 214 ff., 177 n.; vv. 374 f., 37; vv. 376–94, 34; vv. 445–622, 22; vv. 527 ff., 110 n.; vv. 798 f., 34 n.; vv. 824–45, 17, 34, 41; v. 871, 83 f. n.; vv. 1228 ff., 148 n.; vv. 1375 ff., 35 n.

Orestes: 7, 24, 29, 33, 39, 40, 116 n.; chorus, 32; *deus ex m.*, 19–21; epilogue, 102; hypothesis, 21 n.; length, 33 n.; Phrygian, 39 n., 41

V. 128, schol. on, 30 n.; vv. 140–86, 32; vv. 580 f., 156 n.; vv. 675 f., 156 n.; vv. 772–8, 24, 40; v. 981, schol. on, 17 n.; v. 982 ff., 15 n.; v. 1068, 24; vv. 1225 ff., 156 n.; vv. 1231 ff., 156 n.; vv. 1369 ff., 39 n.; vv. 1497 f., 57 n.; vv. 1671 f., 22; vv. 1682 ff., 41 n.

Phoenissae: 27, 31, 33, 44, 117 n.; chorus, 38; compared with *Septem*, 49; interpolations, 36 f., 152, 179; length, 36; melodramatic, 25 f.; messenger's speech, 27, 43; structure, 36 f.

Vv. 10–13, 40; v. 22, schol. on, 38 n.; v. 63, 147 n.; vv. 81–83, 26 n.; v. 88, schol. on, 33 n.; v. 202, 38; v. 208, 38; v. 211, 38; v. 388, schol. on, 14 n.; vv. 515–17, 120 n.; vv. 696–783, 36; v. 751, 15 n.; vv. 1139 f., 16 n.; v. 1147, 38; vv. 1172–86, 127 n.; vv. 1183–5, 157; v. 1430, 22 n.; vv. 1758 ff., 36 n.

Rhesus: 7, 32, 44 n., 150; *deus ex m.*, 7; prologue, 19 n.

Vv. 161–90, 27; v. 304, 38; v. 356, 38; vv. 617 f., 38; vv. 893 f., 97 n.; vv. 906 ff., 97 n.; vv. 938 ff., 97 n.

Supplices: 6, 7, 17, 31, 37, 42; Aethra's speech, 27, 151 f., 161 n., 166, 167, 174; chorus: who are they? 115 f.; classes in the state, 128, 154, 165 n., 177; Epigoni, 14 and n., 116, 143, 149, 152, 160 f.; faults of language or style, 145–9; funeral speech, 117 n., 126–9, 157, 166 ff., 177; handmaids, 113, 153, 155, 160, 166 f., 168; herald, 118, 127 n., 130 f., 142 f., 147, 156, 161, 166, 173 f.; "hitch-thrill", 27; messenger's speech, 114 n.; mothers of the Seven, 115 f., 129, 130, 153, 158 f., 160 f., 162, 167 n., 175 f.; politics and political history, 129–41, 155, 166; rescue, 28 n.; the Seven, 112, 114 n., 126–9, 167; stage-presentation difficulties, 159 f.; suttee, 125 f., 160, 168 f.; Theseus' "sermon", 129 n., 143 ff., 176, 177; urn-bearing, 113 f., 159, 160 f., 162, 166

Who wrote our *Supp.*? 152–81; analysis into Euripidean and anonymous parts, 153–61; anonymous "Supplices" discussed, 166 ff.; Euripidean authorship, arguments for, 149–52; Euripidean portions, 161 f.; fourth-century features, 118–26; sutures, 157

Vv. 1–70, 153; v. 9, 115 n.; vv. 11 ff., 112; vv. 36 ff., 154 n.; vv. 40 f., 117; vv. 71–87, 113 n., 153, 166; vv. 87–194, 153 f.; vv. 100 ff., 112; v. 113, 133; vv. 115 ff., 152 and n.; v. 161, 143; v. 166, 142, 154 n.; v. 170, 144 n.; vv. 171 f., 153 n.; v. 179, 153; vv. 180–3, 153 n.; vv. 184 ff., 166 n.; vv. 184–92, 153; v. 186, 146, 153 n.; vv. 190 ff., 165; vv. 195 ff., 125 n., 170 n.; vv. 195–252, 129, 143–5, 154, 166; v. 209, 146; vv. 216 ff., 125; vv. 219–25, 143, 171; vv. 226 ff., 122 n.; vv. 238–45, 128, 165 n., 168 n.; vv. 240 ff., 123 f.; vv. 246–9, 154; v. 248, 143; v. 249, 122 n.; vv. 250 f., 142, 154; vv. 253–62, 155; vv. 267–70, 118, 155, 166, 167; vv. 271–398, 155; vv. 275 f., 113 n., 153 n., 155; vv. 297–331, 161 n., 167; vv. 314 ff., 152; v. 346, 132; vv. 349–53, 132, 133 n., 135 n., 155

INDEX

Euripides (cont.)
Supplices (cont.)
 Vv. 359–64, 155; v. 365, 115 n.;
vv. 393 f., 132; vv. 399–597, 155 f.;
vv. 403 ff., 133; vv. 403–55, 166;
vv. 404–8, 135, 145, 155; v. 432,
155; vv. 438–42, 138, 145, 155, 166;
v. 452, 146; vv. 454 f., 156; vv.
465–510, 142; vv. 476–93, 146 f.,
156; vv. 481–93, 118, 156; vv. 494 f.,
147; vv. 496–9, 127 and n.; vv.
508 f., 147, 156; v. 513, 173; vv.
513 ff., 142, 156; vv. 528 f., 145; vv.
531–6, 156, 169 and n., 171, 173,
177; vv. 531–58, 173; vv. 533 f., 143 n.
 Vv. 543 ff., 156; vv. 545 f., 156;
vv. 545–8, 125 n.; v. 549, 168 n.;
vv. 549–57, 144 n.; v. 557, 156 n.;
v. 561, 146; vv. 569 f., 156; vv.
584 ff., 156 n.; vv. 586 ff., 173;
vv. 589 f., 122 n., 141 f. n., 145;
vv. 594 f., 156; vv. 596 f., 156 n.;
vv. 598–633, 156; vv. 634–777,
156 f.; v. 661, 146; v. 665, 158 n.;
v. 667, 164 n.; vv. 674 f., 148; vv.
674–9, 164 n.; v. 682, 156; vv.
714–17, 148, 156 f., 167 n.; vv.
725 ff., 151; vv. 734–6, 157, 167 n.;
vv. 744–9, 118, 157, 166 n., 167 n.;
v. 755, 114 n.; v. 764, 148; vv.
774–7, 148, 157; vv. 778–837, 157;
vv. 786 ff., 115 n.; vv. 798–836,
160; vv. 811–17, 162 n.; vv. 838–
954, 157–9; vv. 841 ff., 126, 143;
vv. 844–56, 158, 167; vv. 846–56,
158; v. 858, 129 n.; v. 860, 149 n.;
vv. 860–908, 114 n.; vv. 861–6,
149 n.; vv. 861–71, 127 f.; v. 871,
146; vv. 873–7, 125 n., 127; v. 879,
127 n.; vv. 886 ff., 115, 148; vv.
899 f., 128 n., 147; vv. 901 ff.,
152 n.; vv. 913 ff., 145; vv. 925–31,
114 n., 126, 167 n.; vv. 933–54, 158;
vv. 934–9, 115, 158, 159 n.; v. 936,
160; vv. 949–54, 119, 158, 166 n.;
vv. 955–79, 159; v. 957, 115 n.,
162 n.; vv. 961 f., 159; vv. 963 ff.,
112, 114 n., 162 n.; vv. 974–6, 149 n.
 V. 980, 159; vv. 980–1113, 125 f.,
166; vv. 980–1164, 159, 161; vv.
982 f., 159 n.; v. 1073, 115 n.; vv.
1077 ff., 116; vv. 1080–1103, 160;
vv. 1089 ff., 160, 178 n.; vv. 1108–
14, 124, 149 n., 160; vv. 1115 ff.,
113, 153 n., 160, 166; vv. 1139–42,
143, 160; vv. 1147 ff., 143 n.; v.
1165, 115 n., 145, 162; vv. 1165 f.,
160; vv. 1165–1231, 161; vv. 1188 ff.,
117; v. 1207, 114 n., 115; vv. 1217 f.,
114 n., 162 n.; v. 1219, 147, 148,
161; vv. 1232 ff., 116, 161
 Troades: 9, 11, 15, 25, 42, 43 f., 109,
120 n.; lyric of Troy's downfall, 41
 V. 1, schol. on, 30 n.; v. 62 ff.,
21 f.; v. 91, 40; v. 147, 41; vv.
469 ff., 84 n.; vv. 884–8, 14 n., 144 n.;
vv. 933–50, 83 n.; vv. 985 f., 104 n.;
vv. 987 f., 83 n., 109; vv. 1126–35,
43; vv. 1266 f., 25 n.; vv. 1305 ff.,
156 n.; v. 1327, 25 n.
Andromeda: 28 n., 31, 50 n.
Hippolytus Veiled: 78 n., 93 f., 108 n.
Hypsipyle: fission, 46 n.; lullaby, 50;
rescue in, 28 n.
Peliades: 16 n.
Phaethon: 31
Polyidus: 78 n.
Protesilaus: 126 n.
Stheneboea: 78 n.
Dithyramb for Alcibiades?: 165
Euripides Junior, 18, 60 n.
Eurydice (Hypsipyle), 46 n.
Eurystheus, 21, 46
εὐθύς, 94 n., 95 n.
Exangelos, 83 n.
ἐξοισθήσεται, 146

Fairy Queen, 108
Faust: Goethe on chorus in Helena, 69
Feugère, G., 125 n.
"Fillers", 31
Forgeries of Gk. literature, 136 n., 181
Fortune, 121 f.
Four-horsed chariots, 164 n.
Fourth-century, idea of Fortune in,
121 f.; war and society in, 118–21,
157, 158
Frenzy (Heracles), 46, 103
Freytag, G., 11
Fritzsche, F. V., 13 n.
Frogs. See Aristophanes
Fury (Aeneid), 92 n.; Furies (Eumenides),
114 n.

Galen, 181 n.
Ganymede, 42 n.

INDEX

Geffcken, J., 7 n.
George, Mrs. (*Getting Married*), 81 n.
Gift of Prayers in *Hippolytus*. *See* Eur. *Hipp*.
Giles, P., 128, 164 n., 165 n.
Glamour. *See* Eur. *Bacchae*
Glover, M. R., 65 n., 71 n., 72 n.
Goethe, 1, 47, 69
Gogh, Van, 5 n.
Golden Lamb legend, 103
Gomme, A. W., 120 n.
Goossens, R., 123 n., 132 n., 134, 151, 164 n.
Graham, H. F., 104 n.
Grantly, Major, 91 f. n.
Grégoire, H., 114 n., 117 n., 123 n., 127 n., 129 n., 132 n., 142 n., 151 n., 152 n., 153 n., 155 n., 158 n.
Gregory, St., of Nazianzus, 179
Grillparzer, 34 n.
Grube, G. M. A., 53 f., 55 n., 56, 69, 79 n., 87 n., 89 n., 92 n., 95 n., 98 n., 107, 116 n., 117 n.

Hadley, J., 93 n.
Hadrian, 136 n.
Haigh, A. E., 117 n.
Haliartus, 164
Halicarnassus, 132 n.
Hamlet, 37, 81
Hamlet, 92 n.
Handmaids. *See* Eur. *Supp*.
Hardy, Thomas, 17 n., 108
Harrison, J. E., 6 n.
Hartleton, Lady (Trollope) 92 n.
Hartung, A. J., 94 n., 126 n., 128 n., 159 n.
Headlam, W., 1
Hector (*Rhesus*), 7 n., 22 n.
Hecuba (*Hecuba*), 40, 47 and n.; (*Troades*), 14, 25, 43, 84 n., 109 f., 144
Hecuba. *See* Euripides
Hedda Gabler, 29
Helen, 43; (*Helen*), 24 f., 28 n., 39, 44; (*Orestes*), 22; (*Troades*), 14, 109
Helen (*Helena*). *See* Euripides, Isocrates, Goethe
Hellanicus, 17
ἡνίοχοι, 164 n.
Hera, 103
Heracleidae. *See* Euripides
Heracles, 43, 46, 94 n., 120 n., 134; (*Alcestis*), 12 f., 18, 37; (*Heracles*), 28 n., 47 n., 56 n., 159; (*Philoctetes*), 45
Heracles. *See* Euripides
Heraclides, 135
Herald, Theban. *See* Eur. *Supp*.
Hermann, G., 113 n., 114 n., 115 n., 145
Hermes, 28
Hermione, 3, 39, 46; (*Androm*.), 11, 43; (*Orestes*), 22, 103
Herodotus, 50, 126
Herter, H., 99 n.
Herwerden, H. van, 145 n.
Hesperides, 111
Hesychius, 125 n.
Hicks, E. L., 132 n.
ἱερόν, 92 n., 95 n.
Hill, G. F., 132 n.
Hindu widows, 126
Hippolytus, 6, 28, 58, 74–111; his religion, 74 ff.; his oath, 77
Hippolytus, and *Hipp. Veiled*. *See* Euripides
Hippomedon, 126, 128
Hitch or check in dramatic action, 27 f.
Holzner, E., 145 n.
Homer, 11, 37, 42 n., 50, 56 n., 57 n., 72 n., 94 f., 97 n., 124, 125 n., 135, 148 n. *See also* Hymn to Dioscuri, *Iliad*, *Odyssey*
"Homo ex machina". *See* Deus ex machina
Horace, 11, 20, 53 n., 57
Hound of Hell, 37
Housman, A. E., 40
Hugo, Victor, 41
Hyginus, 136 n., 175 n. (*bis*)
Hyllus, 43, 46
Hymn to Dioscuri, Homeric, 97 n.
Hypnotism. *See* Eur. *Bacchae*
Hypsipyle, 46 n.
Hypsipyle. *See* Euripides

Iago, 24
Iambics. *See* Moschion
Ibsen, 8, 10, 29, 60, 78 n.
Ibycus, 97 n.
Iceman Cometh, The, 12
Iliad, 7, 93 n., 95 n., 124, 125 n., 135, 148 n.
"Imitation", mutual, of Sophocles and Euripides, 10 f.
India, 169
Indians of Virginia, 9

INDEX

Influence on the tragedians: of contemporary events, etc., 8 f.; of the festival, 8; of other playwrights, 10 f.
Ino, 56 n.
Interpolation by actors, 33, 36 f., 179
Iolaus, 43, 94 n., 143 n.
Ion, 27, 37 f., 43, 135
   (of Chios), 10, 11
Ion. See Euripides
Ionia, 17
Ionian Sea, 38
Iphigenia, 17, 45
Iphigenia at Aulis, Iph. in Tauris. See Euripides
Iphis, 116, 124, 160, 177
Iris (*Heracles*), 46
Iscariot, 113
Isocrates, 96 n., 119 f. and n., 125 n., 133 n., 136 f., 139 f., 141
Italy of the Renaissance, 3
Ivanhoe, 48
Ixion, 128

Jason (*Medea*), 5, 22, 34, 101, 109
   (of Pherae), 172 n.
Jebb, Sir R. C., 7, 9 n., 15 n., 32 n., 93 n., 97 n., 107 n.
Jerome, St., 48
Jesus, trial of, 159 n.
Joan of Arc, 131
Jocasta (*Oed. Tyr.*), 26 n.; (*Phoen.*), 44; (Eur. *Supp.*), 115, 162
John Bull, 109
John Bull's Other Island, 101 n., 153 n.
Jonson, 3
Jowett, B., 1 n., 165 n.
Juliet, 81
Julius Caesar, 102
Justin, 164 n.

Kalkmann, A., 80 n.
κάνθος, 178 n.
Kayser, T., 170 n., 172
Keats, 10
King Lear, 180
Kirchhoff, A., 133 n., 153 n.
Kirkwood, G. M., 47 n.
Kitto, H. D. F., 11 n., 42, 44 n., 47 n. (*bis*), 53 n., 55 n., 56 n., 58 n., 106 n., 117 n., 125 n.
Knight, Henry (*A Pair of Blue Eyes*), 17 n.
Knights. See Aristophanes

Körte, G., 170 n.
Kranz, W., 32 n.
κράσπεδον, 146
Kretschmer, P., 76 n.

Labels, value of, 12
Laches, 128
Lamachus, 128
Lamian War, 165
Laodamia, 126 n.
Last Chronicle of Barset, The, 92 n.
Laurentian MS. (Aesch.), 95 n.; (Eur.), 149
"Law for the gods", 98, 100
Lee, Sir Sidney, 9
Length of tragedies, 32–37
Lennep, D. F. W. van, 15 n.
Leochares (pseudo-Demosth.), 146
Leonardo da Vinci, 7
Lesky, A., 99 n., 107, 112, 162 n.
Lions in *Iliad*, 7, 37
Little snags in Eur., 37 f., 154 n.
"Longinus", 11, 61 n.
Love's Comedy, 10, 29
Lucan, 1
Lucretius, 48
Lüders, O., 117 n.
Lycophron, 1
Lycurgus, 61 n.
Lycus, 30 n., 37
Lyrics. *See* Euripides
Lysander, 164
Lysias, 164, 181 n.
Lysistrata. See Aristophanes

Macaria, 35, 46
Macbeth, 5, 24, 33 n., 92 n., 180 n.
Macedonia, 68, 71, 119
McLean, J. H., 36 n.
Maenads, 28
Magi, 159 n.
Magic. *See* Eur. *Bacchae*
Mahaffy, Sir J. P., 118 n.
Man of Destiny, The, 33
"Man of the theatre", 29 f.
Marivaux, 29
Markland, J., 145, 146 n.
Marlowe, C., 11, 37, 127
Marquee (*Ion*), 38
Martin Chuzzlewit, 48, 162
Masqueray, P., 154 n.
Matthaei, L. E., 77 n., 82 n., 86 n.
Mausolus, 132 n.

INDEX

Medea, 17, 18, 21, 28 n., 34 f., 37, 85, 101, 109
Medea (Eur.). *See* Euripides
    (Grillparzer), 34 n.
Megara (*Heracles*), 46
Meineke, J. A. F. A., 164 n., 169 n. (*bis*), 170 n. (*bis*), 172 and n. (*bis*), 175 n. (*bis*), 176 n., 177, 178 n., 179 n.
Mela, Pomponius, 126 n.
Melodrama. *See* Euripides
Menander, 83 n.
Menelaus (*Ajax*), 29; (*Androm.*), 11, 30 n., 43, 51, 69; (*Helen*), 24 f., 36, 39, 44; (*Iph. Aul.*), 24, 44, 101; (*Orestes*), 22, 102; (*Troades*), 14; (*Faust*), 69
Menoeceus, 27, 36
Méridier, L., 106
Merlin, 91
Messengers' speeches, 16 n.; (*Ajax*), 45 n.; (*Bacchae*), 54 f., 59, 64, 66; (*Helen*), 45; (*Hipp.*), 88, 91–95; (*Ion*), 45; (*Iph. Taur.*), 45; (*Medea*), 45 n.; (*Phoen.*), 27, 45; (*Supp.*), 114 n., 151, 162, 164 n., 166
Mewaldt, J. R., 181 n.
Meyer, G. H., 54
Meyer, K. H., 93 n.
Michaelis, A., 169 n.
Michel, C., 132 n.
Middle Comedy, 21
Milton, 10, 152 n.
Minos (pseudo-Plato), 150
Moira, 98
Molière, 25 n., 29
Mon Étoile, 10
Mona Lisa, 7
Monarchy, divergence from, 134 f., 138 and n., 141 f. n., 155 n.
Monopoly, Apollo's, 42
Moreau, Dr. (H. G. Wells), 178
Morgan, C., 100 n.
Moschion, 156, 169–78; date, 169 f.; iambic technique, 169 n., 170 n. (*bis*), 176–8; on refusal of burial, 170–2, 173 f.; style and language, 178; his "Supplices"? 166, 173, 176
Moses Chorenensis, 16
Mothers of the Seven against Thebes. *See* Eur. *Supp.*
Mourning Becomes Electra, 12
Müller, C., 10 n.
Munychia, Munychus, 104 n.

Murray, G., 6–8, 18 n., 20 n., 30 n., 32 n., 33 n., 36 n., 38 n., 47, 54 n., 56, 60 n., 64 n., 65 n., 68, 70 n., 71 f., 76 n., 79 n., 80 n., 85 n., 86 n., 95 n., 104 n., 115 n., 127 n., 133 n., 144 n., 149 n., 150 n., 153 n., 156 n., 157 n., 158 n., 160
Musgrave, S., 128
Musurus, 65 n.
Mylasa, 132 n.
Mystery-plays, 159 n.
Mythology, modern, 109

Naevius, 180 n.
νάρθηξ, 65 f. n.
Nauck, A., 95 n., 133 n., 157 n., 166 n., 173 n., 175 n.
Naxos, 78
Neaera (pseudo-Demosth.), 136, 137 f., 139
Nereids, 114 n.
Nereus, 114 n.
Nestle, W., 49 n., 165 n., 168 n.
New Comedy, 21, 152 n.
Newman, W. L., 166 n.
Nicias, 128, 129; Peace of, 150 n.
Nicomachus, 61
Nihard, R., 65 n., 68 n., 71 n.
Nile delta, 68
Nurse (*Hipp.*), 19, 74, 76 f., 79, 80–83, 87, 90, 95, 107

Ocean-nymphs, 115
ὀχετός, 124
Odysseus, 57, 97 n.
Odyssey, 21 n., 57 n., 72 n., 95 n.
Oedipus, 49, 116, 157, 179; in Sophocles, 107 n.; (*Oed. Tyr.*), 26 n., 121; (*Phoen.*), 36, 179
Oedipus Coloneus and *Oed. Tyrannus*. *See* Sophocles
Oenone (*Phèdre*), 86 n.
Oeta, Mt., 17
οἰσθήσομαι, 146
Oligaethidae, 91 f. n.
Oligarchs, Athenian, 164
Olympia, 165
ὄμπνιος, 178 n.
One-act plays, 33
O'Neill, E., 11 f.
Ophelia, 79 n.
Orestes, 3, 21; (*Androm.*), 43; (Eur. *El.*), 23; (*Iph. Taur.*), 20, 23, 26 f., 28; (*Orestes*), 20 n., 22, 24, 40, 102
Orestes. *See* Euripides

Orgies, Bacchic, 38
Orgon (*Tartuffe*), 25 n.
Orphan, The, 180
Orpheus, 74
Othello, 24, 43
Otto, W. F., 90 n., 96 n.
Otway, T., 180
Ovid, 92 n., 98 n.
Owen, A. S., 38 n.

Paedagogus (*Ion*), 19; (*Phoen.*), 36
Page, D. L., 179 n.
Pagondas, 150 n.
Pair of Blue Eyes, A, 17 n.
Palace-miracle. See Eur. *Bacchae*
Palatine MS. of Eur., 149
Paley, F. A., 15 n., 93 n., 114 n., 125 n.
Pandion, 97 n., 138
Pantomimes, Christmas, 108
Paphos, 68
παραβάται, 164 n.
Paris (Trojan), 204; (*Rhesus*), 44 n.
Parthenopaeus, 126, 128
Pater, W. H., 53 n.
Patin, M., 80 n.
Pattes de Mouche, Les, 29
Paul, St., 15
Pausanias (author), 136 n., 164 n.
    (K. of Sparta), 164
Peace. See Aristophanes
Pearson, A. C., 36 n., 94 n., 123 n., 175 n.
Peasant-husband of Electra, 22
Peisistratid tyranny, 140
Peisistratus, 136 n.
Peleus, 20
Peliades. See Euripides
Pelias, 16 n.
Peloponnesian War, 9, 28, 30, 156 n.
Pentheus, 2, 17, 28 n., 38, 46, 52–67
Periboea, 115
Pericles, 49, 102, 119 (*ter*), 132 n., 133 f., 149, 151
Peripatetic School, 6
Peripeteia, 44, 46; (*Lynceus*), 4 n.; (*Oed. Tyr.*), 4 n.; (original Eur. *Supp.*), 161 n.
Persae. See Aeschylus
Persephone, 42
Persius, 1
Petersen, E., 113 n., 115 n.
Pflugk, A. J. E., 114 n.
Phaedra, 3, 6, 21, 28, 58, 74, 76, 77–80,
    81–86, 89 f., 90 f., 95 f., 99 n., 102 and n., 104 and n., 107 and n., 109 f.
Phaedra (Seneca), 79 n.
    (Soph.). See Sophocles
Phaedrus, 16
Phaethon. See Euripides
Phantom. See Eur., *Bacchae*
Pharae, 172 n.
Pharnabazus, 172
Pheidippides, 13
Pherae, 172
Pheraeans, 172
Pheraeans, 170, 171–3
Pherecydes, 17
Pheres, 12, 13
Philemon, 1
Philip II of Macedon, 119, 125, 164 n., 165
    V of Macedon, 149 n.
Philippic, Fourth (pseudo-Demosth.), 150
Philochorus, 134 n.
Philoctetes. See Sophocles
Philostratus, 123 n.
φόβος, 95
Phocylides, 48
Phoebus. See Apollo
Phoenissae (Eur.). See Euripides
    (Phrynichus), 10
Photius, 94 n., 172 n.
Phrynichus (tragedian), 10
    (scholar), 178 f., 181 n.
Pickard-Cambridge, Sir A. W., 31 n., 117 n.
"Pièce bien faite", 29
Pilate, 159 n.
Pindar, 11, 16, 41, 91 f. n., 121, 150
Piraeus, 164
Pitcher-Feast, 17, 20
Plato, 16, 39, 119, 123–5, 140, 150, 154, 156, 160, 168 n., 181 n.
Platonius, 46 n.
Plautus, 35, 180
Pleiad, Alexandrian, 152, 170 n.
Pleisthenes, 97 n.
Pliny the Elder, 137 n.
Plots, simple and complex, 44
Plutarch, 85 f. n., 133 n., 135, 136, 138, 139, 149 n., 164 n., 165 n.
Plutus. See Aristophanes
Poenulus, 35, 180
Pohlenz, M., 53 n., 79 n., 85 n. (*ter*), 94 n., 105 n.
Politics and political history. See Eur., *Supp.*

INDEX

Polonius, 51
Polybius, 120 n., 149 n.
Polydorus, 47
Polyidus. See Euripides
Polymestor, 21, 35, 37, 47 n.
Polynices (*Phoen.*), 25, 27, 36; (Eur. *Supp.*), 114 (*bis*), 115 n., 126, 157, 162
Polyphron, 172
Polyxena, 37; "Polyxena-tragedy" in *Hecuba*, 35, 47
Pompeius Trogus, 164 n.
Portress (*Helen*), 44
Poseidippus, 120 n.
Poseidon (*Hipp.*), 87, 88, 91, 95, 96 f., 98, 99, 109 n.; (*Troades*), 21 f.
Potidaea, 143 n.
Powell, J. U., 36 n., 179 n. (*bis*)
Prayers, the three, in *Hipp.* See Eur. *Hipp.*
Prior, M., 100 n.
Private performances. See Euripides
Prodicus, 105 n., 168 n.
Prometheus, 170 n.
Prometheus Vinctus. See Aeschylus
Propertius, 126 n.
Prospero, 81
Protesilaus. See Euripides
Providence, 125 n.
Pseudo-Demosthenes. See Demosthenes
Ptolemy Philadelphus, 170 n.
Published texts of plays, 160 n.
"Puppets of Fate", 107 f.
Pylades (*Iph. Taur.*), 23, 25, 26 f.; (*Orestes*), 24, 40
Pylos, 134 n.
Pythia (*Ion*), 21

Racine, 3, 4, 77 n., 80 n., 86 n., 88 n., 100 n.
Reiske, J. J., 153 n.
Repeat performances, 30 f.
Republic (Plato), 119, 123–5, 140, 156, 160
Rescue-plays, 7, 28 f.
Rhesus. See Euripides
Rhetorical or idiomatic blunders. See Eur. *Supp.*
Ribbeck, O., 169 n., 170 n., 171 n., 172 n., 176 n.
Richard III, 44
Riddle of the Bacchae, The, 52–73
Rivier, A., 34 n.
Robertson, D. S., 50 n.
Romeo and Juliet, 180

Ronsard, 2
Rose, H. J., 181 n.
Rosmersholm, 29
Rural Dionysia, 31 n.
Rutherford, W. G., 179 n.

Sabazius, 71 n.
Salaminian sailors, 115
Salamis, 141 f. n., 171
Salter, W. H., 72
Samos (island), 9 n.
  (Macedonian), 149 n.
Sandys, Sir J. E., 67 n., 91 n., 135 n. (*bis*)
Santa Claus, 109
Sardou, 10, 29
Schenkl, K., 155 n., 167 n.
Schiller, 49 n., 50, 131
Schlegel, A. W. von, 1, 4 n., 23, 43 f., 51, 100 n., 108 n.
Schmid, W., 6 n., 7 n., 17 n., 19 n., 20 n., 21 n., 28 f., 30 n., 56 n., 70 n., 93 n., 106, 108 n., 132 n., 149 n., 156 n., 167 n.
Schramm, F., 169 n., 170 n., 175 n., 177 n.
Scopas, 149 n.
Scott, Sir W., 48
Scribe, F., 10, 29
Semele, 70, 82
Seneca, 79 n., 88 n., 92 n., 92 f. n.
Sergius Saranoff (Shaw), 22
Seven against Thebes (*Septem*). See Aeschylus
Seven champions. See Eur. *Supp.*
Sextus Empiricus, 105 n.
Shakespeare, 4, 7, 11, 24, 29, 33 n., 51, 57 f., 180; inscription on his bust, 143
Shallow, Justice, 47 n.
Shaw, G. B., 8, 33 n., 81 n., 101 f., 131
Shelley, 41
Sheppard, Sir J. T., 26 n.
Shield of Achilles (Eur. *El.*), 42
Sicilian Expedition, 9, 119
Sicily, 38
σίδαρος and σίδηρος, 95 n.
Sneller, C. B., 7 n., 38 n.
Socrates, 16, 50, 84, 125 n., 143
Solinus, 126 n.
Solon, 102, 132 n., 133, 134 n., 135 n., 138, 139, 141 and n.
Sophists, 49
Sophocles: 3, 4, 5, 6, 8, 11, 19, 33, 36, 45 and n., 85, 86 n., 90, 92–94, 175 n.; characterization, 6 n.; chorus, use of, 31; devices to heighten suspense,

INDEX

Sophocles (cont.)
26; on Euripides, 14, 94; the hitch, 27; a "man of the theatre", 29; Oedipus a "puppet of fate"? 107 n.; Plato on, 16; his religion, 8; and the sophistic era, 10; style, 39, 92–94
  Ajax: 10, 27, 45 n.; v. 847, 93 n.
  Antigone: v. 352, 91 n.; vv. 126–35, 127 n.
  Electra: 27; v. 121, 93 n.; v. 747, 93 n.; v. 806, 93 n.
  Oed. Col.: 31; episodic? 44 n.; length, 33, 179; vv. 964–73, 107 n.; vv. 1016 f., 32 n.; v. 1116, 15 n.
  Oed. Tyr.: 4 n., 5, 27, 31, 45; v. 264, schol. on, 30 n.; v. 361, 26 n.; v. 558, 26 n.; vv. 717–30, 26 n.; vv. 788–93, 107 n.; vv. 1110 f., 107 n.; vv. 1329 f., 107 n.; vv. 1475 f., 156 n.; vv. 1524–30, 36 n.
  Phaedra: 93 f. n., 108 n.
  Philoctetes: 9 n.; chorus, 31; *deus ex machina*, 19; solution, 11, 45; vv. 410–52, 9 n.
  Thyestes at Sicyon: 175 n.
  Trachiniae: 10, 47 n.; vv. 868 ff., 175 n.
  Fr. 683: 123 n.
Sophrosyne (σωφροσύνη), 67, 78 n., 84 f., 86, 89 f.
Sositheus, 170 n.
Soteria, Delphic, 117 n.
Southey, 10
Sparta, 119, 125
Spenser, 10, 57, 95 n.
Spongy writing, 39, 171 n., 178 n.
Spranger, J. A., 35 n., 37 n., 47 n.
"Stage"-presentation in Eur. *Supp.*, 159 f. *See also* Curtain
Stage villains, 30
Standard of tragedy, none for Greeks, 5 f.
Steinweg, C., 12 n., 68 n., 71 n.
Stesichorus, 11
Stheneboea. *See* Euripides
Stitchery in plays, 178 ff.
Stobaeus, 156, 169, 170, 173, 174, 177
στορέννυμι, 53 n.
Strange Interlude, 12
"Stranger, The". *See* Eur., *Bacchae*
Stratford-on-Avon, 143
Strepsiades (*Clouds*), 13
Sublime, On the, 36 f.
Suidas, 10 n.
Sun-god, 34, 109 n.

συνθρανόω, 52 f. n.
Supplices. *See* Aeschylus *and* Euripides
Susemihl, F., 165 n.
Suspense, dramatic, 25–29
Suttee. *See* Eur. *Supp.*
Sutures. *See* Euripides
Swinburne, 1, 117
Synoecismos, 133, 134, 136, 137, 139
Syracuse, 31

Tableaux, 116
Talthybius, 40
Tamburlaine, 127
Tamburlaine, 11
Tartuffe, 25 n.
Tate, N., 180
Telephus (Moschion), 170, 171
Temenus, 175 n.
Tempest, The, 9, 57 f.
Temple at Jerusalem, 159 n.
Tennyson, 121
Terence, 8, 83 n., 180
Tess of the d'Urbervilles, 108 n.
Teucer (*Ajax*), 29; (*Helen*), 44
Thales, 155 n.
Thanatos (*Alcestis*), 13
Thebes, 5, 119, 122, 132, 149
Themistocles, 171 n.
Themistocles, 170, 171
Theocritus (pseudo-), 150
Theodectes, 4
Theognis, 48
Theonoe, 7, 144
Theophrastus, 133 n.
Théramène (*Phèdre*), 77 n.
Theramenes, 123 n.
Thermum, 149 n.
Theseus (Bacchylides), 97 n.
Theseus (Euripides)
  Heracles: 16, 21, 47 n., 56
  Hippolytus: 19, 43, 74 f., 77, 80, 85 n., 86–89, 97 f., 99 f., 102 f., 105, 107, 109, 111
  Supplices: 27, 112, 114 n., 115, 117 n., 122–9; altercation with herald, 130 f., 142 f.; in political history, 131–41, 155, 168; on politics, 132; prototype of Pericles, 132 n., 133 f., 151; his "sermon", 129, 143–5, 154, 168, 170 n., 177
Thesmophoria, 152
Thesmophoriazusae. *See* Aristophanes
Thespis, 10 n.

INDEX

Thesprotus, 175 n.
Thetes, 134 n.
Thetis, 26, 46, 108, 114 n.
Thoas, 22, 40
Thompson, M. B., 169 n.
Thorne, Mrs. (*Last Chronicle of Barset*), 92 n.
Thrace, 35
θρανεύω and θρανόω, 53 n.
Thrasyllus, 117 n.
Thucydides, 9, 11, 17 n., 114 n., 120, 134, 140, 150, 151, 165 n., 171 n.; account of Delium, 163 f.; speeches in, 119
Thyestes, 175 n.
Thyestes at Sicyon. See Sophocles
Tiresias (*Bacchae*), 2, 22 n., 38, 46, 66, 71 n.
   (*Phoen.*), 27, 36
Toup, J., 158 n.
Trachiniae. See Sophocles
Tragedy: "anagnostics", 118, 159, 167 f.; no curtain, etc., 116, 153, 159 f., 162, 168; *deus* (and *homo*) *ex machina*, 7, 19 ff., 28 f., 35, 102; "economy", 5 f.; episodic scenes, 5 f., 43–45; its genesis, 8–18; 'hitch-thrill", 26 f.; influences on tragedians, of contemporary events, etc., 8 f., of the festival, 30–33, of other playwrights, 10 f.; length of plays, 32–34; "man of the theatre", 29 f.; plots simple and complex, 44; puppets of fate? 107 f.; repeat-performances, 30 f.; rescue-plays, 7, 28 f.; stage villains, 30; no standard, 5 f.; suspense, 25–29; tableaux, 116; Trojan War a favourite theme, 31
Tribes, four Athenian, 134
Trilling, L., 4 n.
Triphylia, 120 n.
Troad, 35
Troades. See Euripides
Trochaics, 63
Trogus, Pompeius, 164 n.
Trojan women, 115
Trojan Women. See *Troades*
Trozen, 80, 90, 95
Tyché, 121 f.
Tydeus, 114 n., 115, 126 (*bis*), 128, 162 n.
Tyrannos, 130
Tyre, 38
Tyrrell, R. Y., 67 n.

Tyrtaeus, 128
Tyrwhitt, T., 54 n.

Uncle Sam, 109
Urn-bearing. See Eur. *Supp.*

Valckenaer, L. K., 95 n., 171 n.
Venice Preserved, 180
Venus (Lucretius), 48
Verrall, A. W., 1, 3 f., 7, 16 n., 20, 29, 33 n., 42 n., 43 and n., 46 n., 52 n., 55, 57 n. (*bis*), 64 and n., 65 f., 68, 71, 72, 80 n., 91, 95 n., 108, 112 n., 179 n.
Villefosse, H. de, A. M. A., 169 n.
Virbius, 99 n.
Virgil, 10, 92 n., 99 n., 107 n., 143
Virginia, 9
Voltaire, 60

Wagner, F. G., 169 n. (*bis*), 172, 175 n. (*bis*)
Walker, R. J., 170 n., 175 n., 177 n.
Wasps. See Aristophanes
Webster, J., 37
Wecklein, N., 119 n., 127 n., 129, 145 n., 146, 149 n., 157 n., 158 n., 160 n.
Weil, H., 27 n., 74 n., 79 n., 92 n., 95 n.
Welcker, F. G., 115 n., 168 n., 172, 178 n.
"Well-made play", 29
While shepherds watched, 180 n.
Wieseler, F., 117 n.
Wilamowitz-Möllendorff, U. von, 28 n., 43 n., 46 n., 79 n., 80 n., 85 n. (*bis*), 88 n., 107, 113 n., 116 n., 123 n., 134 n., 135 n., 141 n., 149 n., 151, 152 and n., 162 n., 165 n., 169 n., 170 n., 181 n.
Willems, P., 76 n.
Winnington-Ingram, R. P., 56 n., 58 f., 65 n., 67 n., 68, 69, 72 f.
Winter's Tale, The, 29
Wordsworth, 10, 17
Wouverman, 48

Xenocles, 61
Xenophon, 125 n. (*bis*), 146, 150, 164, 170 n., 172 and n.
Xuthus, 3, 19, 38

Zeugitae, 134 n.
Zeus, 63, 82, 85, 94, 98 n., 122, 127
ζυγουλκός, 178 n.

www.ingramcontent.com/pod-product-compliance
Lightning Source LLC
Chambersburg PA
CBHW021708230426
43668CB00008B/759